*Strategies of American
Electoral Politics*

*presidential
elections*

strategies of
american electoral politics

presidential
elections

third edition

Nelson W. Polsby & Aaron B. Wildavsky
University of California, Berkeley

Charles Scribner's Sons | New York

For Linda and Carol

preface to
the third edition

Presidential elections are great teachers. We are particularly
well situated to make this observation as authors of a book
which originally, in the early 1960's, attempted to lay out in a
fairly orderly way those strategic considerations which would
in normal circumstances govern the behavior of rational political actors in Presidential elections. While the two intervening
elections have not made utter nonsense of what we tried to do,
they have provided far less in the way of normal circumstances
or rational political behavior than anyone in 1960 could have
predicted. The appearance of a third edition of this book in
time for the election of 1972 is, thus, as Dr. Johnson once said
of second marriage, something of a triumph of hope over
experience. We are still hoping to provide a little guidance for
readers who find Presidential elections as fascinating as we do
and who wonder how these extraordinary events relate to
every-day politics in America.

In this edition we have expanded our discussion of political
reforms, those accomplished (such as in the rules of the Democratic National Convention) and those in prospect (such as
the abolition of the Electoral College). We have added discussions of the Presidency and Vice-Presidency as assets and
liabilities in election-year strategy and paid even greater attention than in the second edition to the problem of explaining the
mobilization of political activists.

We have given greater coverage to the problem of making Presidential elections more responsive to popular preferences. This turns out to have complexities not adequately evoked by the slogans that in recent years have sometimes substituted for political discussion in this country. We have also devoted a new section to the problem of voting participation, since it appears that substantial increases in participation could be achieved by relatively simple changes in laws governing eligibility to vote and practices relating to voting registration. In this edition, like the previous two, we have tried to attend to silent majorities, "real" majorities, emerging (and disappearing) Republican majorities, participatory (and other) Democrats. The Democratic Convention of 1968 gave us an opportunity to do some hard critical thinking about the reform and, we hope, regeneration of that faltering institution.

As usual, we have plagiarized shamelessly (when consciously) from thoughts we have committed to print on subjects germane to this book since the last edition, and we have tried to reflect upon our modestly expanding personal experiences in the politics of Presidential elections. We have also had an opportunity to teach a graduate seminar together on political reform, and in myriad other ways to draw upon the good will of our students and colleagues. We are especially grateful for the collaboration of Bill Cavala and Byron Shafer in the preparation of this edition. They criticized our past words, straightened our circuitous passages, and contributed ideas of their own. We are also deeply indebted to Elsie Kearns of Charles Scribner's Sons for her heroic organizational work and editorial efforts.

Pat O'Donnell and Kathleen Peters gave us secretarial help that made things go smoothly regardless of the difficulties we were creating for ourselves by ripping out the innards of what we think of as a pretty good book and trying to put it all together the right way this time.

N.W.P.
A.B.W.

Berkeley, California
Oxford, England
May, 1971

preface to the second edition

In preparing the Second Edition of this book, we received a great deal of help, mostly intentional and direct, and some hindrance, most unintentional and indirect. In both categories, we place the candidacy of Barry Goldwater for the Presidency. The Goldwater nomination made the 1964 election the most peculiar election of modern times—and it forced us to rewrite the entire book. The silver lining in this black cloud was the fact that the Goldwater candidacy also gave us an opportunity to rethink our interpretation of Presidential elections from start to finish. We believe that, on the whole, what we said in early 1964 stands up well, and we are able to affirm this in the light of a comprehensive consideration of the election of 1964. Our review of the literature has, however, led to certain changes of emphasis. Important recent research and the experience of 1964 have led us to give greater significance to the ideological commitments of party activists. Similarly, we have developed further our views on the reform of the Electoral College, reconsidered the significance of national conventions as decision-making bodies, and examined more closely alternative strategies that may be employed in choosing a Vice-Presidential candidate.

Although for some years we taught on opposite sides of the

continent, it was our good fortune to spend a year as neighbors while this book was being revised. In this connection, Nelson W. Polsby wishes to thank the Center for Advanced Study in the Behavorial Sciences for its hospitality in 1965–66. Our manuscript received a most helpful editorial critique from Miriam Gallaher of the Center and from Jean Zorn; Bryson Collins and Joan Warmbrunn prepared it for the publisher with care and efficiency; Robert P. vom Eigen worked devotedly on our revised and expanded Index.

Both of us have published preliminary thoughts on the 1964 election: Nelson W. Polsby, "Strategic Considerations," in *The National Election of 1964,* ed. Milton C. Cummings (Washington: Brookings Institution, 1966) and Aaron Wildavsky, "The Goldwater Phenomenon: Purists, Politicians, and the Two-Party System," *Review of Politics* 27 (July 1965), 386–413. We want to extend our thanks to the editors of both these publications and to the Institute of Governmental Studies at the University of California (Berkeley) for indispensable financial support that facilitated research on the Goldwater phenomenon.

Finally, to our wives who warned that collaboration with either of us was impossible (and how would *they* know?), we rededicate this book.

N.W.P.
A.B.W.

June, 1967
Middletown, Connecticut
Berkeley, California

preface to the first edition

This book has had a long, and for us a very happy, gestation. Each of us has had over the last decade a chance to watch from a distance several Presidential elections; we have from time to time examined the scholarly literature on the subject, collected data on our own, and tried to think systematically about them independently of one another. In the winter of 1956–57, while we were graduate students at Yale, our collaboration began, with an effort at disentangling the theoretical and practical implications of then current proposals for party reform. Since then, we have repeatedly returned to American electoral politics in conversation and in our thoughts and writing. Despite considerable differences in the ways in which we express ourselves, and occasional differences in the emphases we would give to different events, we have been able to arrive at agreement on virtually all of the issues raised in this book. It is a totally collaborative effort in that we ourselves would have difficulty tracing the genesis or development of ideas contained here to one or the other of us.

Along the way, we have incurred many intellectual debts, separately and jointly. Some of our obligations are mentioned in the footnotes, but others, of a more personal kind, should be noted here. Nelson W. Polsby wants especially to thank Malcolm

C. Moos, Harvey Wheeler, and Ralph M. Goldman, who originally got him interested in Presidential election politics, and who helped to guide his first preliminary researches into the decision-making of the Democratic National Convention of 1952. Robert A. Dahl stimulated an approach to political analysis that led to a paper describing the logic of national convention behavior. This paper appeared as "Decision-Making at the National Conventions," *Western Political Quarterly* 13 (September 1960), 609–619. Lewis A. Froman, Jr., collaborated with him on a paper which served as forerunner and prototype of the treatment in this volume of the Electoral College. He also received excellent assistance from Margaret MacGregor Spellman, Carolyn Stoakes, Sheila Jones, and Martha Leiserson, who typed several versions of our manuscript, and from Bruce Franklin, Paul D. O'Brien, John R. Hanson, Peter Fritts, Charles L. Zetterberg, and Michael Austin, who ran down footnotes, read proof, and performed other odious chores cheerfully and well. Much of this work was made possible by a Ford Foundation Grant to Wesleyan University.

Aaron Wildavsky wants to thank the students in his senior seminar at Oberlin College for their stimulating discussion and for the preparation of a series of papers on past national conventions. He is grateful to the Eagleton Institute of Politics for a National Convention Fellowship which enabled him to study the behavior of the Ohio delegation at the 1960 Democratic Convention. The results of this enterprise were published as "'What Can I Do?': Ohio Delegates View the Convention," in Paul Tillett, ed., *Inside Politics: The National Conventions, 1960* (Dobbs Ferry, N. Y., 1962). While at the convention, he benefited from conversations with James D. Barber.

Together, we are grateful for the lasting inspiration and repeated encouragement of our teachers, David B. Truman and Allan P. Sindler, and, for excellent critical readings of earlier versions of this work, to Richard F. Fenno, Fred I. Greenstein, Lewis A. Froman, Jr., H. Douglas Price, Milton C. Cummings, Jr., Michael Leiserson, Duane Lockard, Allan B. Sindler, Herbert E. Alexander, Elmer E. Cornwell, and Paul G. Willis.

It is customary for joint authors each to receive half the

credit for their work, but to be blamed for all its errors. In this instance, as, we are sure, in so many, the credit deserves to be even more widely dispersed. We need hardly volunteer to our readers information about the sources of error.

N.W.P.
A.B.W.

July, 1963
Washington, D.C.

contents

Preface to the Third Edition   *vii*

Preface to the Second Edition   *ix*

Preface to the First Edition   *xi*

Introduction: Political Strategies and   *3*
    Presidential Elections

Chapter One: The Strategic Environment   *7*

    VOTERS
    INTEREST GROUPS AND VOTING BLOCS
    PARTIES
    NEW PARTY ACTIVISTS: PURISTS VS.
        PROFESSIONALS
        Emphasizing Differences
    THE PRIVATIZATION OF POLITICS: SEMI-PERMANENT
        OPPOSITION
        Whither the Purists?
    THE ELECTORAL COLLEGE
    THE DISTRIBUTION OF RESOURCES
        Money
        Control Over Information
        The Presidency
    INCUMBENCY AS A RESOURCE—A SOUTHERN STRATEGY?

INCUMBENCY AS A LIABILITY—THE VICE-PRESIDENCY
CONVERTIBILITY OF RESOURCES
SUMMARY

Chapter Two: The Nominating Process   *115*

STRATEGIC CONSIDERATIONS
     Goals
     Uncertainty
     Power
PRE-CONVENTION STRATEGIES
     Primaries
     State and District Conventions
AT THE CONVENTION
     Candidates and Their Organizations
     Delegates
     Straws in the Wind
     The Balloting
     The Vice-Presidential Nominee
THE FUTURE OF NATIONAL CONVENTIONS
APPENDIX: SELECTION OF DELEGATES TO NATIONAL
     CONVENTIONS

Chapter Three: The Campaign   *171*

THREE UNDERDOG STRATEGIES
THEORY AND ACTION
INS AND OUTS
FRIENDS, VOLUNTEERS, AND PROFESSIONALS
WHERE TO CAMPAIGN?
DOMESTIC ISSUES
FOREIGN AFFAIRS
LAW AND ORDER
PRESENTATION OF SELF
THE TELEVISION DEBATES
GETTING A GOOD PRESS
MUD-SLINGING
FEEDBACK
APPENDIX: PREDICTING ELECTIONS

Chapter Four: Reform?   *223*

THE POLITICAL THEORY OF PARTY REFORM
THE BIAS BEHIND PARTY REFORM
IS BROAD-GAUGED PARTY REFORM POSSIBLE?
IS BROAD-GAUGED PARTY REFORM DESIRABLE?
    An Appraisal of the Nomination Process
    An Appraisal of Permanent Voting Enrollment
    An Appraisal of the Electoral College
    Party Differences and Political Stability
IS PARTY REFORM RELEVANT?

Chapter Five: The Ballot and the Political System   *293*

COALITIONS IN THE SYSTEM
ELECTIONS AND PUBLIC POLICY
IS PARTICIPATORY DEMOCRACY BETTER?
EXTREMISM
PARTY COMPETITION AND POLICY

Appendix A: 1972 Presidential Primaries   *317*

Appendix B: Convention Delegates and the Electoral   *318*
    College, 1964, 1968, and 1972

Bibliography   *320*

Index   *323*

*Strategies of American
Electoral Politics*

*presidential
elections*

introduction

political strategies and presidential elections

This book is about the winning of the Presidential office. In spite of the great and lonely eminence of the Presidency, this office exists within a cultural and political tradition that guides and shapes the ways in which the Presidency is won and, later, the ways in which Presidential power is exercised. But we will not speak further here about the exercise of executive power. Rather, the task before us is to make plain the context within which the battle for Presidential office is waged, to discuss the strategies of contending parties and, if possible, to explain why some strategies are used by some contestants and other strategies by others. In this way we hope to elucidate a significant area of our common political life.

Our thesis is a simple one: The strategies of participants in a Presidential election make sense once we understand the web of circumstances in which they operate. This principle applies to candidates and their managers, to delegates at nominating conventions, to party workers, and to voters. Strategies are courses of action consciously pursued toward well-understood goals. Watching strategies shows how political leaders use the constraints and opportunities of their environment to achieve their goals.

Both the political strategies of participants in Presidential elections and the circumstances that give rise to them are relatively stable, persistent features of our political system. We have had a two-party political system with the same two major parties for a little over a hundred years. Presidential nominees have been picked by national party conventions for an even longer period.[1] Presidential candidates have always been faced with such problems as deciding whether a greater or lesser emphasis on their party affiliation will help them gain more votes. Contemporary evidence that party preferences are not distributed evenly among the electorate helps explain, for example, why the strategy of recent Democratic candidates has been to place great stress on their party label, while Republicans are normally inclined to minimize their connection with their party.

Political strategies that persist over a period of time are reasonably easy to identify, even when they are colored by the distinctive styles and personalities of particular candidates. We hope, therefore, to achieve a level of discussion that goes beyond the special circumstances of 1972, or any other year, and say something about American Presidential elections in general.

The study of politics has progressed to the point where political scientists can now make available such a discussion. In large measure, an improved description and analysis is possible because of the efforts of dozens of scholars who have reported upon and investigated, with ever-increasing detail and accuracy, the component parts of the American political system. The task of this book will be to synthesize these reports for the enlightenment and use of interested citizens. But we cannot forecast the outcome of any particular election, and we have no desire to advise people how to vote.

In the first chapter we identify characteristics of the American political system which make up the strategic environment within which the pursuit of the Presidency takes place. The would-be President must come to terms with voters, who enter each election period as complex bundles of already-formed habits, attitudes, and loyalties. The ways in which interest groups and parties activate these habits are largely out of the hands of any single participant in the process. Another element, the rules by which votes are counted, is also beyond any participant's control. Finally, we discuss the comparative availability to candidates of certain key resources, such as money and control over information.

The first chapter lays out a framework for much that follows in the second and third chapters. The latter deal, successively, with the various steps of the nomination and election processes. At this point in the book, we discuss a variety of classic strategic "moves," such as entering or not entering primaries, the candidacy of favorite sons, the starting and stopping of bandwagons at national party conventions, the selection of areas to campaign in, and the selection of issues to emphasize. In Chapters 2 and 3, we try to relate these moves to their necessary preconditions in terms of resources, and also to relate them to their probable consequences.

In the fourth chapter, we discuss significant proposals for altering the strategic framework of Presidential elections—proposals for reform that would in some respects reconstitute the party system and redistribute resources among contestants for the Presidency. Reform proposals are often debated rather abstractly on their presumed merits, without being related to any concrete consequences. We hope to provoke fresh insight on the subject by looking at these reforms in the light of the new distribution of benefits and handicaps which they propose to allocate to various participants in Presidential elections.

Finally, in Chapter 5, we attempt to state in general terms what the ballot means in a political system like ours. Here we urge reconsideration of two stereotypes: one which insists that democracy cannot exist without strict majority rule, and another that suggests that public officials in our system receive many specific and meaningful policy directives from the electorate. We try to show that while our political system discourages both strict application of majority rule and mandates on specific policies, it is still meaningful to speak of our form of government as democratic, open and responsive—as well as flexible, tough, stable, and resourceful.

Presidential elections are important to us as citizens. They determine who will guide our future. They also remind us of our heritage of political responsibility and freedom, a heritage which, in a troubled world, seems to us increasingly precious.

NOTES

1. See Paul T. David, Ralph M. Goldman, and Richard C. Bain, *The Politics of National Party Conventions* (Washington, 1960) for a lengthy treatment of the history of national party conventions.

chapter one
the strategic environment

All political strategies are worked out within a framework of circumstances which are in part subject to manipulation but to even a greater degree are "given." Needless to say, this fact of life also applies to the strategies of aspirants to the Presidency, who must construct extremely complex plans of action within a context of hundreds of thousands of relevant circumstances, most of which lie beyond their control. Some of these circumstances are contingent and relate to the strategies being pursued by other active participants in the election process and to the resources at their command. Other circumstances are more stable and have to do with features of the American political system that have persisted over time. These features provide advantages and handicaps differently to Democrats and Republicans, to incumbent Presidents and challengers. In this chapter we shall deal with these relatively persistent "givens" of the political system to show how they shape the decisions of Presidential election strategists.

VOTERS

Precisely what part does the voter play in American politics? This depends entirely on his interest and activity. Most people, however, are not interested in most public issues most of the time.[1] In our society, it is apparently quite possible to live comfortably without being politically concerned. Political activity is costly. It eats up time and energy at an astounding rate. To be informed on strategic problems in nuclear politics or on the operations of a municipal electric plant is not a matter of a few moments of reflection; many hours must be spent. One must ordinarily attend meetings, listen to or participate in discussion, write letters, attempt to persuade or be persuaded by others and engage in other time-consuming labor. This means foregoing other activities, like devoting extra time to the job, playing with the children, and watching TV. So far as we can tell these other activities rather than public affairs are the primary concerns of most people, and the costs of participation in public affairs appear, for most people, to be greater than the returns. Only a few people receive financial rewards or hold jobs or are acclaimed in the public arena—considerations which might lead them to devote the time and effort required to participate. It is only in regard to a few issues at best, that most citizens find it worthwhile to participate in politics rather than do other things.

Even so, there are a few people who are continuously interested in a wide variety of issues. These are usually public officials, interest group leaders, newspaper editors, and academics —all people whose occupations require their interest. There are a larger number who have specialized interests in specific policy areas. These may include public and private officials, members of civic organizations and interest groups, citizens who are directly affected, and a sprinkling of others who make a hobby of being interested, including seekers after causes and people who like to get their names on letterheads. These political activists, who may or may not themselves be political leaders, are different from ordinary voters, as we shall see.

The fact that individuals do vary enormously in their degree of interest has profound implications for political life. For interest is a necessary condition of influence. The interested tend to go to meetings where public affairs are discussed and decided. They tend to belong to political parties and to work in various ways to help the party of their choice. They cultivate their access to public officials. They tend to care more about the outcomes of public policies and to communicate their concerns to decision-makers. And so, they become more influential.

Differences in interest also influence voting behavior: People who are interested in politics tend to vote and those who are uninterested tend not to vote.[2] Who are in these two groups? In general, the better educated people are more active and interested in public affairs. They also tend to be people who are better off financially.[3] This is, of course, also the population from which the Republican party draws disproportionate support, which consequently gives a substantial advantage to that party among voters who tend to turn out most reliably for Presidential elections. On the other hand, the low turnout groups (normally Democratic) tend to be numerically greater than the high turnout groups. Furthermore, traditionally Democratic groups may be clustered in such a way as to maximize their strength in Presidential elections by being located in areas which are favored by the Electoral College system of vote-counting. We shall return to this topic later.

How do voters make up their minds whom to support? By far the majority of people vote according to their habitual party affiliation.[4] In other words, most people will have made up their minds how to vote in 1972 before the candidates are chosen, because they always support a particular party. These party regulars are likely to be more interested and active in politics and have more political knowledge than the "independents."[5] But they rarely change their minds. They tend to listen to their own side of political arguments and to agree with the policies espoused by their party. They even go so far as to ignore information which they perceive to be unfavorable to the party of their choice.[6]

If party is so important in giving a structure to a voter's picture of reality, and in helping him choose a Presidential candidate to vote for before the candidate is even nominated, we had best inquire where people get their party affiliations from. There seems to be no simple answer to this. The party affiliations of most voters seem to be governed by a number of forces. An individual lives in a social context and inherits a social identity from his parents that contains a political component. People are Democrats or Republicans, in part, because their families and the other people they interact with are Democrats or Republicans.[7] Most individuals come into close contact only with people who are predominantly one or the other.[8] And just as people tend to share characteristics with their friends and families such as income and educational level, religious affiliation, area of residence, and so on, they also tend to share party loyalties with them, too.[9]

Of course, we all know of instances where people do *not* share various status-giving characteristics with their parents and at least some of their friends, and so it should come as no surprise that sometimes children do not share the politics of their parents. In fact, political differences tend to run together with the other kinds of differences as well. But, by and large, voters retain the party loyalties of the primary groups of which they are a part.

The result of this process is to give each of the major political parties reservoirs of voting strength they can count on from year to year. Republicans traditionally do well in the small towns and rural areas of New England, the Middle Atlantic states, and the Middle West. They draw their support from people who are richer, better educated, occupy managerial or professional positions or run small businesses, tend to live in or to move into the well-to-do suburban areas, and are predominantly Protestant. Democrats draw great support from the large cities outside of the South. Wage earners, union members, Catholics, Negroes, Jews, and the new (that is, since 1880) immigrant populations of Irish and Polish ethnic origins —all contribute disproportionately to the Democratic vote.[10]

One may ask how did these particular groups come to have these particular loyalties? We must turn to history to find answers to this question. Enough is known about a few groups to make it possible to speculate about what kinds of historical events tend to align groups with a political party.

Let us take a few examples. We all know about the "Solid South," which from the Civil War until the era of George

Wallace and Barry Goldwater was predominantly Democratic in its Presidential voting. For all those years, resentment against the harsh Reconstruction period under the leadership of the Republican party was reflected in the election returns. Less well known is the fact that the South was not unanimous in its enthusiasm for the Civil War, or in its resentment of Reconstruction. In many states of the old South, there were two kinds of farms: plantations on the flat land that grew cash crops, used slaves and, in general, before the Civil War, prospered; and subsistence farms in the uplands that had a few or no slaves and, in general, were run by poorer white people. This latter group formed the historical core of mountain areas that year after year voted Republican in Presidential elections in western Virginia and North Carolina, eastern Tennessee and Kentucky, and southeastern West Virginia.[11]

The voting habits of black citizens, where they have voted, have been shaped by several traumas. The Civil War freed them and made them Republicans. The Counter-Reconstruction disenfranchised them, and the industrial revolution brought them North, where a crushing burden of economic destitution was added to racial discrimination. The differing effects of the Great Depression of 1929 on black voters in the North brought them into the New Deal coalition, and the Northern black voter has remained Democratic ever since.[12]

If, for some people, the historical events of the Civil War and the Depression shaped their political heritage, for others the critical forces seem less traumatic and more diffuse. It is possible perhaps to see why the poor become Democrats, since the Democratic party has in recent years been so welfare-minded, but why do the rich lean toward the Republicans? Perhaps, in part, this is a reaction to the redistributive aspirations of some New Deal programs and the inclination of Democratic Presidents to expand the role of government in the economy. But in all probability it is also a response to the record of the Congressional wing of the Republican party which so thoroughly dominated the post-Civil War era of industrial expansion. In this era, Republican policies vigorously encouraged risk-taking by private businessmen, granted them Federal aid in a variety of forms, and withheld Federal regulation from private enterprise.

Sometimes party affiliation coincides with ethnic identification because of the political and social circumstances surrounding the entry of ethnic groups into the country. In southern New England, politics was dominated by the Republican party and by "Yankees" of substance and high status during the decades following the Civil War. During these decades, thousands of Irish people streamed into this area. The Democratic party welcomed them; the Republicans did not. Soon the Democratic percentage of the two-party vote began to increase, and Irish politicians took over the Democratic party.[13]

In the Middle West, events such as the American involvement in two wars against Germany under Democratic auspices seem to have shaped the political preferences of Americans of German descent.[14]

Specific *candidates* of special attractiveness may under certain circumstances sway voters to leave the party of their choice. The extraordinary elections of President Eisenhower are a recent example of this. His appeal to Democrats was quite amazing. But this was possible partially because these Democrats did not perceive President Eisenhower as a partisan figure, and so it is not surprising that his personal popularity did not greatly aid other Republicans who ran with him, or the Republican party, once he no longer headed the ticket.[15]

Most of the time *issues* have much the same sporadic and peripheral effect as candidates. Let us see why. We can say to begin with that at least three preconditions must be satisfied for a voter's opinion about an issue to change his vote.[16] First, a voter must know about the issue; second, he must care about it at least a little; and third, he must be able to distinguish the positions of the parties and their candidates on the issue. Data from public opinion polls tell us that most people are not well informed about the content of issues most of the time.[17] All but major public issues are thus eliminated for most people. And even these major issues may enter the consciousness of most people in only the most rudimentary way. It makes a difference whether a person has a weak preference on an issue, or whether he breathes fire when the subject is mentioned. The number who care, even a little, is substantially less than those who know about issues.

Once a voter has some grasp of the content of a public policy, and learns to prefer one outcome rather than another, he must also find public leaders to espouse his point of view. Finding differences on policy issues between parties is not always easy. Party statements on policy may be vague because leaders have not decided what to do. They may deliberately obfuscate an issue for fear of alienating interested publics. They may try to hold divergent factions in their parties together by glossing over, as best they can, disagreements on many specific issues. Even when real party differences on policy exist, many voters may not be aware of them. The subject may be rather esoteric to the common understanding, or the time required to master the subject may be more than most people are willing to spend. By the time we get down to those who know *and* care *and* can discriminate between party positions on issues, we usually have a small proportion of the electorate, rarely larger than 30 per cent.[18] What can we say about these people?

Their most obvious characteristic is interest in and concern about issues and party positions. But these are precisely the people who are most likely to be strong party identifiers, men and women who are characterized by a deep devotion to party, which makes it most unlikely that they will shift allegiance just because of a disagreement on one or two issues.[19] The number of issue-oriented "independents" who are left must be very small. And it is not unlikely that these people are distributed about equally on both sides of major policy questions so that the total number of votes changed by the impact of any specific issue is bound to be minute.

We still have some preconditions to satisfy, however, before even these changes can be accepted as certain. One is that there must not be other issues which are also highly salient to voters and which work the other way. For if voters were willing to change their votes on one particular issue, why should they not switch their support back because of another? There are usually many issues in a campaign; only if all or most of the issues pointed voters in the same direction, would they be likely to switch their votes. But what is the likelihood that parties will arrange their policies along a broad front so as to force large numbers of "independent" voters from or into the fold? It is low—but not impossible. In 1964 the Republicans may have done so.

Although it is true that the less knowledge a person has about public affairs, the more likely he is to vote for a candidate of the opposite party, it is important to distinguish between those who only have a little knowledge and those who have none at all. For the man utterly without any contact with the political world, except at the polls, has no reason whatsoever to change his customary party vote. Thus changes in vote from one party to another are likely to be concentrated among those who receive a little but not a great deal of information about parties, issues, and candidates.[20]

A recent study seeks to demonstrate that there is considerable issue content in the citizen's behavior at the polls, by showing that those who change party from one election to the next are generally sympathetic to some key policies of their new party. The standpatters, on the other hand, generally are in sympathy with major policies of their party.[21] Whether the citizen is taught what to believe by his party or finds a party in accordance with his beliefs cannot be determined from evidence presently available.

We can now see that a strong issue orientation is likely to guide voting decisions under some circumstances. One set of circumstances occurs when one issue becomes so intensely important that the voter is willing to lay aside his party preferences and his preferences on other issues. An unpopular war, severe economic deprivation (whether or not it is related to governmental policies), a fixation on a subject like keeping water free of fluoride have at times led to the required intense feeling. The pocketbook nerve seems especially sensitive.[22] Another possibility occurs when a party is seen to change across the spectrum of policies or the voter himself undergoes such a broad-scale change of heart. Finally, in a historical sense we can say that issues may have a lasting impact on voting behavior through the ways in which they shape the party affiliations of whole generations of voters. But if parties and their leaders make the issues and give them meaning for most people, then fundamental *changes* in party allegiance among large numbers of people are not likely to arise from their own reasoned look at issues. A depression, a civil war, events felt immediately and personally by millions have precipitated the great changes in party allegiances, not debates on the merits of this or that comparatively minor matter. The sheer, brute impact of great events does more to change votes over the long run than any single policy problem.

This picture of the relation between voters and issues is somewhat unreal in any case. For as far as we are able to tell, voters adopt most of their issue orientations at the instigation of the parties: strong party identifiers are more likely to learn more about issues and to care more about them, in part, precisely because it reinforces their party identification.[23] This means that there are few issues that are not made by parties and political leaders, and hence few party identifiers are lost as a result of the policies adopted by the party of their choice.

The complex relationship between issues and electoral outcomes was illustrated by two issues in the 1968 election: the war in Vietnam and what was delicately called the social issue —racial conflict, crime, and law and order. Both issues had enormous public exposure and excited the passions of the politically aware. Yet the most sensitive and sophisticated analysis we have of these issues and public opinion shows that party identification had "fifty times the net impact of the Vietnam issue"[24] in determining the relative favorability of voters toward Nixon and Humphrey. Party was so powerful that it cannot be considered on the same scale with other forces. The figure, which summarizes the impact of various issues on the 1968 Presidential vote, shows that domestic policy issues (the bread-and-butter matters of social welfare, employment and prosperity) were considerably more important than the Vietnam and social issues combined. Like other Democrats before him, Humphrey gained on domestic policy because voters saw themselves as closer to him than to his Republican opponent. Richard Nixon gained on the foreign policy side because of the Democratic image as the party of war.

Why was the Vietnam issue so unimportant? Most voters found Senators Robert Kennedy and Eugene McCarthy too "dovish" for their taste and Governor George Wallace much too "hawkish." The candidates of the major parties were rather close to the voters' preferences, with Nixon coming in a little ahead. It is difficult for an issue to have a major impact on an election outcome when the voters do not differentiate greatly among the candidates with respect to that issue. So, once again, we come back to party as the great organizer of voters' ideas and sentiments.

Merely to list the functions which party identification performs for the voter—reducing his costs of acquiring political

Domestic Policy More Important Than Vietnam and Urban Issues Combined: Issue Forces and the Presidential Vote, 1968

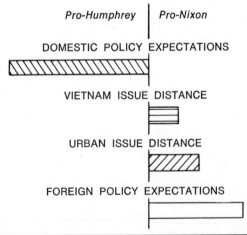

Source: Richard A. Brody, Benjamin I. Page, *et al.*, "Vietnam, the Urban Crisis and the 1968 Presidential Election: A Preliminary Analysis," prepared for delivery at the 1969 meeting of the American Sociological Association, September, 1969.

information, telling him what side he is on, organizing his information, ordering his preferences, letting him know what is of prime importance—is to suggest the profound significance of parties in the voter's mind. Politics is amazingly complex; there are scores of possible issues, a myriad of relevant political personalities, and often many choices to be made on election day. The voter who follows his party identification, however, can vastly simplify the choices he must make and thus reduce to manageable proportions the amount of time he spends on public affairs. He need only follow his party's nomination to arrive at a voting decision. When issues arise, the voter with strong party identification need not puzzle over each and every one. He can, instead, listen to the pronouncements of his party leaders who inform him what issues are important, what information is most relevant to these issues, and what position he ought to take. Of course, the citizen with greater interest in public affairs will want to investigate matters for himself. Even so, his party identification provides him with important guides for the many matters on which he cannot possibly be well informed. Indeed, all of us, including full-time participants like the President, have to find ways to cut information costs on some issues.[25] For most people who vote, their identification with one of the two major political parties performs that indispensable function.

INTEREST GROUPS AND VOTING BLOCS

Interest groups are collections of people who are similarly situated with respect to one or more policies of government and who organize to do something about it. The interest groups most significant for elections in our society are those having the following characteristics:

1) they have a mass base, that is, are composed of many members;

2) they are concentrated geographically, rather than dispersed thinly over the entire map;

3) they represent major resource investments of members—such as in the case of the *producers* of bicycles, whose entire livelihoods

are tied up in the group involved, as against the *consumers* of bicycles, for whom investment in a bicycle is not anywhere near as important;

4) they involve those characteristics of people which give them status in society—such as their race or ethnicity.

Interest groups may be more or less organized, and more or less vigilant and alert on policy matters that concern, or ought to concern, them. They are not necessarily organized in ways that make them politically effective; very often the paid lobbyists of interest groups spend more time trying unsuccessfully to alert their own members to the implications of government policies than they spend lobbying with politicians.[26]

In American politics, interest group activity is lively and ubiquitous, even when it is not particularly effective or meaningful in terms of policy outcomes. We shall be concerned with interest groups in three ways: First, we must recognize that membership in these groups may be quite important in giving voters a sense of affiliation and political position. In this respect, interest groups act much the way parties do, helping to fill in the voter's map of the world with preferences, priorities, and facts.

Second, interest groups are important because of their partisan political activities; they may actively recruit supporters for candidates and aid materially in campaigns. Third, interest groups may influence party policy by making demands with respect to issues in return for their own mobilized support.

The extent to which interest groups can "deliver" the votes of their members, however, is always problematic; to a great extent interest group leaders are the prisoners of past alliances their group has made. Even so, the Negro vote, the farm vote, the labor vote, and many other "votes" are bandied about as though they were political commodities which could be manipulated easily in behalf of one or another candidate for public office. So long as the use of election statistics and opinion polls was in its infancy, claims to guarantee support or threats to withdraw it could be accepted or rejected on intuitive grounds where no man could claim much greater competence than another. The appearance of voting studies and the development of the arts of statistical manipulation have created new opportunities for the purveyors of bloc votes and new difficulties for the interested but necessarily amateur citizen and public official. How are they to evaluate these important political claims backed up by impressive and complicated arrays of data?

The usual argument is that if one or another candidate captures the allegiance of a particular bloc, that bloc's pivotal position in a state or large population will enable the fortunate aspirant to capture all of the electoral votes and thus win the election. It is incorrect to speak of any one combination of states totalling more than a majority of electoral votes as in any sense more critical, valuable, or pivotal than any other such combination. In a fairly close election the defection of any number of combinations of states to the other side would spell the difference between victory or defeat.

An important point to remember is that appeals to various groups are necessarily conditioned by time, place, and circumstance. There is little doubt that under *some* conditions during *some* elections *some* social characteristics of voters and candidates may have *some* relevance to the polling results. Finding the conditions under which specified social characteristics become relevant to voter choice is most difficult. We know that in a competitive political system various participants (parties, interest groups, leaders) put forward candidates and issues designed to capture the allegiance of various groups of people. Rarely is it possible to appeal to one group and one group alone, not only because there are so many different groups, with all sorts of conceptions of policy, but also because each individual may have many social characteristics which are potentially relevant to his voting decision. While some men may be so single-minded that they have only one interest that is important in determining their vote—color, religion, ethnic background, income—most of us have multiple interests which sometimes conflict. Much depends on the movement of events which may bring one or another interest to the forefront of the voter's consciousness and incline him toward the candidate he believes best represents his preferences on that matter.[27] In addition, the more directly pecuniary appeals which were relevant at the turn of the century have slowly lost their effectiveness and have given way to a period when national, economic, and foreign policy issues have assumed primary importance to many children of immigrant parents. Long-term social trends, as well as the strategies of candidates, have much to do with the impact of appeals to bloc votes.

In each election members of the various groups that make up the American voting population turn out to vote, dividing their loyalties in varying ways between the major parties. To determine the contribution that a particular group makes to a party, it is necessary to know three things: how big is the group, how many of its members actually vote, and how devoted they are to one party or another.

For example, let us look at the contribution of poor people —defined as those whose incomes are $3000 a year or less—to the Democratic party. Basing his analysis on Survey Research Center polls, Robert Axelrod [28] has shown that the contribution of the poor to the total Democratic vote has fallen from 29% in 1952 to only 12% in 1968. This trend can be accounted for in any—or all—of three ways: 1) More of the non-poor are voting Democratic these days, diluting the contribution of the poor. 2) Fewer poor people are voting Democratic these days. 3) There are simply fewer poor people, by the standard definition, and this dilutes their vote. This last is certainly true: in 1952, poor people made up 35% of the U.S. adult population; in 1968, the proportion defined by the standard measure as poor had sunk to 16%.

While the poor have not really been an important part of the Democratic coalition in recent years, black people have established themselves as a substantial component. "Their contribution has grown substantially from 5% to 7% in 1952–1960 to 12% in 1964, and 19% in 1968." Since the black population has remained a relatively constant 11% of the total population, their vastly increased contribution is due to a near doubling of their turnout throughout the nation and high loyalty to the Democratic party.

While union members and their families made up a third of all Democratic votes in the 1950's, their contribution fell slightly to 28% in 1968. They are important to the party because a quarter of all adults are in union families, their turnout is reasonably good, and they vote more Democratic than other people. The decline in their contribution is due to a small decrease in size and a considerable drop in loyalty to the Democratic party.

Where union families contributed four times as many votes as black people to the Democratic party in 1960, the unionists contributed only one and a half times as many votes as the blacks in 1968.

Although Catholics are just a quarter of the population, they still provide a third of all Democratic votes. In 1952 and 1956 Southerners still voted about 10% more Democratic than voters in the rest of the country, but in recent elections they have been slightly more Republican than other people. They gave a quarter of their votes to the third party movement of George Wallace in 1968. Black Southerners stayed with the Democrats, but white Southerners split their Presidential vote among all three parties.

There is much misperception of the role of youth in party voting. Young people between twenty-one and twenty-nine make up about 18% of the population but they provide the Democrats with approximately 13% to 15% of the votes because they have low turnout. Actually, in 1968, the youth of the nation was somewhat pro-Wallace and pro-Republican compared to the nation as a whole.

Thus, the Republican coalition appears to be as follows: White people, who comprise approximately 90% of the U.S. population, vote anywhere from 1% to 3% more Republican than Democratic. The comparatively small size of the black population means that even in 1960, when Nixon got about a quarter of the black vote, 97% of his total came from whites; 99% of his vote came from whites in 1968. If one can conceive of non-union families and Protestants as "groups" in the usual sense, they make up about 75% of the population and vote 5% or 6% more Republican than the nation as a whole. Those who are not young divide their vote relatively equally between the parties. The Republican party gets its vote then from white

TURNOUT VARIES GREATLY AMONG GROUPS

	% of eligible who voted	% of total vote
Age:		
18–20	33%	
21–24	51	
25–29	60	17% (under 30)
30–65	72	68
65–	66	15
Income:		
under $3000	54%	9%
3–5,000	58	13
4–15,000	72	66
15,000 +	84	12
Race:		
White-National	69%	91%
White-Southern	62	
White-Northern	72	
Non-white, National	56%	9%
Non-white, Southern	51	
Non-white, Northern	61	
Education:		
College educated	88%	
High school educated	76	
Grade school educated	68	
Occupation:		
Professional and managerial	85%	
Other white collar	84	
Farm operators	81	
Trade union members	80	
Non-union members	75	
Skilled and semi-skilled workers	73	
Unskilled workers	67	

Sources: Age, Income and Race, Richard Scammon and Ben J. Wattenberg, *The Real Majority* (New York: Coward McCann, 1970) pp. 46, 48, 54–6; Their figures are for the election of 1968. Education and occupation, Survey Research Center, University of Michigan, reported in Fred I. Greenstein, *The American Party System and the American People* (2nd edition) (Englewood Cliffs, N.J., 1970) p. 19. These figures are for the election of 1964.

people, non-union members and Protestants. The youth and the poor split their votes between the parties and fail to vote in disproportionate numbers.

We can also say a word about the coalition that supported George Wallace. The only group in the country that gave him substantially more support than his 14% national total was the South, including the border states, which provided 28% of his votes. The poor, youth and union families gave him on the average a few more percent than he got from the nation as a whole.

As the table indicates, *turnout* varies enormously among different groups in the population, rising with income, occupational status, education, and, in general, with age. Since Republicans are disproportionately located in the high turnout groups and Democrats in the low, this tends to give Republicans electoral advantages that in some measure—varying from election to election—makes up for the preponderance of Democrats in the potential electorate.

It is possible, then, to analyze party coalitions in terms of the group memberships of the people who vote regularly for one party or another. Likewise, it is possible to consider the differential impact of different candidates on these various groups.

In this context we can appraise the impact of John F. Kennedy's appeal to his fellow Catholics in the 1960 election.[29] Let us distinguish between two kinds of claims. One is the minimal claim that Kennedy's Catholicism helped him more than it hurt him in the election. This is correct. And it is largely correct because Catholics are disproportionately located in areas where they could contribute to Kennedy's majorities in states with large electoral votes.[30] If the claim is expanded to state, however, that something called the "Catholic vote" was the single factor which gained Kennedy his victory, then it is incorrect.

Two hard facts stand out from the welter of imponderables in the 1960 Presidential election: (1) there was probably a Catholic vote of some magnitude; (2) the increase in the votes of Catholics as compared to 1956 was not sufficient in and of itself to ensure Kennedy's victory. He also needed increases in the Democratic votes of Negroes, Jews, and other groups.

Both poll and electoral data strongly suggest that there was both a Catholic vote and an anti-Catholic vote in the 1960 election. According to the Gallup poll, the percentage of Catholics supporting the Democratic candidate rose from 51% in 1956 to 78% in 1960. Moreover, 62% of the Catholics who voted for Eisenhower in 1956 actually voted for Kennedy in 1960, while only 3% of the Catholics who voted for Stevenson in 1956 switched to Nixon in 1960. Although we do not know how many of the Catholics who voted for Eisenhower and Kennedy would also have voted for a Protestant Democrat in 1960, it seems safe to assume that by no means all would have done so. The presumption that there was a Catholic vote is further strengthened by the 1960 election returns which show that there is a high and positive correlation between the percentage of Catholics in a state and the percentage gain for the Democratic party over 1956. While part of these results may be accounted for by other demographic variables such as urbanization, it appears unlikely that this conclusion about the Catholic vote will be shaken.

These figures, it must be said, do not necessarily validate the claim that Catholics had been moving from the Democratic party and that the presence of a Catholic candidate brought them back into the fold. Another Gallup poll shows that 75% of the Catholics who voted in the 1958 Congressional election supported Democratic candidates, a total just three percentage points less than Kennedy received in 1960. It is possible, therefore, that the relatively low vote of Catholics for Adlai Stevenson represents a switch to the magical name of Eisenhower rather than a permanent desertion of the Democratic party.

It takes a rather complicated analysis to ascertain whether Kennedy lost many votes from Protestants, as seems to have been the case.[31] Gallup tells us that Kennedy received 38% of the votes by Protestants, while Stevenson received only 37% in 1956. But we know from other surveys that Stevenson's overall personal popularity in 1956 lost ground from 1952. In addition, he faced the handicap of running against the extraordinarily popular incumbent, President Eisenhower. Any Democratic candidate in 1960 was expected to do better than Stevenson did in 1956. Since we are not permitted the luxury of running a laboratory test in which a Protestant Democrat runs against the Nixon of 1960, there appears to be no certain way of determining how many Nixon voters who are Protestant would have gone Democratic if Kennedy had not been on the ballot. The closest thing to such a test is a study done by the Simulmatics Corporation which predicted electoral outcomes from survey data on voting intentions carefully broken down into the characteristics of voters. The analysis concluded that:

> The religious issue cut both ways. Not only did some Protestants reject Kennedy but also some Catholic Republicans swung to him. . . . The shift of one in ten American voters on religious grounds cost Kennedy one and a half million votes, or 2.3% of the total vote. But while Kennedy lost in the popular vote, he gained in electoral votes on the religious issue. The best-fit simulation indicates that Kennedy achieved a net gain of 22 electoral votes because of the religious issue. . . . The bunching of the Catholic shift in large, closely fought, industrial states and the location of much of the Protestant shift in "safe" Southern states gave Kennedy this net advantage despite a popular vote disadvantage. By our calculations, Kennedy lost, by the religious issue, the following states he otherwise would have won: Kentucky (10), Tennessee (11), Florida (10), Oklahoma (8), Montana (4), Idaho (4), Utah (4), California (32), Oregon (6), Virginia (12), and Washington (9). He won the following states he would otherwise have lost: Connecticut (8), New York (45), New Jersey (16), Pennsylvania (32), Illinois (27), and New Mexico (4).[32]

A study has also been made which shows that Democratic candidates for Congress in Wisconsin suffered defeat in close districts probably because of Protestant defection due to Kennedy's candidacy.[33] Finally, a plausible guess has been made by the Michigan Survey Research Center. It estimated what the "normal" votes of Catholics and Protestants for Democratic Presidential candidates would be. Then, calculating the 1960 divergence from this hypothetical "normal" pattern, they concluded that Kennedy was shy about 2.2% of the two-party vote, a large proportion of the defections coming from the

South.[34] On balance, it appears that Kennedy was hurt somewhat in the Southern and border states and perhaps in the Midwest and Mountain states as well, but he more than made up for it in the Northern and Midwest industrial states whose electoral votes were far larger.

In terms of popular votes, Kennedy received 49.7% to Nixon's 49.6% out of a total vote of 68,832,670, a hair-breadth margin if there ever was one. The exceedingly close popular and Electoral College vote makes it unlikely that increased votes by Catholic voters alone could have been sufficient to give Kennedy victory. Virtually any group—Jews, or Negroes, for example—could claim that a shift of their few thousand votes in a few critical states made the difference between victory and defeat.[35]

Two brief examples may be cited to support this conclusion. Illinois and Texas together accounted for 51 electoral votes. Out of the approximately 4.7 million votes cast in Illinois, Kennedy's margin of victory was 8,858. Where a shift of 4,500 votes by any group would have been enough to spell the difference, it would not be difficult to find any number of groups which could be considered necessary for the victory. Gallup reports that on a national basis the votes of Jews increased from 75% to 81% Democratic over 1956 and the votes of Negroes from 61% to 68%. Evidently Kennedy needed the additional votes from the Jews and the Negroes who live in Illinois in order to have won there. In Texas, Kennedy's margin was 46,233 out of 2.3 million votes cast. There could easily have been a shift by as many as 25,000 Texas Negro voters toward Kennedy.[36]

What, then, do the 1960 election returns have to teach us about the requirements for future non-incumbent Democratic Presidential candidates? If a candidate wants to get elected President on the Democratic ticket he had better get many more votes from Catholics, Jews, Negroes, and other groups traditionally providing support for his party than was the case in 1956. If the best he can do is to get 38% of Protestant voters, he had better look for exceedingly strong support from other groups. Common sense suggests that if a candidate can increase his support among Protestants he need not be so dependent upon other groups. As a postscript to Kennedy's victory we might add that it is also advisable to be personally attractive, energetic, photogenic, wealthy, skillful, determined, and to run against Richard Nixon rather than Dwight Eisenhower.

The picture of voters and interest groups we have drawn thus far can be generalized. Presidential elections and election campaigns are events which activate the personal loyalties of voters. The amount of new information about candidates or issues which citizens need in order to participate at the minimal level of voting, or in order to hold casual conversations about the election, is slight, because the political component of their personal identities is reasonably stable and familiar to them. Party loyalty and membership in interest groups provides a short cut to voter preferences, and minimizes the costs of getting information about the specifics of the issues and candidates in any particular election years.

Interest groups act as intermediary agencies that help voters to identify their political preferences quickly—by actively soliciting their members' interest in behalf of specific candidates and parties, and, more importantly, by providing still another anchor to the voter's identity. This helps the voter fix his own position quickly and economically, in what otherwise would be a confusing and contradictory political environment.

PARTIES

A third aspect of the social framework which will help us to account for the strategies of participants in Presidential elections is the nature of political parties in this country. These can best be explained as organizations devoted to maintaining or increasing their own opportunities to exercise political power.

By "political power" we mean the ability to make decisions, or to influence decision-making by governments. Instrumental to this goal is access [37] to those offices and officials legally entitled to make such decisions. Access, in turn, depends in part upon one's participation in staffing the government, either by selecting officials to fill appointive offices (patronage) or by significantly influencing the nomination and election of elected officials. Since elected officials are usually empowered to select appointed officials, access to them is often instrumental to the dispensation of patronage. There are, of course, numerous ways of gaining access to public officials, but the original selection of these officials is the primary avenue of access used by political parties.[38]

At each level of government, the elected chief executive (Mayor, Governor, President) generally has the most political power, and as a result the party organizations depend more upon controlling these offices than on any other source for their political power. In addition, parties are accountable for the activities of chief executives elected under their endorsement. Accountability means that when the party endorses a man, it designates him as its agent before the electorate. The fortunes of the party depend on the success of party candidates. Candidates come and go, but parties and electorates remain. The party organizations, therefore, are quite concerned about selecting suitable officeholders since it is assumed that the actions and identities of these men will in the long run marginally determine the extent and location of the party's appeal within the electorate, and its record of success at the polls.

Just as the party is greatly dependent, at any moment, upon its incumbent officeholders for its political power, these officeholders in turn often have great discretion in the distribution of rewards to the party, and it is expected that they will seek to strengthen themselves within the party organization by the judicious dispensation of favors and patronage. As men who have won office at the head of party tickets, elected chief executives will probably come closer than other individuals to possessing the kinds of control over the party organization that will make it possible for them to impose their own preferences on party organizations.

State party organizations are not simple in their internal

workings. Sometimes elected chief executives run them; sometimes they are run by coalitions of party chieftains representing the local organizations of several large cities or counties. Sometimes party officials and elected officials work cooperatively; sometimes they work at cross purposes. A strong national committeeman in a state party organization whose party, nationally, occupies the Presidency may find his position amplified as *the* avenue of access in the distribution of Federal largesse if there are few elected officeholders in the state with whom he might have to share power. On the other hand, there are instances of Governors who felt their chances of continuing personal victory would improve if they thoroughly disassociated themselves from the party whose label they nominally bore, causing the party organization in the state to shrivel on the vine. A strong party organization, well led, can enforce on an executive choices suitable for the party's purposes that conflict with alternative choices more likely to enhance the executive's position regardless of its effect on the party. Leaders of party organizations are frequently at odds with the party's elected officeholders for a variety of reasons. Many elected officials see their party leaders as potential threats to their positions; many party leaders see the officeholders as ungrateful louts with whom the organization is unfortunately saddled.

Even so, what party leaders ordinarily care about most is getting their men into office and keeping them there. Other considerations are usually secondary. Party leaders are neither for nor against policies in the abstract; they are concerned with policies as means to the ends of officeholding. If new policies help win elections, they are for them; if they help lose elections, they are against them.

Though party leaders try to espouse policies which they believe will enhance their political power and try to avoid very unpopular points of view, this does not mean that they are necessarily indifferent to the substance of policy questions. Because they are more interested and active than most citizens, they also tend to care more about the policies with which they have to deal. In fact, some politicians who hold public office make a specialty of being policy-oriented. At times they may deliberately incur some unpopularity in order to serve their policy preferences, although they are unlikely to go so far as knowingly to lose the election for which they are a candidate. The heavy losses of the Republicans in the 1964 election provides an extreme case, which is instructive in this connection. But in general, party leaders regard policy to a certain extent as a result of an interaction among legitimate political demands —as a bargainable product—and not as an inflexible set of logical or ideological imperatives.[39]

Political parties in America are not organizations with elaborate procedures of membership, dues, and formal organizational structure. They are constituted differently in different localities and exist primarily to make nominations for and elect candidates to a variety of state and local elective offices. They are regulated by state law, and are often quite cohesive up to the state level. But the state parties are joined together nationally only in loose federations. The most obvious indicator of this decentralization is the way the national parties are organized on a geographical basis with the state units as the constituent elements. The state party organizations meet formally by sending delegates to national committee meetings, and most importantly, by coming together at national conventions to nominate a President.[40] They choose their representatives to national party bodies; the national committees and conventions do not choose officers of state parties. In a negative sense, the permanent national party organizations are not in a position to help the state parties; they have neither the funds, nor personnel, nor contacts to contribute substantially to the nomination or election of candidates for Congress or local offices who must run within state boundaries. The operation of the so-called Presidential coattail is problematical:[41] it does not help state parties and candidates who must try to win every year in numerous elections at the state and local level. With all of Richard Nixon's intensive campaigning in the 1970 Congressional elections, for example, the results were probably not significantly different than they would have been without his participation. At best, coattails operate every four years and then only if there happens to be a strong Presidential candidate on the ballot.

The state parties, however, have substantial powers enabling them to share in the making of national policy. Their Representatives and Senators in Washington compete for the distribution of Federal resources and for assignments to advantageous positions on Congressional committees. The states have their own sources of patronage and, through their Congressmen and Senators, a share in Federal patronage. The very circumstance that the states are separate legal entities engenders a drive for autonomy as those who hold places of prestige and profit in the state governments and parties seek to protect their jurisdictions, much as the framers of the Constitution hoped they would. Federalism, however, is much more than a legal fact. The states have great vitality because there are distinct, numerous, and vigorous ethnic, religious, racial, and economic groups that are disproportionately located in specific geographic areas and that demand separate recognition. State organizations, therefore, become infused with the purposes of groups of citizens who use their state parties for the recognition and enhancement of their separate identities and needs. Italians in Rhode Island, Jews and black people in New York, dairy farmers in Wisconsin, wheat growers in Kansas, and many others make the idea of a decentralized party system a living reality.[42] The state parties are composed of different personnel, with somewhat different interests to protect and demands to make. Control over these organizations must be exercised from within each state, since the various states do not control one another, and the national party cannot exercise this control. This, we take it, is the essence of what is meant by a decentralized party system in which power is dispersed among many independent state bodies.

Thus, our national parties are coalitions of state parties which meet every four years for the purpose of finding a man and forging a coalition of interests sufficiently broad to win a majority of electoral votes. This means making a coalition of state parties and party factions—Southern and Northern

Democrats, coastal and Midwestern Republicans—who disagree on some major policy issues. As a result, it is necessary to compromise and, sometimes, to evade issues which would split the parties and lead to drastic losses of support. A man and a set of policies, however, loosely joined, must be found that can blend disparate party elements for the purpose of securing electoral victory.

The major parties, as we have seen, cull their electoral support from somewhat different groups in the population, *But,* no party has a monopoly of support from any of these groups; each party draws significant, and often indispensable, support from almost all the categories.[43] How could Republicans hope to win without some support from wage earners, or Democrats without some votes from business and professional people? The parties are sufficiently variegated to draw support from many quarters. In a close election the ability of a party to increase its support within one group from, say, 20% to 30% may be crucial, even though that group still votes overwhelmingly for the opposition. The strategic implications of these remarks color all of national campaign politics: the parties try to do things which will keep happy the groups consistently allied to them without alienating other groups unduly.

Thus the temptation for parties to avoid specific policy commitments in many areas is very great. The American population is so extraordinarily varied—crisscrossed by numerous economic, religious, ethnic, racial, sectional, and occupational ties—that it is exceedingly difficult to guess at the total distribution of policy preferences in the population at any one time, except for questions that have already been settled between the parties like Social Security and unemployment compensation. It is even more difficult to predict how these aggregations of actual and potential interest groups might react to shifts in party policy positions, and still more hazardous to prophesy what different policy commitments might do to the margin of votes required for victory. This pervasive problem of uncertainty makes the calculation of gain from policy positions both difficult and risky and suggests that the self-interests of the parties and candidates in keeping office might best be served by vague, ambiguous, or contradictory policy statements which will be least likely to offend anyone. The advantages of vagueness on policy are strengthened by the facts that the vast majority of citizens are not interested in policy or are narrowly focused on a few things, and that only a few groups in the population demand many specific policy commitments from their parties and candidates.

Yet, despite all this, political leaders and parties do make policy commitments which are often surprisingly precise, specific, and logically consistent. Thus, we must consider not only why the parties sometimes blur and avoid commitments on issues, but also why they often commit themselves to policies more than their interest in acquiring or retaining office would appear to require.

Part of the answer may arise from the fact that the parties serve slightly different functions for their own activists than for people who vote but are otherwise largely disengaged from politics. Party activists are people who are much more interested in politics and attentive to political issues than the general population is. The interest and attentiveness of political activists leads them to formulate and elaborate political opinions and preferences. Their desires to make these preferences internally consistent and consistent with the preferences of the party of their choice and the mutual reinforcement of activist opinions when activists interact with one another would certainly lead to demands upon the party leadership for policy positions which are reasonably clear and forthright.[44]

There are notable differences between the parties in the social identities of party activists. Activist Democrats are far more likely to come from working-class backgrounds; activist Republicans, on the other hand, are disproportionately middle class. These differences may be reflected in the noticeable tendencies for the two parties to support policies intended to benefit the members of the social strata from which their active members are drawn.[45]

The interest groups most closely allied with each party also make policy demands upon them which must be met to some extent. While it is true that voters are generally disinterested in specific policies, interest group leaders and their paid bureaucracies are manifestly concerned. If they feel that the interests they represent are being harmed, they may inform their members or even go so far as to withdraw support from the party at a particular election. Should voters find that groups with which they identify are opposed to the party with which they identify, they may temporarily support the opposition party, or they may withdraw from participation and not vote at all. Consequently, the party finds that it risks losing elections by ignoring the demands of interest groups. Since the demands of many of these groups conflict, however, the parties have no choice but to mediate among them, hoping to strike compromises which, though they give no one group everything, give something to as many groups as they can.

Finally, throughout the years the opposing political parties have become identified with somewhat different policies. When new candidates arise they may bring with them somewhat new policy preferences. But there are bound to be many areas of policy on which they are not informed or do not have strong preferences. In such cases the existing set of policies traditionally associated with the parties provides the candidates with a useful economizing device. They can accept the going positions and concentrate on the policies which they may wish to revise, supplant, or present anew. This tack is bound to be popular with the party faithful who have been brought up on the rallying cries of the past, who have learned to prefer what their party prefers, and who respond with vigor and enthusiasm to the cues provided by mention of their party's chief stocks in trade. Just as voters commonly use parties as a means of cutting their information costs on issues and candidates, and activists use them as reference groups, so may candidates use the parties' traditional policy positions to ease their burden of calculation.

Political parties today, however, are not as reliable guideposts for their candidates as they once were. For the past thirty years the New Deal structured the nature of political conflict in the United States. Those who were for or against a greater role for the Federal government, for or against public or private power, for or against medical care for the aged and a host of other issues knew immediately where they stood. When the Republicans nominated Barry Goldwater, however, huge Democratic majorities were elected in both houses of Congress, and the 89th Congress effectively enacted the agenda of the New Deal. Both of these episodes sharply altered the content of partisan conflict at the national level. Since then new issues have arisen in bewildering profusion and new groups have come to public attention, clamoring to determine the shape of public policy. It is no longer clear that Republicans stand for local control and Democrats for central direction. Issues from pollution of the environment to law and order have not yet taken on firm identification with either of the major political parties. Hence there is more fluidity in political life, more leeway for the Presidential nominees to set their party's course, and less opportunity for them to rely on the past policy positions associated with their respective parties.

NEW PARTY ACTIVISTS: PURISTS VS. PROFESSIONALS

Through the efforts of journalists like Theodore H. White and Jules Witcover, more and more is known with each passing election about the goals and maneuvers of political leaders. Correspondingly impressive work has been done—mostly by academic survey researchers—on the attitudes and political views of the voting masses. Much less, however, is known about the people in between who have played such important roles in the last two presidential elections. What motivates these people to become politically active? We have noted some of the things which are important to regular party workers, and some of the traditional appeals that are made by and to them; doubtless there is a great variety of reasons which drew them into political activity originally and continues to draw them year after year. But hundreds of new recruits to political activity seem to have been made by the candidacies of Barry Goldwater in 1964 and Eugene McCarthy in 1968. Were these

new activists likely to remain in the years to come, joining the
ranks of party workers? Or would they fade like the "morning glories" that Plunkitt of Tammany Hall long ago observed
in the New York reform movement? Because the requisite
work has never been done, it is impossible to do more than
guess at the staying power of new activists in national politics,
but their influence over the short run is quite impressive. The
presence of a large number of activists with intense personal
loyalties is an important resource which a candidate can to
some degree substitute for money, incumbency, or years of
party service.

Obviously, Goldwater and McCarthy recruits are not similar
in every way. They certainly do not agree about the substance
of governmental policy, at least on most issues.

Goldwater's supporters captured their party machinery and
then lost roundly at the polls, while McCarthy supporters were
at their strongest in the various state primaries, but had little
luck in their party convention. But the similarities between
the two groups are also striking, as we discovered by conducting interviews with numerous Goldwater and McCarthy delegates at the 1964 and 1968 conventions. The same concerns,
the same perceptions of their man and his opponents, recur
again and again, arguing that what we have in the presence
of these new activists is a phenomenon which is not best seen
as a matter of right versus left, or organization versus anti-
organization, but rather in terms of political purists (found
among both the Goldwater *and* McCarthy people) versus professional politicians.

Whatever their disagreements on specific policies, left- and
right-wing activists both excoriate the immorality of men
in office. These political purists consider the stock in trade
of the politician—compromise and bargaining, conciliating the
opposition, bending a little to capture public support—to be
hypocritical; their style relies on the announcement of principles and on moral crusades. Since it is difficult to make
public policy or to win elections without compromising one's
self in some way, there is an understandable tendency for purist political leaders to adopt a highly critical view of the main

activities of American politics. Politicians have been accused of many things; until now it has not been usual to accuse them of wishing to lose elections. But perhaps in specifying only the paramount goal of winning, we have been taking a narrow view of the matter. Interviews held with Goldwater delegates to the Republican Convention of 1964 and with McCarthy delegates to the Democratic Convention of 1968 illustrate this problem.[46]

One Goldwater delegate said: "The delegates are for Goldwater because they agree with his philosophy of government. That's what you people will never understand—we're committed to his whole approach." He was undoubtedly correct. There was a remarkable fit between Goldwater and a substantial majority of his followers. What they liked about Goldwater, however, was not merely or even primarily his policy positions but rather his "approach," his style of operation. When we asked Goldwater delegates to tell us what they most liked about their candidate only a few mentioned his position on the issues, and those who did were content with brief references to constitutional principles like state's rights.

By far the most frequent delegate characterization of Goldwater referred to his consistency, honesty, integrity, and willingness to stick by principles.[47] It was not so much his principles (though these were undoubtedly important) but the belief that he would stick to them that counted most with his supporters. "He can be trusted." "He is straightforward." "He does not compromise." "He doesn't pander to the public; he's against expediency." "He is frank." "He has courage." "He stands up for what he believes." "He won't play footsie with the people." "He votes his convictions when he knows he's right." "He doesn't go along with the crowd." "He meets issues head-on." "Goldwater speaks about things others avoid. Most politicians like to avoid issues." "He keeps promises." "He doesn't change his mind." "He is not confused." As one of Goldwater's supporters perceptively observed, "He's different from most politicians." And so were most of Goldwater's followers different from most politicians.

Many Goldwater delegates held attitudes quite different from those characteristic of American politicians. We can refer to these delegates as "purists"—political activists whose attitudes about politics have strongly moralistic overtones. Here is an example. This Goldwater purist was a delegate from a rural area in Pennsylvania attending his first convention.

Interviewer: What qualities should a Presidential candidate have?

Delegate: Moral integrity.

I.: Should he be able to win the election?

D.: No; principles are more important. I would rather be one against 20,000 and believe I was right. That's what I admire about Goldwater. He's like that.

I.: Are most politicians like that?

D.: No, unfortunately.

I.: What do you like about Goldwater?

D.: I am in sympathy with many of his philosophies of government, but I like him personally for his moral integrity. I always believed that a candidate should carry out his promises. Scranton didn't do that. But now, for the first time in my life, we have a candidate who acts as he believes. He doesn't change his position when it is expedient.

I.: Do you think that if the party loses badly in November it ought to change its principles?

D.: No. I'm willing to fight for these principles for ten years if we don't win.

I.: For fifty years?

D.: Even fifty years.

I.: Do you think it's better to compromise a little to win than to lose and not compromise?

D.: I had this problem in my district. After we fighters had won [the nomination for] the Congressional seat the local [Republican] machine offered to make a deal: they wouldn't oppose our candidate if we didn't oppose theirs. I refused, because I didn't see how I could make a deal with the men I'd been opposing two years ago for the things they did. So I lost, and I could have won easily. I've thought about it many times, because if I had agreed I could have done some good at least. But I don't believe that I should compromise one inch from what I believe deep down inside.

At this same convention an observer remarked, "I've talked to some of the California delegates, and I don't understand them at all; they talk like they don't care if we win." In a sense he was wrong, because the delegates desperately wanted Goldwater to win. But our informant was essentially correct in the sense that these delegates cared more about maintaining their purity—"I would rather lose and be right" —than about winning. The essential element of this style is a devotion to principles, especially the principle that men in politics should have, maintain, and cherish their principles.

When asked why they entered politics, Goldwater delegates often answered, "For the same reason as any man—principles." When asked if the party should change some of its policies if Goldwater lost badly, the delegates responded by reiterating their devotion to principles. "God, no. These are American principles; these are what we stand for." "No, we want a clear party which will represent principles to the people." "I'd rather stick by the real principles this country was built on than win. Popularity isn't important; prestige isn't important; it's the principles that matter."

Here we begin to see the distinguishing characteristics of the purists: their emphasis on internal criteria for decision, on what they believe "deep down inside"; their rejection of compromise; their lack of orientation toward winning; their stress on the style and purity of decision—integrity, consistency, adherence to internal norms.

The professionals looked at politics quite differently. Here is a California delegate strongly for Goldwater, with more than fifteen years in party work, attending his third Republican Convention.

Interviewer: You seem different from many of the Goldwater supporters. How would you characterize your position in comparison with them?

Delegate: Yes, I'm more practical. I realize you have to live together. For example, I'm going up now to a meeting of the California Republican committee and we've got to handle a liberal candidate and an ultra-conservative. I'm going to urge them to accept the liberal because we've got to work together. We [the Republicans] are a minority party in California and we can't afford to squabble amongst ourselves. The art of politics is the art of compromise. If I can get a whole loaf, I'll take it. If not, I'll take half rather than lose it all.

I.: What would Goldwater do about the Cuban situation?

D.: Well, it's there now, and we'll just have to live with it.

I.: The Berlin Wall?

D.: He won't tear it down; I know him very well.

I.: Social Security?

D.: We've had it for a long time. It's part of our system. That's something some of these Goldwater people don't realize. They're a new breed and sort of naive on things like this. They think you can suddenly shift the whole range of government to the right. What they don't realize is that you can only bend a little back away from the left.

I.: What if Goldwater loses by a landslide?

D.: Well, I don't think that will happen.

I.: Suppose it does?

D.: Well, then, maybe the people aren't ready for a change. . . . Yes, we'll have to try to change, maybe a little more toward the liberal side.

Although professionals like this delegate put a high premium on popularity with the electorate, there were things that even they would not do and ways they would not prefer to win. A Scranton delegate, in politics for many years in Philadelphia, pointed out that in his white, upper-class ward he and his party had benefited from a white backlash issue in a local election. "But we don't want that; that divides the country. We don't want whites and blacks to fight; it's not good for the country."A New Jersey delegate with many years of political experience did not really like any of the candidates for the nomination and feared that the party would fare badly at the polls if Goldwater were nominated. Yet he felt that things could happen: "a white backlash building up if the Negroes have a lot of big demonstrations in the cities; or if Vietnam blew up in our faces. But I'd rather lose than have those things happen. I'd rather lose than have race fights or war."

One great difference between the purists and the professionals lay in what they considered valid grounds for preferring not to win. The professionals emphasized specific unfortunate consequences, such as race riots and war. The purists emphasized departures from internal principles—such as consistency, integrity, and standing firm—held by their party leaders. The professionals were oriented toward what might happen to other people, the purists toward their own consciences.

If it comes as something of a surprise to discover that even to Goldwater partisans the man who promised "a choice, not an echo" was seen as offering more a choice of style than of issues, it is more of a surprise to find that the analysis can be extended to McCarthy delegates. One major issue—the Vietnam war—was the galvanizing force for the McCarthy campaign, and nearly every piece of literature distributed by McCarthy supporters dealt also with a variety of urban issues, but the "new politics" about which one heard when interviewing delegates seemed long on the principles and conscience of the candidate (and his followers) but short on issue content. For many followers of Senator McCarthy there would be no point in taking over the Democratic party if it were to become just like it was in the past. There had to be a new politics to give life to a new party. But no one was successful in defining what that new politics might be. It had to do with enlisting greater citizen participation in public affairs. There was talk about democratizing party procedures. Aside from avoiding future Vietnams, however, there was little specific content to give substance to the future polity. Our interviews suggest that the meaning of the new politics lay not in substance but in style, not in policies but in people, not in what McCarthy did but in what his actions symbolized for his followers.

McCarthy's great attraction was his political style. From the comments of his supporters he emerges as the antithesis of the unscrupulous politician who changes his views on public policy in order to curry favor with the electorate. He opposed the Vietnam war before it was politically popular to do so. He is pictured as a man outside the ordinary political framework who holds the morally bankrupt politicians to account. When asked why they liked McCarthy, his supporters would say, "He's sincere and honest. He opposed the war in the primaries, and he's not a bullshitter."

Since McCarthy's integrity was his stock in trade, his supporters were concerned that he remain pure at all times. Many of his supporters eagerly assured us that "McCarthy wouldn't sell out. He wouldn't compromise. He won't accept the Vice Presidency with Humphrey." On hearing McCarthy say that he would support neither Humphrey or Nixon, a delegate leaped up and cried out, "What a man! What a man! What guts he has!" Telling established powers where to go was dear to the hearts of McCarthy men. This style went beyond McCarthy, as could be seen in a delegate's comment about the Democratic candidate for Senator from Ohio: "I like what Gilligan has done, more or less saying to organized labor, 'To hell with you.'"

The McCarthy people wanted very much to win, but only on their terms; they had no desire to fight their fight and then fall into line behind Hubert Humphrey for a November Democratic victory. One of the most revealing outcomes of our interviews was the insight it gave into the extraordinarily high sense of political efficacy manifested by the McCarthy forces. Their work at the local level convinced them that the regular party was terribly weak and they were amazingly strong. They were young and energetic and the party regulars were old and tired. Probing the personal experience of McCarthy delegates generated many stories like this one: "Humphrey's organization is an empty shell. I found that out when I ran against these people for committeeman for my township. I won two-to-one with the help of the kids. I wish I were your age. What a political future there is for young people."

The McCarthy people believed that the era of a "new politics," built on youth, the poor, plus all those who believed in disengagement abroad and tackling problems at home, was at hand, and all that remained was to offer a candidate who would put this coalition together. Secure in their vision of future triumph, the McCarthy delegates knew what would happen after Hubert Humphrey was nominated. "First off," a typical McCarthy delegate predicted, "a crashing and complete defeat this fall. And I'm glad of that. Get rid of a lot of deadwood. Then we can really take over."

The same emphasis on internal criteria for decision, the same rejection of compromise, the same absence of an orientation toward winning, the same stress on style and purity—all are there.

For the McCarthy people, the young are the hope of the

future because they represent a counterweight to the elements traditionally strong in the Democratic party. Observe how delegates in California and Ohio made young people the engine for gaining party control.

In the last few years, with the waning of the power of the Young Democrats and the California Democratic Council, and even organized labor, which I think is overestimated, the real power has been the big money men. Savings and Loans, wealthy men, have become very powerful; some are liberal, others are not, but they are all powerful because they have a lot of money. The kids could offset their influence—and they still can; I hope that Humphrey's nomination won't drive them out.

The party is controlled by people with money and the moneymakers that operate through the party. The Republican Party in the late 19th century was too often a business venture for people who wanted to make a buck. The Democratic Party is too much like that right now. For instance, I could name you fifty people in Ohio politics who are there only to help their business. So the party is in bad shape this year, because there is a sudden swell of young people coming in who are interested in principles and in issues.

Democratic professionals, not surprisingly, looked askance at this whole development. To the regular delegates with long years of service the McCarthy supporters were like spoiled children, an analogy party regulars themselves used several times: "The McWhinnies [McCarthy supporters] are like little boys with marbles: you don't play by their rules—they want to break up the game."

Party regulars insisted that the party was the domain of adults, and in the adult world norms of apprenticeship are observed. But youth is not only a matter of chronological age; delegates saw it also as a question of whether one takes a short- or long-run perspective on party affairs. Consider the views of a 27-year-old committeeman. His understanding of party politics is that "this is just one inning of a long game. One goes into politics to increase one's influence over decisions, but that takes time. If one doesn't win one year, [he] can try again the next year. People that jump in and out don't understand this basic fact of political involvement." He was saying that McCarthy supporters should wait their turn and that he did not expect them to stay in politics. "They just came out of the woodwork this year," he observed, "and now they'll go back." Because they were never really in the party, never served their apprenticeship, the McCarthy people were judged by regulars as not important to it. "Many of them are under 21 and can't vote anyway. A lot of whooping and hollering doesn't matter much."

The regulars confessed to being hurt and bewildered when faced with demands for immediate access to positions of party power. "The party structure is always open to people who are interested in working," said one party loyalist. "It's just that we have a sort of seniority system like Congress; those who make the most contribution get the largest say in what we do. That's only fair." Those who do most for the party are those who worked their way up from the bottom. "The problem," as one Humphrey delegate viewed it, "is that while the McCarthy kids want into the party they want in at the top. They aren't interested in the status which the beginner usually gets licking envelopes and things like that, which we did, all of us, when we were coming up."

The norm of apprenticeship means more than just telling newcomers they have to wait their turn; it is based on years of struggle and sacrifice for the party. "I worked for the coal company for 18 years," said a man who served his party for five decades. "But when I put my hat in the ring for Democratic councilman, I was thrown out of my job by the coal company who controlled everything in town." Another old timer recalls that it cost him a "fortune to fight the vested interests . . . to build a Democratic Party. . . . I was running a trucking company, and they attacked me by revoking the license. They spread rumors against me. There were protests even within my family. You should tell the young people who are demonstrating that they are not the first people to try to change things." The feeling that youth gave no credit to their personal hardships rankles these party regulars. "My son, who is 17, takes all the advantages of the affluent society for granted. He does not realize what we went through to get them for him." "In my day," an old timer said, "your father told you what to vote. Nowadays it's your son who tells you how to vote."

Over and over again party regulars contended that McCarthy supporters would not retain their party strength because they were one-issue types. If the Vietnam war were over they would leave because they got what they wanted and if the war continued they would desert the party because their policy had been defeated.

It would be difficult to overemphasize the importance of loyalty to the party faithful. This is not, as their detractors would have it, a mere question of unthinking obedience. Nor is it, as the more sophisticated regulars would say, a matter of the requirements of effective party organization. Party loyalists identified themselves with the party and the party with the nation. "The Democratic Party is the people," they said. "The Democratic Party is the real majority party."

The McCarthyite challenge, it must be understood, was quite different than the assault of the Kennedy forces on the bastions of party power. The Kennedy people (those who would have supported Robert Kennedy had he lived) were young in years but not in adherence to party norms. They impugned neither the party nor its activists. When the Kennedys challenged the party regulars in 1960, they told the party men to deal with them or be run over. However distasteful the prospect, the party loyalists understood the danger and could accommodate themselves to it. They made adjustments, and the party continued along familiar lines. The McCarthy forces, however, said that the party was not good and its regulars were even worse.

When a person believes that the Democratic party in and for itself is an important institution, that "without the Democratic Party you would never get any good policies," it is difficult for him to understand how people who profess to belong to the party could willfully hurt its electoral chances. If you came of age in the depression years of the 1930's when the Democratic party meant hope and progress and even life, the idea of abandoning its candidates is virtually incomprehensible.

This wounded air of outrage was expressed by a Humphrey delegate from New York who asserted his unswerving loyalty: "I would never support a fourth party. I will work energetically for the ticket whatever it is. McCarthy people won't tell you that. [They] will only elect Republicans. Is that what they want? I just don't know about them; they say they are liberals, but they hurt the party. It just doesn't make any sense." Another delegate—"you can classify me as an old-line, hard-core party man"—said that "I could talk for two hours as to why I prefer Humphrey, but I'll tell you something that is a deciding factor: McCarthy's disloyal because he won't support the ticket." For delegates who believe that the Democratic party is the American people, an attempt by others to orient that party to a whole new constituency, and concomitant argument that it is the Democratic party which blots out the voice of the American people, are not going to sit well.

The charge that McCarthyites would leave the party at the end of the Vietnam war had broad ramifications. It was tied to the belief that successful party activity required an adult ability to live with disappointment. "In politics you win and lose," a party regular commented, "sometimes mostly lose. But you can't give up, you must keep at it." The McCarthy "kids" did not have what it takes, the regular asserted, because they played the political game like little children who quit the "football team after losing one game."

The predominant focus of the McCarthy forces on the issue of the war in Vietnam was widely seen as preventing the normal give-and-take through which internal party differences should be resolved. When many issues are at stake, support for one can be traded for help on another. When issues are strung out over a period of time, early losses may be accepted as the price for later gains. According to exponents of party unity, McCarthy's men "pursue the single issue so hard that they become intolerant." A single issue of overriding importance at a specific moment in time breaks party solidarity.

The belief in compromise and bargaining; the sense that public policy is made in small steps rather than big leaps; the concern with conciliating the opposition and broadening public appeal; and the willingness to bend a little to capture public support are all characteristic of the traditional American politician.

Emphasizing Differences

An important component of the Goldwater style was the guiding principle that the parties ought to be different. The maintenance of wide and sharp differences between the parties was seen as a fundamental purpose of engaging in politics. As an enthusiastic woman from New Jersey put it, "I think everything should be an issue, civil rights should be an issue, Cuba should be an issue. This is the first time a campaign will be on issues; I think it's wonderful. It's just terrible the way personality has been in politics, like Kennedy winning on his hair and teeth and Nixon losing because there was a shadow on his chin. . . . It's ridiculous."

Hence when Goldwater supporters were asked whether they should balance the ticket with a liberal as Vice-President, they replied: "We don't want a blurred image, we've been a 'me-too' party for too long. We want to take a clear position." If, in order to provide clear differences between the parties, the Republicans lost, that was all right. For "even if the party loses at least we have presented a clear alternative to the people. At least we'll have a strong party." What is meant by "strong"? "Cohesive, united on principles." The chorus of Goldwater purists rose to a crescendo when they insisted, in almost identical words, "We don't want to become a 'me-too' party; we don't want to be the same as the Democrats." There is a definite possibility, therefore, that, if they had been offered accommodations or compromises on issues, they would have rejected them because they wanted to be different.

The ideal party of the Goldwater purists was not merely a conservative party; it was a distinct and separate community of co-believers who differ with the opposition party all down the line. To this extent their style merges with that of the liberal Democratic reformers in some cities who wish to see the parties represent clear and opposing alternatives

and to gain votes only through appeals based on policy differences rather than on such "irrational" criteria as personality,
party identification, or ethnic status.[48] But the Goldwater
purists went even further in their willingness to cast aside
whole groups of voters who did not agree with them. "We
won't get Negro votes anyway, so there's no point in trying."
They can vote for the other party for all I care." "We won't
change our principles just to get a few votes from Negroes."
In the same spirit, Barry Goldwater suggested that people
who favored the kind of government the United States has had
since 1932 should not vote for him.

For the professionals, the desire to win is intimately connected with the belief that a political party should try to get as
much support from as many diverse groups as possible. In
describing the qualities a Presidential candidate should have, a
professional would say, "He should be diplomatic. He should be
able to gather support from a lot of groups underneath him.
That's what Eisenhower had, that's what Kennedy had, and
that's what Johnson has. You know there's one thing about
politics, there's no such thing as second place, you don't get
anything for coming in second."

Hence the professionals were concerned with the possible
loss of a substantial part of the small Negro vote they had
received in the past. "You just can't go around throwing away
votes. The object of a party is to draw voters together to the
party, not to push them away." A delegate from Philadelphia
was more specific. He had "nothing personal against Goldwater" but feared that if Goldwater were to run "we'll get the
hell kicked out of us. We've been out of [state] power for ten
or twelve years. Now we're getting some of the Polish vote
and the Italians don't treat us too bad. The Jews and the
Negroes go about 75% against us, but at least we get part of
the Negro vote and that helps us hold the line in the state
generally."

To their dichotomous view of political parties and their belief
that issue preferences are the only moral way to choose between the parties, the Goldwater purists added a strong desire
to simplify political choice: a party for the growth of govern-

ment and a party against; a party which believes in standing up to the enemy and one which believes in appeasement; a party which believes in private initiative and one which wishes to stifle it; a party of free enterprise and a party of socialism. The desire to dichotomize and simplify found expression in ways of locating political supporters and opponents. Perhaps the most charming example came from a California delegate who expressed the wish to see all liberals in the East and all conservatives in the West. Presumably then, if one knew where a man came from, one could immediately discern his political tendency. Many delegates voiced the desire to divide friend from foe by simple criteria and then do joyous battle.

In addition to their emphasis on making the public decide about a variety of foreign and domestic issues, there was a very practical reason for McCarthy delegates to emphasize differences—they needed a way of breaking up the Humphrey coalition. The Goldwaterites had come into their convention four years earlier as at least the clear plurality faction, and the differences they emphasized were largely with the other party. Hubert Humphrey came into the 1968 Democratic Convention as the clear favorite, however, and therefore the differences that the McCarthy forces emphasized had to be differences, real or imagined, between themselves and Humphrey. In their attempt to do this, they attempted to challenge the credentials of nearly half of all state delegations, and conducted a floor fight over the Vietnam plank of the platform.

The division which they created which was most indigestible for party regulars, however, was one that was intimately linked with the question of "the new politics"—youth versus age.

McCarthy people saw themselves as the wave of the future. The McCarthyites claimed they understood the changes that are taking place in America and their opponents did not. "We know what's on the news programs. The Humphrey people don't." Their knowledge of emergent conditions provided McCarthy's supporters with an important link to youth. "The kids are part of what's happening. Like us, they see the changes that have to be made."

The supporters of Senator McCarthy accepted with considerable pride the charge that they were new to the party. Youth and newness were, to them, indications that they would inherit control of the Democratic party. "To the extent that the party draws on youth," a delegate said, "it ensures its position as the party of the future."

The confidence of McCarthy forces in eventually gaining control of the Democratic party rested squarely on the idea of youth. They were the new men to whom the party would belong. They would make use of the energies of youth—new ideas and young bodies—to revitalize the party and bring it to victory. Whenever supporters of Senator McCarthy talked about giving youth its rightful voice or the danger of youth leaving the party, they meant that *they* must be given a dominant voice and *they* must not be compelled to leave the party. "The big change in the country," McCarthy delegates insisted, "is the rising youth interest in government and their own destiny. The Democratic Party better wake up to this or it will be in real trouble."

One possibility that McCarthy delegates considered as it became clear that their credentials challenges, their Vietnam plank, and their candidate for the nomination would fail, was the alternative of starting a fourth party splinter movement. Many delegates spoke interchangeably about the influx of new McCarthy people and of youth into the party as vehicles for change in party control. The great question was whether they should seek to make the Democratic party "young" or try to build a fourth party made up of "youth" like them.

McCarthy's followers were certainly not tempted to remain in the Democratic party by their attraction to the candidacy of Hubert Humphrey. Only about one out of four of those we interviewed would even suggest that he might consider supporting Humphrey in the election. The Vice-President's position on the Vietnam war was unacceptable. He reeked of party regularity. As a delegate put it, "I feel like a party hack just saying I might vote for him." These views were reinforced by the scars of internal party conflict that McCarthy delegates had picked up in the pre-convention period. "I dislike the regular party types," a McCarthy activist reported. "They are immoral and fought in a petty fashion in Long Island. We had a hard time even getting registration lists."

Despite their evident unwillingness to support the party's nominee for President, however, many of the McCarthy people had no intention of leaving the Democratic party. Some delegates were tempted to leave but they could not stand the thought of indirectly helping Richard Nixon get elected President of the United States. "This is a tough one. Yes, I would work for a fourth party. This answer troubles me because it means Nixon would get in. Change that—I'd say no, I wouldn't work for a fourth party." Other McCarthy supporters were kept in the party by their ability to work for a local candidate. Question: Would you support a fourth party? "I doubt it. I am a Democrat. I will work for [Paul] O'Dwyer [running for the Senate from New York] this year." Senator McCarthy's refusal to endorse a fourth party movement undoubtedly had great influence with his followers. "Gene says no." By far the most important reason McCarthy people had for rejecting a fourth party, however, was that they expected to take over the party themselves.

THE PRIVATIZATION OF POLITICS: SEMI-PERMANENT OPPOSITION

We may sum up the purist style by saying that it represents a virtually complete privatization of politics. The private conscience of the leader—rather than his public responsibilities—becomes the focal point of politics. Internal criteria—possession of, devotion to, and standing up for private principles—become the standards of political judgment. Constituents disappear, and we are left with a political leader determining policy on the basis of compatibility with his private principles. From this perspective we can better understand why Goldwater voted against the Civil Rights Act of 1964 despite his agreement with the view that the race issue should not become a matter of political partisanship. Goldwater's conscience dictated that he vote against an Act which contained two sections that he believed violated the Constitution. Although he knew that the Act would pass anyway, he was simply unwilling to sacrifice his private conscience in order to achieve what he agreed was the public good. Nor would he or his supporters agree to make rather innocuous concessions in the civil rights plank of the Republican platform in order to placate Negroes because that would have suggested compromise; and compromise suggests that one has not stuck to one's principles. Once the platform became identified as a Goldwater platform, presumably derived from careful scrutiny of conscience, it became a matter of principle not to permit any alteration whatsoever, even if this refusal to compromise meant rejecting important segments of the party.

Conspicuously missing from purist thought is any consideration of the voters. The political party is defined entirely without reference to the people who would have to vote for it. To be sure, the purists believed that there was a hidden Republican vote, and they fully expected a huge upsurge of support as these Americans discovered that a party embracing their most cherished principles had at last appeared on the scene. But the "real Republican party," as they were fond of calling it, did not have to be summoned by vulgar pandering for votes. It stood on its principles. It did not change to attract votes. Voters would be attracted to it when people changed.

One can see the privatization of politics at work when Goldwater delegates expressed their feelings about President Johnson and former President Eisenhower. Extremely hostile feelings were voiced about both men because they were seen as traditional politicians, given to compromise. Goldwater's castigation of Johnson as a "faker," for example, was regarded by the delegates interviewed as accurate and appropriate. "Originally and historically," a delegate told us, "Johnson was a conservative, but he's willing to do things, to change to stay in power. This shows weakness of character."

The purists did not think it appropriate for a man to act differently as President than as Senator: if a public official need consult only his private conscience, of course, there should be little change in his actions in different offices. If Johnson acted differently in the two offices this could only be because "he has no principles. L.B.J. is a consummate politician. He is inconsistent and immoral." Goldwater was different: "He doesn't talk from both sides of his mouth."

If the essence of politics is to be found in the relationship between leaders and their principles rather than between leaders and constituents, one would ask quite different questions and give much different answers to queries about the positions taken by candidates. When we asked delegates about Goldwater's position on racial matters, the purists would always respond by saying that Goldwater himself was not bigoted. They knew the exact percentage of employees in the Goldwater department store in Phoenix who were non-Caucasians and pointed with pride to this statistic as evidence of their candidate's favorable disposition toward Negroes. There was no mention of what Goldwater might do as President; there was no understanding that the public role of a Presidential aspirant might be of interest. The Negro delegates we interviewed, to be sure, could not have cared less about Goldwater's personal predilections. They wanted to know what he would do for Negroes in his capacity as President of the United States. That Goldwater shared his supporters' perspective became evident during the campaign when he asked if Negroes would not rather have a President who dealt with race relations as a matter of conscience than as a political football. Since political action is a major method of redressing Negro grievances, it is not surprising that Goldwater failed to get his conscience accepted as a substitute for favorable Presidential action.

Goldwaterite activists brought with them a purist stance in which the leader's attachment to private moral values took precedence over political agreement on feasible public policy. Goldwater as a Senator had been in nearly total opposition to presidential activism and liberalism on the part of President Kennedy and even President Eisenhower; indices of liberalism and conservatism usually gave him a "perfect" conservative score.

McCarthy people had much the same things to say about

President Johnson four years later. Like the Goldwaterites, they assumed that character, not role, determined behavior; just as McCarthy had been an early and unbending opponent of the war in Vietnam, now that he might need to build a national coalition in order to accomplish anything as President he would not be less unbending.

It should be clear by now that a central part of McCarthy's appeal to his style-oriented followers was that he did not act like a politician. He wrote poems, he was too reflective, he was too frank, he refused to bargain. He would not make the traditional gesture of supporting the party's nominee after he had lost. He attracted the political innocents rather than the worldly. His followers took all this as a sign that he was, like themselves, an outsider to the party who refused to become just another politician.

Yet the aspects of McCarthy's style that appeared attractive in a candidate led many delegates to wonder whether they were appropriate in a President. A Kennedy man insisted that "Presidents have to exercise power, not just pick flowers." There was no doubt about McCarthy's personal appeal, but as one respondent put it, he was "lacking in—I want to choose this word carefully—dynamics. He looks as if he were President somebody would steal the gavel away from him before he had a chance to use it."

McCarthy's supporters recognized that he might have difficulty in acting like the powerful Presidents of the past. Those whose affection for him was greatest wondered whether it was fair to send him out into the cruel political world. But in the end, the style-oriented McCarthyites consoled themselves with the thought that they did not want their candidate to be like other Presidents. He would raise their self-esteem instead of his own. If there were a new breed of party activists, why shouldn't McCarthy be a new kind of President? The fact that his devotion to internal conscience rather than constituents, coalitions, or even, in the end, his own followers,[49] plus pronouncements about the need for less Presidential initiative, might make him the first true conservative President in 40 years, did not seem to receive serious consideration.

The contention by McCarthy's followers that McCarthy's style is part of a trend in American political life is supported by an interesting finding: contrary to what we would expect, numerous polls reveal that approximately twenty percent of those who supported Senator McCarthy during the primaries ended up voting for Governor Wallace.[50] In what ways might Wallace and McCarthy, despite their vast differences appear to be similar? Perhaps voters who were disgusted with the major parties were attracted to leaders outside the system who stood up for what they believed and told off people in power. Wallace, who had no hopes in the regular political system, castigated the major parties for failing to represent citizens who were opposed to growing lawlessness and compulsory integration; McCarthy, who hoped to reconvert the Democratic party, blasted its leaders for failing to meet the aspirations of the young. Neither man had use for the people in control of party decisions. For much the same reasons the supporters of Barry Goldwater found his purist stance—no bargaining, compromise or pandering for votes—especially attractive as they attacked the Eastern "Establishment" of the Republican party. No one is suggesting that McCarthy, Goldwater and Wallace are perfectly equivalent, but they do share a common characteristic that gives them appeal to people for whom the ordinary processes of political adjustment have become distasteful.

Where Goldwater sought to save a fundamentally sound political system by bearing witness to its potential purity, however, McCarthy took the position of an outsider who was in semi-permanent opposition to it. He apparently sensed the impatience of his followers with normal politics and yet knew that he must at times take an active position within existing political institutions. So he talked of basic changes in political processes but moved into action only when this consisted of a form of opposition.

McCarthy's style may best be appraised through an understanding of his followers. He did not find them, they adopted him when he expressed willingness to make opposition to the war in Vietnam an issue in Democratic primaries. McCarthy's followers liked him best when he attacked the "Establishment" or led a moral crusade. They wanted him untainted, so he had to be careful about the company he kept and the commitments he made. This must have been what was meant by commentators who explained that McCarthy did not endorse Humphrey after the nomination because he "couldn't."

This style of what we have called "semi-permanent opposition" springs from the privatization of politics, for to such an opposition, coalition building in order to win ceases to be important. Thus the legitimacy of the American political system comes under attack. Such attacks change the incentives for public activity and political leadership. If a politician fails in the difficult task of organizing disparate coalitions to support social legislation, he has little to show for his labors. If he succeeds, he may be told that he has not accomplished anything worth doing. This suggests a situation where whatever the "Establishment" does is by definition small and inconsequential; in that case the only way of knowing whether a policy is significant is that it does not gather support.

The greater the attack on the legitimacy of the political system, the less the willingness to accept responsibility for it. The greater the rejection of modest improvements in favor of wholesale changes, the less the ability of the political system to meet these requirements. Indeed, the more requirements are stated in stylistic terms, the less it is possible to know whether they have been met at all. As demands for governmental performance become ever larger and more indefinite, the likelihood of any action receiving widespread approval decreases. Under these conditions, the temptation to engage in semi-permanent opposition is bound to increase. No doubt there will still be a preponderance of governmental officials who will concentrate on the substance of public policy, but we can expect increasing numbers of them to seek what the French call "the cure of opposition." Those who are deep-dyed conservatives in the Goldwater mold have in fact been in near total opposition since New Deal days. Should a significant number of politicians on the left also choose "semi-permanent opposition," the room for constructive coalition building could be severely curtailed. Whether such dire consequences are even remotely likely depends first of all on whether the purists are likely to remain in politics, and, should they remain, whether they will continue to behave as they have.

Whither the Purists?

There is no evidence that permits more than a guess at the staying power of purists. We have seen that the party regulars felt that the McCarthy people were "one-shot" and "morning glories"; McCarthy delegates, on the other hand, clearly felt they would "be around." A heightened sense of future power explains much of their reluctance to walk out of a Democratic Convention where they were losing the fight for the nomination. At a caucus of McCarthy delegates a speaker put it this way: "I think we must remember that the vehicle for change in the United States is the Democratic Party. We're part of it. If we walk out, we say we're not going to be part of that process at a time we are close to success . . . . The day is near when the party will return to its basic liberalism. (Loud applause)." McCarthy supporters were optimistic to the end. "I think we came off pretty well. We have a horrendous ticket, but I think these [McCarthy] guys—Peterson, Hoeh, and so on—are going to take over the party."

At first glance it would appear difficult for McCarthy supporters to accept central leadership. Their stress on individual conscience and personal participation might lead them to reject attempts at organization into a solid bloc. This is certainly the way they describe themselves. "McCarthy people represent a new type of worker and voter. They are different. They desire participation, dislike tight control. Every one must have his say."

Whatever their original predispositions, however, their experience at the convention led some McCarthy delegates to value leadership and solidarity. They learned how difficult it was for the ordinary delegate to exert influence on behalf of his candidate. The conclusion they arrived at was well put by a delegate who said, "Who am I, that I can persuade other delegates to vote with me? I just don't have enough clout. What we ought to do is to use some of our really big names." Participatory democracy was beginning to give way to centralized leadership.

As the convention wore on with its votes on contested delegations and the platform, McCarthy delegates began to see the value of central organization. They were dismayed by their inability to communicate with each other and with other delegates. They were delighted with the impact made by the large bloc of votes that a virtually unanimous California delegation delivered to the cause. Our report of the discussion at a caucus of the McCarthy delegates in the California delegation reveals a drastic change in the value these people put on the leadership provided by Speaker Jess Unruh. The change is the more remarkable because these political men had long been known as his opponents in state politics. As one important McCarthy delegate told his fellows, "We have to have Jess. The floor operation last night was murder. We might have won some votes if we had a decent operation, but we had nothing. You have to have someone with clout; Jess is the only one who could put together the kind of operation we need. Without him, nothing. It would be nice to have a lot of votes for McCarthy, but I think it's even more important to have Jess." These delegates had learned an important truth under fire. They would still prefer their kind of leadership to other people's in the future, but they were not likely to believe they would prevail without any kind of leadership at all.

It might be possible to judge the likelihood that these lessons will mean something to the future of the Democratic party by looking at what happened to the Goldwater activists in the Republican party. What little we know suggests that the purists could not sustain their dominance over the party in the face of defeat. The nomination of Goldwater did not affect the "Eastern Establishment" states of New England and the Middle Atlantic area much; Goldwater activists never controlled the party machinery there. Goldwater's national party chairman, the conservative Dean Burch, did not last until the next convention; the Republican National Committee replaced him with Ray Bliss, an unideological organizer, chosen for his non-purist talents at winning elections and healing differences. In some states, however, the Goldwater people did maintain control of the state Republican party machinery; California, where they nominated one of their own for Governor in 1966, is an example.

There is, of course, one fundamental difference between Goldwater purists and McCarthy purists. Goldwaterites were and are party insiders; McCarthyites, with rare exceptions, are not. The Goldwaterite sentiments of Republican activists sharply differentiate Republican activists from the bulk of the American population, and make winning difficult for the Republican party. If Democratic activists became more purist in their orientations, they too would part company with most Americans on at least some issues. If Democratic leaders became more purist and less concerned with winning, we believe they would win less often, elections would be more bitterly contested than they now are, the costs of losing would rise, and the complex tasks of governing would become even more difficult.

THE ELECTORAL COLLEGE

Another element of the strategic environment within which the drama of a Presidential election is played is that peculiarly American institution, the Electoral College. American Presidential elections are not decided by popular vote, but rather popular votes are collected within each state, and each state casts all of its electoral votes for the candidate receiving the most popular votes within the state. This "winner take all, loser take nothing" approach is called a "unit rule."[51] We will explain some consequences of this rule presently.

Each state is allowed as many electoral votes as it has Senators and Representatives in Congress. Thus, all states, no matter how small, have at least three electoral votes. This means that mathematically, sparsely populated states are overrepresented by the Electoral College. In 1968, 72,951 Alaskans influenced the disposition of three electoral votes, which gives a ratio of one electoral vote for every 24,317 voters. In New York, on the other hand, 6,386,408 voters went to the polls and voted for 43 Electors, a ratio of one electoral vote for every 148,521 voters. In California, 6,711,962 voters for 40 Electors produces a ratio of one electoral vote for every 167,799 voters. One might conclude, therefore, that each Alaskan had about eight times as much influence on the final outcome as each Californian. But this is not entirely valid.

Why not? Because the unit rule of the Electoral College provides that the candidate having the most votes in a state receives the entire electoral vote of the state. This means that each Alaskan was influencing the disposition of all three of Alaska's electoral votes, and each Californian was helping to decide the fate of all *forty* of California's votes. Ask any politician whether he would rather have three votes or forty— the answer is immediately apparent. In fact, the present method of electing the President tends to give greater power to the large, urban states, not the small, rural states, because the large states can deliver to the winner large blocks of the votes he needs to win. Consequently, Presidential nominees tend to come from big states and tend to run on platforms likely to appeal to big city interest groups. They concentrate their campaigns in the big centers of population, and, as politicians know, they stand or fall on the big state votes. This feature, interestingly enough, is the mirror image of the situation in Congress. Whereas the unit rule of the Electoral College gives extra weight to the voices of large, urban, two-party states in the Presidential nomination process, the seniority rules of Congress and the rules strictly allocating jurisdiction to Congressional committees have over the years worked to give one-party areas the most power, and these have, until quite recently, tended to be disproportionately rural and small-town in their composition.

THE DISTRIBUTION OF RESOURCES

Certain resources which, at any given time, are disproportionately available to Democrats and Republicans play a significant part in the strategic environment. For example, possession of the Presidential office, skill in organization, knowledge of substantive policies, a reputation for integrity, facility in speech-making, ability to devise appealing campaign issues, wealth, stamina—all can be drawn upon to good advantage in a Presidential campaign. There are, it is clear, more resources available to the parties than any one book could deal with exhaustively. But some resources are obviously going to be more important than others, and the importance of different resources varies from occasion to occasion. It would be sensible to regard as especially important those resources which one side effectively *monopolizes*—such as the Presidential office—and those resources which can be easily *converted* into other resources, or directly into public office—such as money, which can be used to buy competent staff, newspaper space, and so on.

Although political resources are distributed unequally between the parties, in a competitive two-party system such as ours the inequalities do not all run in the same direction. Sometimes the Republicans reap the benefits; sometimes the Democrats do. One result of these inequalities of access to different resources, however, is that different strategies are more advantageous to each of the two parties. Let us examine three resources commonly held to be extremely important in the strategic environment of the Presidential election—money, control over information, and the Presidential office—in order to see what effects they have on election strategies.

Money
Presidential campaigns are terribly expensive. Radio and tele-

vision appearances, newspaper advertising, travel for the candidate and his entourage, mailings of campaign material, buttons and placards, maintaining a network of offices to run the campaign, taking polls—all cost a great deal of money. It is estimated that the various committees (the Republican and Democratic national committees, the House and Senate campaign committees of both parties, and various *ad hoc* volunteer committees that spring up in each campaign) at the national level spent approximately $25 million in 1960, $29 million in 1964, and over $52 million in 1968.[52] There is no sign that costs are decreasing. And substantial sums were also spent by state and local organizations in behalf of the Presidential candidates. Total political costs for all candidates at all levels of government amounted to something like $140 million in 1952, $155 million in 1956, an estimated $175 million in 1960, $200 million in 1964, and approximately $300 million in 1968.[53] The huge costs involved inevitably raise serious questions about the relationship between wealth and decisions in a democracy. Are Presidential nominating and electoral contests determined by those who have the most money? Do those who make large contributions exercise substantial or undue influence as a result of their largesse? Is the victorious candidate under obligation to "pay off" his major financial contributors? Do those who pay the piper call the tune?

First, let us establish some basic facts. Republicans do spend more than Democrats in most places, but the difference is not as overwhelming as some would suppose. The Democratic percentage of major party expenditures from 1932 to 1968 has varied from a low of 31% in 1968 (when Humphrey lost) to a high of 49% in 1932 (when Roosevelt won).[54] Although the Johnson forces spent more money in 1964 than Kennedy's had in 1960 (the Democrats in 1964 managed to spend $12 million), Goldwater's forces spent $17.2 million, significantly more than Johnson's.[55] Thus, total expenditures of both parties are high in absolute terms, but outlays per voter per party are quite modest, running in the 1960 election to about 16 cents for each of the 68.83 million voters.[56] "Contrary to frequent assertion," says an author who has made a comprehensive study of party finance, "American campaign monies are *not* supplied solely by a small handful of fat cats. Many millions of people now give to politics. Even those who give several hundred dollars each number in the tens of thousands."[57]

Since 1956, roughly 10% of the population has been contributing in Presidential election years. Data from the Survey Research Center show that 10% of a national population sample said they had contributed in 1956, 12% in 1960, and 11% in 1964. Translating these numbers into individuals, we find that 8 million people in 1956, 10 million in 1960, and 12 million in 1964 contributed to political campaigns.[58] It remains true, however, that the bulk of the money to run campaigns comes from people who contribute over $100. For the years before 1956, two-thirds of the campaign war chests at the national level were made up of contributions of over $500, and an additional one-fifth came from contributions of over $100. At the local level, where approximately six-sevenths of election expenses are met, the proportion of gifts over $500 declines to one-half or one-third. The figures on contributors for 1952 will perhaps give some idea of the numbers. Around 3 million people made some contribution. At least one gift of $100 was made by 150,000 contributors, $500 by 20,000 of these people, and $10,000 or more was given by 200 of these individuals.[59]

The most obvious and most important conclusion in our view is that money does not buy election victories. The candidates and party with the most money do not always win. Otherwise, Republicans would have won every election in the last forty years, and we know, in fact, that the Democrats have won seven of the ten Presidential contests from 1932 to 1968. Nor does there seems to be a correlation between the amount of money spent and the extent of electoral victory in national elections.[60] In 1968, for example, the Republican party outspent the Democrats by more than two to one, yet won the election by a mere half million votes out of the 72 million votes cast. One would expect that money would flow into the coffers of the party which was believed to have the best chance of victory. Yet with the possible exception of 1968, there does not seem to be a single Presidential election in this century which any competent observer believes would have turned out differently if the losing candidate had spent more money than the winner. We can at once eliminate all the Democratic victories because the Democrats spent less than the Republican losers. Dwight Eisenhower was so popular that his two elections now seem to have been certain, whether he had a substantial campaign surplus or not. No doubt part of the reason he had as much money to run with as he did was his personal appeal to the people who contribute to campaigns, and they might well have given to him even if he had run as a Democrat. Nixon in 1968 had a great deal of money—indeed, probably a surplus—and Humphrey had less than he needed to make an effective race. Because the final outcome of the election was so close and the financial situations of the two major parties so disparate, 1968, it may be argued, is the single exception to the rule, even though it seems more plausible to argue that it was not lack of money but rather the deep divisions within the Democratic party (only trivially reflected in a diminution of contributions) that hurt even more. The Republicans who won in the period from 1900 to 1928 did so with substantial majorities as befits the party which then enjoyed the allegiance of a preponderant part of the voting citizenry. The problem, then, is not to explain why money is crucial but, on the contrary, to explain why it is not.

No one doubts that money is important; parties and candidates, not to speak of ordinary mortals, can hardly function without it. If a candidate could not raise any money, or only a pitifully small amount, he would be dreadfully handicapped and might not be able to run at all. But this situation has never arisen—Humphrey in 1968 came close—after the national convention has made its choice. The crucial question is not the total spent by each candidate but the *difference* in the amounts they spend. The first part of our explanation, therefore, is that the differences in spending have ordinarily not been so great as to give any candidate an overwhelming advantage. So long as the poorer candidate can raise the minimum amount necessary to mount a campaign—that is, to hire employees, distribute literature, go on the radio and television a few times, get around the country, and so on—he can do most of what he has to do. Another way of putting this would be to say that above the minimum amount necessary to run a campaign the additional expenditures do not appear to confer significant advantages. Like other goods, money is subject to diminishing returns. People may get tired of being bombarded with literature and harangued by speakers. The candidates sometimes worry about over-exposure lest they go the way of certain television celebrities who were seen once too often. Criticism of "trying to buy the election" may arise if too much time is taken on television. Indeed, there may be resentment if favorite programs are taken off the air to accommodate a candidate who seems to have had more than his say. We know that many voters are relatively impervious to bombardment by the opposition, and all the handouts in the world will not make them change. The actual result of extensive assault by the richer party may be to increase the polarization of the electorate as those who oppose that party find additional reasons to intensify their opposition.

Hubert Humphrey's general election campaign presented a number of unusual problems from the standpoint of finance. The Chicago convention brought more than bitterness and disunity. It also made Humphrey's campaign appear a poor investment to those seeking access to a future President. In addition, of course, the lateness of the convention provided little time for wounds to heal among disaffected liberals—especially troublesome in a year when the wounds were deeper than normal. Finally, Humphrey began his campaign with a pre-convention debt and with no clear plan for raising the $10 to $15 million he required.

In the light of these problems, the striking fact remains that the Democratic expenditures "in the general election period in 1968 were at about the same level as for Johnson in 1964 and Kennedy in 1960, in the $10 to $12 million range."[61] This is not to say that the Democrats would not have liked to raise more money, or, more importantly, to have raised it early enough to have allowed for better efficiency in its use and the use of the candidate's time. But even in 1968, the scarcity of money was not the chief problem for the ultimate loser.

A more difficult problem, in fact, will probably be faced by the candidate in 1972. As of March, 1969, the Democratic party was faced with a campaign deficit in excess of $8 million—almost double the record deficit left by John Kennedy's successful effort in 1960. This time they will not have the advantages of incumbency, and the problem of raising the money will understandably be more difficult.

However, given the necessary minimum amount of money on his side, the less affluent candidate can count on a good deal of free publicity. Presidential campaigns are deemed newsworthy by the press and are extensively reported. While Democrats may get somewhat less space than Republicans in papers, they still get some, and they do better in the magazines and on the air. Thus, they get through to their supporters. To some extent the candidates can make news. John Kennedy's grappling with the religious issue, Harry Truman's assaults on the opposition, Dwight Eisenhower's dramatic promise to go to Korea made headlines at little or no financial cost. The television debates in 1960 between Nixon and Kennedy attracted millions of viewers, numbers far in excess of the usual political broadcasts for which fees have to be paid.

The factor of skill must also be considered. Money can be spent for unrewarding purposes which actually rebound against the candidate. Democratic strategists during the 1930's were delighted at the expenditures made by the Liberty League on behalf of the Republican candidate, because they considered it to be an ideal target for their charges that the Republicans were the party of privilege. Money may be expended unwittingly getting the opposition to the polls. A poor performance on television may do the candidate no good no matter how much is spent. The man who says the wrong thing may deeply regret the wealth which made it possible for him to disseminate his statement widely.

Other things being equal, of course, it would be nice to have more money to spend than the other fellow. But conditions are rarely, if ever, equal. The fundamental party allegiances of the population, the state of the economy, religious and ethnic affiliations, the personalities of the candidates—all appear to be more significant in determining the outcomes of elections than the differences in total party spending. Despite the understandable cries of harried party money-raisers, the Democrats always seem to come up with enough to get by. There is always the hope of victory. The winner can expect to have his deficits covered at the next round of party "victory" fund-raising drives. It remains true that the most expensive election is the one you lose.

Money is probably more important at the nominating rather than the electoral stage. Eisenhower and Taft spent about $2.5 million each on their nominating campaigns in 1952.[62] The candidate who wishes to enter primaries and conduct a national drive to obtain delegates may be dissuaded through lack of the minimum amount necessary to get started. The lower visibility of primaries and the lesser attention paid to them by citizens may give an advantage to those with more to spend. Money, however, is only one factor. Estes Kefauver put on a vigorous campaign despite his relative lack of wealth. Had he not been bitterly opposed by party leaders, or had he won all the primaries he entered, as Kennedy did, he might have won the nomination. As it was, Kefauver lost to Stevenson whose command of wealth was the least of his political assets. In 1968, Nelson Rockefeller spent over $7 million in his effort to impress Republican delegates with his strength in the public opinion polls, but the effort was fruitless.[63]

Other candidates may, however, have been adversely affected by lack of funds. Nelson Rockefeller in 1960 is a curious example. Apparently he decided not to contest the Republican nomination that year in part because he could not raise the cash, or, one assumes, the enthusiasm among like-minded party financiers that cash contributions symbolize.[64] During the 1960 Kennedy-Humphrey primary campaigns in West Virginia, charges of vast Kennedy spending were made. Certainly, Kennedy's ready cash did him no harm. In retrospect, however, it does appear that he was decidedly more popular with the voters than his rival, Hubert Humphrey. Would more money have enabled Humphrey to turn the tide? Humphrey's campaign was badly managed and severely underfinanced and in part this led the press to accord him less serious treatment than he might otherwise have merited. Had Humphrey had as much money to spend on campaigning as Kennedy, for as long a period of time, the tide might conceivably have run in the other direction. There were, nonetheless, other candidates—Johnson and Symington, for example—who had plenty of money but who chose not to contest the primaries.[65]

It is exceedingly difficult to get reliable information on an event that involves a decision *not* to act. Such an event would be a decision by a political candidate not to run because he could not raise the money. There is, of course, no literature on this subject. But there have undoubtedly been some men whose inability to raise the cash has proven fatal to their chances of being considered for the nomination. While this is most regretable, a more important question concerns whether there has been systematic bias in favor of or against certain kinds of men that consistently alters the outcome of Presidential nominations. We can immediately dismiss the notion that the richest man automatically comes out on top. If that were the case, Rockefeller would have triumphed over Goldwater in 1964 and then again over Nixon in 1968, Taft over Eisenhower in 1952, and neither Humphrey nor Stevenson would have been nominated.

The ability to raise money is not only a matter of personal wealth but of being able to attract funds from others. Does this mean that only candidates attractive to the wealthy can run? It might be said that the problem is not so much whether it helps to be rich but whether men who favor the causes of the rich have the advantage over those who favor the poor. There is little evidence to support such a view. Given the nature of the American electorate, no candidate would openly admit to being the candidate only of the rich. Candidates holding a variety of views on economic issues—most of which are highly technical —manage to run for the nominations of both parties. If candidates are generally chosen from among men who differ but little on most substantive issues the reason is not because the rich are withholding their money from more radical candidates but rather because the distribution of opinions in the electorate renders the cause of such men hopeless. Our conclusion is that it is nice to be rich; some men who lack funds may be disadvantaged. From the standpoint of the total political system, however, the nomination process does not appear to bar men who are otherwise acceptable to the electorate. Although the difference in ability of the two parties to raise money is not in any sense a critical determinant of national elections, large sums of money are necessary to run campaigns. May not those who contribute or raise money in large amounts thereby gain influence not available to others? Aware the answer to this question is not a simple one, we would say, "Yes, but not overly much." What contributors or fund-raisers (the financial middlemen) get to begin with is access to centers of decision-making. Control over money certainly makes it easier to get in and present one's case. Men of wealth, however, are likely to have substantial economic interests which would provide them with good access whether or not they made contributions. If no significant interest feels disadvantaged by what these contributors want, they may well be given the benefit of the doubt. But in matters of great moment, where the varied interests in our society are in contention, it is doubtful whether control over money goes very far with a President. There are many reasons for this.

In the first place, there are many issues on which a candidate is likely to be already publicly committed. Suggestions that he change his position during the campaign are likely to be met with little favor. If the matter is important enough to be mentioned it has to be considered in relation to its vote-getting potential. Forced to make a choice, nominees are far more likely to prefer votes to dollars. And even if a miscalculation is made *in public*, candidates generally prefer not to reverse their field and appear vacillating and inconsistent. Money may be given in the expectation of future favors. To spell this out in detail would appear unseemly, however, and is likely to be rejected outright.[66] The moral sense of the candidates would most likely forbid such a thing. If not, the good political sense of their advisors would suggest that the consequences of discovery are much worse than any possible benefits. Thus, any strings attached to a gift are likely to be vague and cloudy, subject to all sorts of interpretations.

Once a President assumes office, he is in a much stronger bargaining position. Contributors are likely to need him much more than he will need them; he can do more to affect their fortunes than they can to affect his. A President may at that point refuse to acknowledge any alleged agreement of policy concessions in return for contributions. Wealthy contributors frequently give to both parties and, in any case, are often found on opposite sides of public issues. For candidates to give in to one of them may simply incur the wrath of others.

A decline in contributions from one source may be made up by funds from another. The President's need to gain or maintain support from the voters, the limits placed on his powers of decision by what Congressmen, bureaucrats, and interest groups will accept, his own preferences, all serve to place drastic limits on benefits contributors get from campaign contributions. In brief, money simply becomes much less important to the things a President needs to do while he is in office. Contributors may be heard to complain in the hurt tones of Henry C. Frick, who after visiting Theodore Roosevelt at the White House, said, "We bought the son of a bitch and then he did not stay bought."[67] The foregoing analysis should help to explain why Presidential politicians do not "stay bought" whatever their debt to their financial supporters.

Though it is true that the parties usually seem to raise enough money to get by, finding money is likely to be a traumatic experience. There is a day-by-day scramble which must be enervating. The Republicans are somewhat better off, not only because of their ability to collect in the business community, but also because they go about the task much more systematically than do the Democrats. Personal solicitation has been found to be the best method of collecting funds. So Republicans arrange for comprehensive coverage on a local basis of all likely contributors, and they have a good deal of central coordination which assures that the national organization receives its share. Democratic efforts are, to say the least, chaotic. Aside from the union strongholds, contractors, and textile people, they do not have a visible group in many parts of the country whom they can count on to give a little. Unlike the Republicans, they have not hired a professional money-raiser, sympathetic to their cause, who will take on the job over a long period of time.[68] As a result, each financial campaign tends to be run by different people who have to start from the beginning. Experience is not accumulated as it might be. When Adlai Stevenson was nominated in 1952, he down-graded large contributions and appointed Beardsley Ruml who tried to get most of what he needed from small contributions. Ruml did get more than usual from that source but not nearly enough.[69] Edwin Pauley, who raised funds for Truman, was an oilman who had a wide acquaintanceship among men of wealth and who was adroit in having his claims recognized by groups like road builders and construction firms who could expect to benefit from Democratic policies. Until the Kennedy campaign, the Democrats continued to live, at best, from hand to mouth, day to day, crisis to crisis. President Truman in 1948—few wished to contribute to a sure loser—found himself stranded without funds in the middle of Oklahoma on his campaign train, whereupon the Governor and a few others on that train decided that this could not be allowed to continue and found the money. Humphrey was nearly out of money in the midst of his seemingly hopeless 1968 campaign when as an afterthought a plea for funds was inserted at the end of his nationwide television speech from Salt Lake City in which he pledged a bombing halt in Vietnam. Enough money came in to pay for the program twice over. Again, the essential wherewithal was forthcoming but the attendant tension is hardly the best atmosphere in which to conduct a political campaign.[70] In 1964, "when Republican chances of victory over Johnson were never rated much brighter than those of a snowflake in Austin," the Republicans raised more money than they had in any previous campaign. And, contrary to previous campaigns, the money came not from big business but primarily from "small donations sent in by hundreds of thousands of contributors, many of whom had never before contributed to a national campaign." The GOP collected 651,000 small, individual contributions in 1964.[71]

The fund-raising dinner has in recent years become a major source of money. To the accompaniment of rubbery chicken or, in the more affluent affairs, good steak, the well-heeled come to listen to exhortations at up to $1000 a plate. The advantages of this system to the parties are many. Attendance is visible. Those who do not come may be conspicuous by their absence. Those who wish to be regarded favorably by the parties' office-holders may decide that it is a good idea to come. Dinners are easy to organize, and a large profit is usually cleared. Such disadvantages as there may be to this system do not seem to accrue to the party coffers so much as to the party faithful. These loyal souls may, if fund-raising meals continue to proliferate, find it necessary to give up one of their expensive hobbies, politics or eating.

One of the more promising fund-raising gimmicks, the selling of advertisements in the program book of the Democratic National Convention at $15,000 a page, had to be abandoned in 1965 because of adverse publicity. Lacking this source, Humphrey turned in 1968 to the device of securing loans to cover campaign expenses as they arose. Prominent contributors would sign notes with banks and would then be paid back as funds from more traditional sources (dinners, etc.) arrived. Most of the debt left by the Democrats in 1968 involve these outstanding loans.[72]

After the election of 1960, President Kennedy shifted the emphasis in fund-raising from numerous small contributors to a few large ones. A Presidents' ($1000 a year) Club was formed, whose members were rewarded with invitations to White House social functions and other notable occasions. Under LBJ this club became the primary source of Democratic fund-raising to the detriment of formerly broad-based efforts (Dollars for Democrats). The plan worked well in 1964 (when 4000 members joined), but as Johnson's popularity declined, so did the membership (to 2000 in 1966). From 1966 to 1968,

Johnson was involved too deeply in other problems to concern himself with party affairs and the decline continued.[73]

Control Over Information

Control over information is another major political resource. Information does many things besides help voters to change their minds—that rare phenomenon. It helps people keep in touch with the progress of the campaign, gives the party faithful indications of the effectiveness of their side, acquaints voters with the major arguments that the candidates are making. Information helps to guide and channel both the enthusiasm and content of participation, and therefore control over information and its dissemination is a significant political resource.

As we scan the major media of information it appears that, generally speaking, newspapers are a good deal more partisan in their straight news coverage than are the radio and television stations. A political party that feels discriminated against over the air can take its case to the Federal Communications Commission which may require the offending station to make a prompt restitution of the balance of coverage, on pain of removal of the station's license to broadcast.[74] There is no such legal limitation on the "freedom" of newspapers and magazines to be one-sided in the presentation of the news, and, indeed, it has again and again been discovered that the printed media avail themselves rather extensively of this freedom. Many newspapers enjoy monopoly positions in their communities, and much of the political information available comes from the press. For these reasons the character of press coverage of Presidential elections is a matter of strategic importance.

It will come as no surprise to regular readers of the newspapers to learn that partisanship in news coverage generally tends to favor that side which is most often endorsed editorially by the press, namely the Republicans. Repeated studies have shown that the Republicans are normally the favorite party of the newspaper executives who determine editorial policy in most newspapers. And they have also shown that whatever biases exist in news reporting, in the placing of stories in the papers, in the location and size of headlines, and so on systematically favor the Republicans.[75] The election of 1964, with a slight edge to President Johnson, provided the only exception, and in 1968 the newspapers returned to form.

Yet, paradoxically, Democratic candidates for President do not seem to be harmed excessively by pro-Republican sentiments in the press, even among voters who rely heavily upon newspapers as sources of civic information. In recent decades Democrats like Franklin Roosevelt, Harry Truman, and John F. Kennedy have gained office despite the fact that a vast majority of the press was against them. If electoral votes had been apportioned within each state by the number of newspaper endorsements for each candidate, the 1968 count would have been Nixon 521, Wallace 17, Humphrey 0; if they were apportioned on the basis of the circulation of these papers, the count would have been Nixon 471, Humphrey 60, Wallace 7; the actual result, of course, was Nixon 302, Humphrey 191, Wallace 45.[76]

Despite the seeming Republican edge, the days of the crusading editor who owned his own paper and used it as a vehicle to propagate his own political doctrines are largely gone. In our time, newspapers with substantial circulations are much more likely to be part of a corporate chain devoted primarily to making money for their stockholders.[77] The costs of publication are high. In order to show a profit, papers must have a substantial circulation and a good deal of advertising. This is difficult to achieve in the midst of competition among several papers and accounts for the trend toward consolidation. Reader attention is gained by emphasizing stories with high human interest appeal—sports, crime, local personalities, and the high jinks of movie stars. Political news, though it does have a place, is subordinate because most readers are not terribly interested in politics. An excessive emphasis upon public affairs, therefore, is unlikely so long as appeal to readers is a prime consideration. This factor certainly has drawbacks for civic education. But for present purposes, it means that the possibilities for political propaganda are much less than they otherwise might be, because public affairs do not get much space.[78] Advertising is gained by convincing businessmen that it will pay them in terms of increased sales. The periodic appeals of conservatives requesting businessmen to place or withhold advertising as a form of political coercion usually fall on deaf ears, because the motives of those who pay are commercial rather than political. Both the paper and its advertisers are likely to shy away from many forms of political controversy; it tends to make enemies rather than friends and is commonly believed to be "bad for business." The result is that much of the time newspapers are rather bland. Such political opinions as they do express are watered down so as not to give offense. Their political opinions, far from being their central concerns, tend to be sporadic and aimless, rather than representing a coherent political ideology.[79]

These tendencies are strengthened by a prevailing belief that papers ought to be nonpartisan in their news stories and present both sides of the issues of the day. However much the norm of impartiality may be honored in the breach, it provides a standard which serves to some extent to hold down partisanship. More than that, the belief that it is a newspaper's function to report what happens rather than to editorialize in its news columns has many other attractions for editors. It enables them to escape to some extent from the hostilities engendered by political controversy; it lessens problems of editorial judgment, thus decreasing the amount of work they have to do; it enables them to select items that they think will enhance their readership; it provides editors with a rationale for defending themselves against the charge of giving too much prominence to causes and candidates which may be unpopular with advertisers or some influential readers. This norm leaves the papers open to manipulation by political strategists who can create sensational news stories. During the heyday of Senator Joseph McCarthy, for example, newspapermen slowly became aware of the extent to which they had aided him by publicizing his charges, because they were "news," rather than ignoring or carefully evaluating them.[80] During Presidential campaigns, application of the same standard gives the candidate who is opposed by newspapers the opportunity to enter at least some of its news stories because whatever he says is "news." If he should be an incumbent, his exposure will be greater because the President of the United States, as the outstanding public official and symbol of the nation, gets attention for the smallest things that he and his family do.

The desire to cut costs has at least one favorable consequence for increased impartiality in news stories. There is today increasingly greater reliance on material put out by the giant news services, the Associated Press, United Press International, and to some extent the New York *Times,* Los Angeles *Times,* Washington *Post,* and Chicago *Daily News* news services. These newsgathering agencies serve an exceedingly wide clientele which includes a broad spectrum of opinion. They are instructed, therefore, to prepare stories which will prove acceptable to various shades of opinion.[81] Presenting what happened with a minimum of slanted commentary is a good way to do this, though the wire services are by no means perfect in this respect. The final product, however, is closer to the canons of impartiality than would be the case if each paper prepared stories in accordance with its editorial position.

While it remains true that candidates favored by newspapers receive better treatment and somewhat greater coverage than others, there is one compensating factor in Presidential campaigns which has not received the attention it deserves. If the papers are generally conservative and Republican, political correspondents are comparatively more liberal and Democratic.[82] The stories they send, though subject to the mercies of the rewrite man in the home office, serve to a certain extent to redress the balance on the paper. This is particularly the case in the rather subtle question of how candidates are portrayed. The feeling that some candidates are more responsive, more open, more friendly, more intelligent than others may get communicated through little human interest stories and result in an impression contrary to that preferred by the owners of the paper. Such appeared to be the case in 1960 with John F.

Kennedy, who was popular with the reporters; and the extra attention he received resulted in complaints from Richard Nixon, who was not so popular with them.[83] By 1968, Nixon was a battle-scarred veteran who could watch with grim satisfaction as the press pursued the early Republican front-runner, the relatively inexperienced George Romney. Jules Witcover comments:

> Romney, Nixon reasoned correctly, had not yet learned the lessons about the press that Nixon's experience had taught him, and even if he had, he could not go into hiding. A moratorium on politics by a former Vice-President, Presidential candidate and conspicuous globe-trotter would make little difference, since his face and his views already were widely known in the country; Romney, however, needed exposure in large doses on the national scene if he hoped to graduate to the status of a national candidate. That exposure, Nixon was confident, would be Romney's downfall. . . . Meanwhile, Nixon himself could sit back, let Romney's destruction happen, and emerge all the stronger by virtue of the contrast between the way he and Romney conducted themselves in the pre-election year shakedown.[84]

But it is a far cry from acknowledging this situation to a conclusion that ordinary citizens are actually influenced in their opinions and voting choices by the newspapers they take. We use the word "take" advisedly because the fact that a newspaper enters a home is no guarantee that its political news and editorials will be read. Most people pay little enough attention to politics; they often read nothing or just scan the headlines without taking away much of an impression. Analyses of tons of newspaper clippings showing political propaganda by newspapers means nothing insofar as the effect is concerned if these stories are never read.

When stories and editorials are perused with some care, the reader's perception of what has been written may differ markedly from the intentions of the writer on the newspaper. An editorial may not be clear in intent, particularly if it is hedged by qualifications or watered down to minimize offense as is often the case. Frequently, the reader pays attention only to those parts of the piece which substantiate his own opinions. Opinion studies have demonstrated the remarkable capacity of people to filter out what they do not wish to hear and come away with quite a different impression than an objective analysis of an editorial or article would warrant. Indeed, the reader may interpret the story to make precisely the opposite of what it intends; a criticism of Harry Truman for being vituperative, for example, could be taken as a commendation of his fighting spirit.[85]

Stories and editorials may also be interpreted as they were meant to be and still be rejected as invalid. There is a great deal of suspicion of the press in the United States. Party identification is so powerful a force that it is likely to overwhelm most anything a paper says. Obviously, millions of citizens have no difficulty remaining and voting Democratic while reading Republican newspapers. Group loyalties are another force which may lead to rejection of opinions in newspapers. Face-to-face groups in unions, on the job, in fraternal, religious, and ethnic organizations may generate opinions of their own. If these differ from those in the newspaper, the members of the groups are provided with defense against the persuasion of the press. Group pressures of this kind are likely to be far more influential than what is written in a paper. The group may also reinforce what the paper says, but this represents an intensification rather than a change of opinion.[86]

No doubt the monopoly position of most newspapers in local communities makes the dissemination of opposing views more difficult than it might be in the presence of competition from a newspaper of a different outlook. But there are ways of getting around this. Other publications may enter the home: magazines and pamphlets which are religious, ethnic, union, fraternal, and even political in their focus, and these may contain contrary notions of public policy and candidate preference. True, only a relatively few persons read the political magazines. But these people are likely to be opinion leaders, people who take an active interest in public affairs and who are looked up to by others for advice. The availability, therefore, of little magazines of many shades of opinion permits the opinion leaders to receive and then disseminate on a personal basis information which may counteract whatever is in a newspaper.

Consider a puzzle concerning the political impact of the New York *Daily News*, a sensational tabloid with a circulation in the millions. It is apparent that if those who read the *News* all through the 1930's and 40's had voted against Franklin D. Roosevelt, as the paper repeatedly recommended in vitriolic terms, Roosevelt would certainly never have carried New York City by the huge margins he did. At the same time it seems strange that so many people who not only voted for but revered FDR in New York continued to read a newspaper whose editorials bitterly attacked their hero. The Democratic readers of the *News* apparently managed to get the best of both possible worlds. They read the paper they liked and voted for the man they favored without noticing the apparent contradiction —because, for them, there was no contradiction. They either did not pay attention to the editorials, or blocked out the unfavorable ones completely, or interpreted them to mean something favorable to FDR. Voting studies document instances where people who wanted to vote for Harry Truman in 1948 convinced themselves that the incumbent President was against price controls; some people who preferred Dwight Eisenhower in 1956 apparently had no difficulty in believing that he surely favored medical care for the aged.[87]

Or, let us consider the case of the opposite of the New York *Daily News*, the good, gray, sober, responsible New York *Times*. After the *Times* came out for John F. Kennedy in the closing weeks of the 1960 Presidential campaign, various political pundits speculated as to the probable impact of the fact of this endorsement by so august and respectable a source. Our theory about voting behavior would lead us to be wary of claiming much influence for the *Times*, not because its readership was too indifferent to heed this call to reason but because of the kind of people who read this paper. One has to be terribly interested in politics to read through the *Times* as far as the editorial page. People who read that far are among the small, interested minority who comprise the core of the strong party identifiers. Precisely because of their interest, they are likely to identify with a major party and to resist changing their allegiance. A call from the *Times*, therefore, however respectable, could hardly shake these devoted party people in their fundamental loyalty. The vacillating, the doubtful, and the uninformed who cannot make up their minds are far more likely to read comic books or *Modern Romance* than the New York *Times* with its surfeit of news about seemingly dull political events.

What, then, is the significance of newspapers in Presidential campaigns? We have suggested that the press is by no means immensely influential. Its major importance probably lies in two directions: presenting some kind of information about the candidates and the campaign to its readers, and intensifying the predispositions held by people who tend to agree with the paper's preferences. If one asked the candidates, they would undoubtedly prefer to have the press on their side instead of against them. But they can and do win in the face of opposition from the press. It may be that the newspaper a person reads subtly conditions his attitudes in ways now unsuspected, and that this has some effect on his opinions and voting choice.[88] There is no evidence, however, to indicate that this point has much force in Presidential elections, and evidence does exist which suggests severe limits to what newspapers can do. Undoubtedly whatever impact the press has varies enormously with circumstances. Against a well-known and immensely popular President like Franklin Roosevelt in 1936 or Lyndon Johnson in 1964, with substantial publicity resources of his own, the impact of the press may be negligible. Against a little-known candidate like Adlai Stevenson in 1952, the attitudes communicated by the press—say, aloofness, over-intellectuality, indecisiveness—may be more significant. Yet we know from voting studies that in 1952 Stevenson was favorably regarded by Democrats who identified him with his party.[89] Perhaps the press counts for more on issues that are relatively far removed from the direct experience of the voters, such as corruption in government (where voters are prepared to believe the worst), and which may be blown out of proportion by hostile coverage. But the sheer number of different issues which may become relevant during a Presidential campaign, especially if they are "pocketbook" issues that are grasped with relative ease by voters, may also neutralize the influence of the press.

The Presidency

The Presidency is one resource which, in any given election year, must of necessity be monopolized by one party or the other. When an incumbent President seeks re-election, he enjoys many special advantages by virtue of his position. He is, to begin with, much better known than any challenger can hope to be. Everything the President does is news and is widely reported in all the media of information. The issues to which the President devotes his attention are likely to become the national issues because of his unique visibility and capacity to center diffused public attention on matters he deems important. To this extent, he is in a position to focus public debate on issues he deems most advantageous. The President can act and thereby gain credit. Should he face a crisis in foreign affairs, and there are many, he can gain by doing well or by calling on the patriotism of the citizenry to support its Chief Executive when the nation is in danger. An example of this occurred during the 1964 campaign, when United States vessels in the Bay of Tonkin were fired upon, and President Johnson took to the airwaves to promise rigorous defensive measures. In late July, just before the incident, he attracted 59% of the voters to 31% for Goldwater; in early August, just after the incident, the President's score went up to 65%, and Goldwater's declined to 29%.[90] The Bay of Tonkin episode also shows that the President cannot count on continued popularity if his policies do not appear successful to the electorate. President Nixon, to make a similar point in a different context, made repeated use of national television to mobilize support for his Vietnam policy. So long as his administration's actions were in accord with general public desires for withdrawal, even if gradual, the President did well in the polls. When he sent troops into Cambodia, instead of withdrawing them from Vietnam, however, it was less clear that his fellow citizens approved of that course of action.[91]

As the symbol of the nation, the President can travel and make "nonpolitical" speeches to advance his candidacy subtly, while his opponent is open to charges of "blind partisanship" in what are becoming unceasingly troubled times. Should his opponent claim that he can do a better job, the President need hardly make the obvious response that he is the only candidate who has had experience in a job for which there exists no completely appropriate prior training.

The life of the incumbent, however, is not necessarily one of undiluted joy. If the economic situation takes a turn for the worse, if a race riot erupts, if another nation comes under Communist influence, he is likely to be blamed as the man who was in office at the time. Whether he is really to blame or not, he is deemed responsible and has to take the consequences. Herbert Hoover felt the sting of this phenomenon deeply when the people punished the "ins" for a depression which Hoover would have given much to avoid. Moreover, the incumbent has a record. He has or has not done things, and he may be held to account for his sins of omission or commission; not so the man out of office, who can criticize freely without always presenting viable alternatives or necessarily taking his own advice once he is elected. The "missile gap" turned out to be something of a chimera after Kennedy got into the White House, and he never found it possible to act much differently toward the Matsu-Quemoy situation than did Dwight Eisenhower, despite their over-publicized "differences" about this question during the campaign. Richard Nixon could complain about the problem of "law and order" in 1968 without promising anything more concrete than a new attorney general, which he would have appointed anyway. The incumbent is naturally cast as the defender of his administration and the challenger as the attacker who promises better things to come. We cannot expect to hear the man in office say that the other fellow could probably do as well or to hear the challenger declare that he really could not do any better than the incumbent, although both statements may be close to the truth.

While his opponent can to some extent permit himself to be irresponsible or carried away by exuberance, the President cannot detach himself from office while campaigning, however, and he must recognize that other nations are listening when he makes statements. The President's very superiority of information may turn out to be a handicap as he cannot make certain statements or reveal his sources for others without committing a breach of security. His opponent can attack his record, but the incumbent may have difficulty finding a comparable record to assail on the other side.

INCUMBENCY AS RESOURCE—A SOUTHERN STRATEGY?

The Presidency as a resource is particularly meaningful to Richard Nixon because he was elected in 1968 by less than a majority at the head of a party which is itself not the choice of the majority of U.S. voters. Throughout his term of office, President Nixon has had to wrestle with the problem of finding a majority constituency to which he could appeal for support in 1972.

Perhaps the most significant and systematic attempt to influence President Nixon's strategic thinking on this problem has been Kevin Phillips' book *The Emerging Republican Majority*.[92]

The apparent purpose of this weighty volume is to demonstrate that the "research directors, associate professors, social workers, educational consultants, urbanologists, development planners, journalists, brotherhood executives, foundation staffers, communications specialists, culture vendors, pornography merchants, poverty theorists, and so forth"[93]—whom Phillips identifies as the main beneficiaries of the New Deal era —are numerically too few to elect a President in the near future. Moreover, it seems unlikely that even the addition of pointy-headed bureaucrats and intellectual morons would put the Democrats over the top. Thus, Phillips reasons that President Nixon should pay no attention to those who argue that he should move leftward in search of a secure Republican majority. The true majority, as Phillips sees it, is already both Republican and conservative, and is likely to become more so in the future.*

Phillips—a political columnist, former Nixon campaign worker, and special assistant to Attorney General Mitchell— is frank to say that this majority stands for policies that he himself prefers, and that his interpretation is offered as a lawyer might tender a brief.[94] Because his brief is so long, so copiously decorated with facts and factlets, statistical tables, maps, and other paraphernalia that may be mistaken for empirical demonstration, and because his argument may find favor with persons on the right seeking comfort, persons on the left seeking alarm, and persons in the middle seeking information, it seems worthwhile to give it more than a passing glance.

Like the New Deal alliance that it is supposed to replace as America's ruling coalition, the emerging Republican majority has a large number of disparate components:

1. *Sun Belt conservatives.* All across the South, the Southwest, and on into southern California, there is enormous urban and suburban population growth. These "new cities are centers of commerce, light industry, military preparedness, defense production and space-age technology, vocational seedbeds of a huge middle class." "The very areas of greatest population explosion," says Phillips, "are the demonstrated strongholds of Reagan, Goldwater, Gurney, and Tower, the vanguardmen of the new conservative sun politics."[95] At one point Phillips argues that much as Al Smith prematurely consolidated the urban poor and brought them into the Democratic party, Barry Goldwater in 1964 did the same for middle class sun belt conservatives.[96]

---

* This paragraph and the following few pages originally appeared as "An Emerging Republican Majority?" by Nelson W. Polsby in *The Public Interest* 17 (Fall 1969), pp. 119-126. Copyright © 1969 by National Affairs, Inc.

2. *Backlash urban voters.* Phillips sees the race issue as the millstone of the Democratic party, and he argues that many major population groups are likely to turn or remain Republican as a result of the Democratic commitment to racial equality. One such group will be the urban Catholics, who learned how to vote Republican in the Eisenhower years, and switched back only temporarily because Kennedy was Catholic. These groups are located mostly, but not exclusively, in the Northeast.[97]

3. *The Heartland,* an area that takes in the Midwest, the mountain states, and the trans-Appalachian border states. The features of the Heartland that make it prime Republican territory are, first, that large parts of it are small town conservative or German Catholic and Republican anyway; second, that other parts of it were settled by southerners who will turn Republican as a result of the race issue; and third, that in the cities of the Heartland, there will be backlash voting much as in the cities of the East. "During the mid-nineteen sixties . . . the urban Catholics of the Great Lakes began to turn conservative in response to liberal Democratic politics reflecting a large influx of poor Negroes from the South."[98]

4. *The Old South.* Here George Wallace is the transition figure as Goldwater was elsewhere. Phillips confidently adds Wallace voters to Nixon voters to get a resounding 57 per cent majority in repudiation of the Democrats in the 1968 election. The Democrats, he believes, have permanently alienated white southern voters in national politics, whether from the black belt or from subsistence farming areas where there never have been many Negroes. "Quite simply, as liberalism metamorphosed from an economic populist stance—supporting farm, highway, health, education and pension expenditures against conservative budget-cutting—into a credo of social engineering, it lost the support of poor whites."[99] "Whereas the 1948 Dixiecrats revolt—the first wave of Southern Democratic deterioration—left about half of the white Southern electorate in the Democratic presidential column, the 1968 Wallace candidacy broke loose all but 10 to 15%, including the upcountry and pineywoods poor whites who had hitherto

spurned both Dixiecrats and Republicans. There is a strong precedent for this 1968 estrangement of previous loyal Democrats persisting beyond one election. . . . From the best suburbs of Dallas to the darkest Black Belts of South Carolina, the Dixiecrat party served many conservatives as a way station between a no longer appealing Democratic Party and the increasingly Southern-concerned GOP. History will doubtless label George Wallace's party a similar way-station for another element of Southern voters."[100]

5. *Remnants of the Republican establishment.* Phillips predicts that the trend in the Northeast for the Republicans to get a smaller share of the vote will continue. He is consoled by the facts that the percentage of the nationwide vote cast in the Northeast is on the decline, and that, within the Northeast, the cities are losing out to the suburbs. The suburbs, it is true, are becoming less Republican, but backlash Catholics should provide some suburban Republican and conservative growth. And while the conservatism of traditional Republican strongholds in New England is weakening, Republicans may inherit Wallaceite voting blocs in Maryland, Delaware, and New Jersey. Phillips has very few good words to say regarding "silk stocking" Republicans' influence on the future of the party. Since nationwide they haven't got the votes and take the wrong (which is to say, liberal) side of most issues, their share in the new coalition will have to be small. "The Republican Party is no longer the party of the Northeast—and an increasing part of its Northeastern strength is rooted in voting streams like the urban Catholics and rural non-Yankee who have historically been allies . . . of the South and West."[101]

How plausible is all of this? If we grant Phillips' main premises, quite plausible indeed. But are there any good empirical grounds for granting his premises? Phillips himself devotes surprisingly few pages to their support. Much of the book, in fact, is taken up with entertaining digressions into the minutia of local political lore: migration patterns across the Appalachians, the contrast between northern and southern Ohio, how settlers in Washington and Oregon differed, and so on. This is, in general, not the sort of information one would need in order to test the truth of Phillips' argument. A skeptic might look at the coalition he has in mind and see things quite differently.

Consider the Sun Belt. It is not true that all growing Sun Belt cities are traditionally conservative. Over the last decade, for example, most of the liberal Democratic Congressmen from Texas have represented the growing cities of Houston, Galveston, Fort Worth, Austin, Beaumont, and San Antonio. In the second place, Phillips' belief that traditionally conservative cities of the West and Southwest will necessarily remain so as people from all over the country pour into them is based on a simple confusion between container and contents—a mistake he does not make when contemplating the migration of southern whites into the liberal industrial cities of the North. An influx of northeners is changing Florida from a one-party to a two-party state, and the largest growth of all has been in liberal, metropolitan Dade County. Likewise, the state of Virginia has become more competitive between the parties, and, if we can judge by the results of primary elections over the last few years, its Democratic party is becoming more liberal. Or take the case of California. Owing to the weakness of its political parties, it will undoubtedly continue to show very volatile patterns of voting. Under these circumstances, if Phillips is right, it is peculiar that George Wallace did so badly in California in 1968. And if conservatism is as popular as Phillips says, why does he seek to explain away Max Rafferty's resounding defeat for the Senate on the ground that his campaign was "marred" by "ideological stridency"?[102] Perhaps Los Angeles is not quite as conservative a city as Phillips paints it. He ignores support for liberals in such burgeoning places as central Los Angeles and even the San Fernando Valley (as well as San Jose and Oakland in the north), though he pays close attention to conservative Orange County and San Diego. And he writes off Hawaii—also rapidly growing, in the Sun Belt, and liberal—as insignificant. What all this suggests is that as the Sun Belt becomes more populous it does not necessarily grow uniformly more conservative. Republicans do have a chance to win in previously one-party

Democratic areas, but liberal Democrats now also have a chance to compete in previously conservative Demoratic strongholds.

The Heartland component of Phillips' case seems even weaker. It is true that in 1968 Nixon won all the Heartland states except Minnesota and Michigan. But in doing so he had immense help from George Wallace, who made the difference in all the border states. These Wallace voters had been Democratic, Phillips argues, but are on their way to becoming Republican. Perhaps; but party tradition and pocketbook issues would work in the other direction. Throughout the farm belt, Nixon did less well in 1968 than he did in 1960, whereas in most of the mountain states, he gained slightly over his 1960 showing. There is simply no basis for Phillips' proclamation of a "united Heartland."

On the other hand, there is some reason to concede the Old South to the forces Phillips seems intent upon consolidating under the banner of the Republican party. Anti-Negro feeling does run high there. So, of course, does anti-Republican feeling, but Goldwater did carry five southern states against Lyndon Johnson, and it is easy to imagine Richard Nixon's having done so against Humphrey if Wallace had not been on the ballot. Phillips recognizes, however, that the South as a distinctive political entity is shrinking in size; Texas and Florida have been overrun, and Georgia, Tennessee, Virginia, and North Carolina are not far behind. This will certainly create opportunities for the Republican party (as it will also for liberal Democrats) where none existed before 1948.

A look at the men southern electorates are sending to Congress helps to make the point that the South is becoming more like the rest of the nation in voting behavior rather than simply more conservative. Sun Belt population growth in Texas and Florida has more than balanced the loss of Congressional seats in the less urbanized of the eleven former Confederate states. In 1961, the South held 105 seats in Congress; in 1969, 106. Over the eight year period, Republicans have gained sharply—from 6 to 25 seats, nearly a quarter of the total, and many of them from urban and suburban areas. The growth of southern

bipartisanship and the redistribution of the southern population works two ways: liberal Democrats (Carl Elliott, Clark
Thompson, Frank Smith) have been squeezed out in redistrict-
ing maneuvers, but so have conservative Democrats (Frank
Boykin, James Davis, Dale Alford). Republicans have replaced
conservative Democrats more often than they have replaced
liberals; by a rough count, there are about as many liberal
southern Democrats in Congress today as there were in 1961.
An incidental, but rather important, consequence of the rise
of Republican fortunes in the South is that so long as Democrats control the House, the net effect is to reduce the influence
of the South in Congress. This is not only of great significance
to the Democratic caucus, but to the standing committees as
well. At the start of the decade, southerners held 11 committee
chairmanships; today they hold 8, which is roughly proportional to the percentage of southerners in the House Democratic party.

Concerning the backlash voters, Phillips' premise is quite
clear: anti-Negro feeling will drive large numbers of urban
Catholics and blue collar workers into the Republican party.
It is easy enough to document the existence of these feelings
(though Phillips does not do so), but there are a number of
factors that militate the other way: Democratic party loyalty
for some voters, the political activity of unions for others, and
the salience of economic issues in general. It is not easy to
predict the ultimate decision of a voter torn between what he
conceives to be his economic self-interest and his racial preju-
dices. For many voters, especially those not reached by labor
union campaigning in 1968, a vote for Wallace avoided the
dilemma, since Wallace was neither a plutocrat nor an inte-
grationist. But future Republican Presidential candidates may
or may not come to be seen in that light. In some respects,
1968 combined all the elements least favorable to the Democrats for this group of voters—high prosperity, depressing the
salience of economic issues; extremely visible urban turmoil,
increasing the salience of race and law-and-order; and the
availability on every ballot of a populist, racist alternative.
What about the future? Phillips counts heavily on the race

issue having the same powerful long-term impact on the basic loyalties of voters as the Civil War and the Great Depression once did. For some voters it well may; this certainly will be one of the main questions analysts will be asking as they comb through the attitude and opinion surveys on the election.

Just as party loyalty, habitual allegiances, and tradition will undoubtedly play a part in retarding the movement of some antiliberal voters into the Republican party, so, we must assume, will corresponding forces prevent the wholesale capture of the well-educated, the liberal, and the altruistic by the Democrats. Thus Phillips is undoubtedly right that silk stocking, Wall Street liberals, and their Yankee and suburban cousins, will continue to contribute to the Republican vote.

They will also continue to have a say in party policy-making. This prospect Phillips clearly finds distasteful on what appear to be prudential grounds. If there is, as he implies, a strong tendency for American voters to align themselves with parties according to their current convictions about public policy, and if most Americans are middle class, conservative, and anti-Negro and will vote that way if the Republican party gives them the chance (it being plain that the Democrats are hopelessly committed otherwise), then the existence within the Republican party of an eastern establishment that is liberal, upper-class, and pro-Negro is an embarrassment and a nuisance.

One would have thought that Republicans would have found the 1964 election an adequate test of this choice-not-an-echo reasoning. But hope springs eternal—as well it might, since five years later they were in the White House, and presumably intelligent people were squabbling over whether or not to award President Nixon an honorary title to George Wallace's votes.

Phillips gives no data that will settle the question of the Wallace vote. Aggregate voting statistics do not lend themselves to inferences about second choices. Meanwhile, readers and politicians will want to know whether it is true that the voting behavior of the American electorate is issue-oriented, or becoming more so. Two decades of survey research indicates that, on the whole, it is not. Are anti-Negro feelings associated with economic conservatism? Apparently not. Bigotry and approval of the welfare state are not logically incompatible, nor is it unusual to see them conjoined in the attitudes of Americans. Are Americans actually conservative in their dispositions toward the broad range of economic and social domestic policies? That is not the way they respond when asked directly. How, then, will Phillips effect the trade between Republican upper-class liberals and Democratic working-class authoritarians if the players refuse to report to their new teams?

If economic issues, interest group activity, party loyalty, and inertia still count along with race prejudice in determining partisan alignments, is there in fact a Republican majority? Again, evidently not. Richard Nixon, after all, received 43% of the popular vote—well under a majority. He never went much above that in public opinion polls, while during the unusually short campaign Hubert Humphrey steadily eroded the Wallace vote and, even more significantly, gained heavily among the "undecideds." Year after year voters are asked, what political party do you belong to? By a bit less than two to one, those who declare a party preference say Democratic. The figures in the table on party identification on page 214 include findings for October 1968, when party defections should have surfaced if short run decisions to desert the Democratic party were in fact a down payment on a long run commitment. But the figures show essentially no movement in that direction.

Some of these Democrats do not vote Democratic, and some of them do not vote at all. In 1968, the Survey Research Center found that about 18% of the Democratic identifiers deserted to Nixon and 11% to Wallace, while Nixon only lost 7% of the Republican identifiers to Humphrey and 5% to Wallace. About 60% of the Wallace vote came from Democratic identifiers and leaners. So, manifestly, in a truly bad year for Democrats, a Republican can win.

But long-term patterns of party affiliation seem remarkably stable. Over the whole sixteen-year period, there is a slight increase in voters' tendency to classify themselves as politically unaffiliated. This parallels the massive influx of post-World War II babies into the electorate, and we assume that a large proportion of the rise in non-affiliation can be explained by the changing proportion of young people who affiliate and vote at a much lower rate than their elders. In spite of these small changes, there is a discernible long-run Democratic advantage in Presidential elections. This is also sometimes visible in voting for offices other than the Presidency. Even in a year like 1968, when, according to Phillips, a Republican majority (Wallace plus Nixon) emerged, the Democrats won by a large majority in the House of Representatives. Since then Democrats won special elections for the Heartland Republican safe seats of James Battin of Montana and Melvin Laird of Wisconsin and held the late Robert Everett's Democratic seat in Tennessee by a very wide margin. And, of course, they maintained that majority in the election of 1970, although they lost a few seats in the Senate.

How, then, may President Nixon cause a Republican majority to emerge? There is little beyond public policy that a President can manipulate. Given the improbability that American voters will overhaul their basic long-run commitments in response to most policies, four years is not much time to make an impact, no matter what he does. But following Phillips' reasoning at least part of the way, President Nixon can make the Republican party more hospitable to working and lower middle class people whose anti-Negro feelings are balanced by their beliefs that Republicans are the "party of the rich." Encouraging racial backlash, however, is the hard way to do it because such a strategy would probably entail an increase in violence that would jeopardize a lot more than the effectiveness and good reputation of the Nixon Presidency. A less hazardous course would be to woo the lower middle class by making economic concessions to them. Nixon's initial tax reform policy and (to a lesser extent) the welfare proposals of the new administration seemed reasonably well adapted to this strategy, provided he could get Congress to support them, and appropriate enough money to make them work. But again, it is unlikely that anything the President can do over the short run will drastically affect the party allegiances of the vast majority of Americans.

Even if Phillips is wrong in suggesting that the race issue

has already remade the American electorate, it may yet do so. If this happens, the majority Phillips identifies may conceivably emerge. But whether a Republican administration—or any administration—can govern effectively, or wisely, by catering to the impulses that would mobilize such a majority may well be doubted.

INCUMBENCY AS A LIABILITY—
THE VICE-PRESIDENCY

Yet the incumbent President does have some advantages; it is the candidate who seeks to succeed an incumbent of his own party who suffers the most. His is the unhappy lot, as Stevenson discovered in 1952, Nixon in 1960, and Humphrey in 1968, of getting the worst of all possible worlds. He suffers from both the disadvantages of having to defend an existing record and of being a new man. He cannot attack the administration in office without alienating the President and selling his own party short, and he cannot claim he has experience in office. It may be difficult for him to defend a record he did not make and may not wholly care for. His is the most difficult strategic problem of all the candidates.[103]

Thomas Riley Marshall, the genial Hoosier who was Woodrow Wilson's Vice-President, once observed that the office he had in the U.S. Capitol was so little protected from tourists that they used to come by and stare at him like a monkey in the zoo. "Only," he complained, "they never offer me any peanuts."

This is the way Vice-Presidents have viewed their constitutional office, not just its physical setting, for a long time. "Not worth a pitcher of warm spit" was John Nance Garner's rueful conclusion in the mid-'30s. "A mere mechanical tool to wind up the clock" was the way the first Vice-President, John Adams, described himself. "My country has in its wisdom contrived for me the most insignificant office that was the invention of man."

The main constitutional function of the Vice-President is

to wait. Clearly this is not much of a job for a major political leader, used to active leadership. Yet suppose a sudden tragedy should befall the President. Can we afford in the inevitable days of uncertainty and national bereavement that follow upon such an event to replace him with anything less than a major political leader who can step into the breach immediately, do the President's job and do it well?

This is the first and fundamental dilemma of the Vice-Presidency, and as the quotation from John Adams amply testifies, it has been with us since the founding of the Republic. From this dilemma flow the problems characteristic of the modern Vice-Presidency.

We can date the modern Vice-Presidency from April 12, 1945; the day Franklin Roosevelt died. The next day his successor remarked to some newspapermen. "Boys, if you ever pray, pray for me now. I don't know whether you fellows ever had a load of hay fall on you, but when they told me yesterday what had happened, I felt like the moon, the stars and all the planets had fallen on me."

Harry S. Truman had been a respected but not a leading senator before he assumed the Vice-Presidency. In his three months in that office Vice-President Truman saw President Roosevelt only a few short times. As Vice-President he had not been told of the Manhattan Project to build the atomic bomb. Sticking closely to the duties prescribed under the Constitution, Mr. Truman spent the vast bulk of his time on Capitol Hill, presiding over the Senate.

His knowledge of the affairs of the executive branch and of foreign and military operations was the knowledge of an experienced legislator and not the inside information routinely available to top policy-makers in the Roosevelt administration. Mr. Truman wrote later "It is a mighty leap from the vice presidency to the presidency when one is forced to make it without warning."

Since Harry Truman made the leap in the waning days of World War II the world has grown more complicated, and so has the Presidency. Efforts have accordingly been made to update the Vice-Presidency to meet modern conditions. The

Vice-President now sits with the National Security Council as a matter of right: under President Eisenhower, the Vice-President attended all meetings of the Cabinet at the President's invitation and presided in the President's absence. In addition to his Capitol Hill quarters Vice-President Johnson had a suite of offices in the Executive Office Building adjacent to the White House. For a while President Nixon moved Spiro Agnew to an office down the hall from his own.

Moreover, since 1945, Presidents have made greater efforts to involve Vice-Presidents in various administrative activities: good-will tours abroad, occasional attempts to promote legislation on Capitol Hill, honorific jobs "coordinating" programs to which the President wants to give a little extra publicity, and, especially, political missionary work around the country— speeches and appearances in behalf of Presidential programs.

These are the tasks of the modern Vice-President. In return for continuous briefing on the entire range of problems confronting the government, vastly improved access to the ear of the President and a closer view of the burdens of the Presidency, the modern Vice-President must carry some of these burdens himself.

Which burdens he carries, how many, and how far, are up to the President. Naturally a Vice-President may withhold his cooperation: but if he does, he impairs his relationship with the President. This is bound to affect adversely his capacity to fulfill the constitutional obligation of the Vice-Presidency, to be genuinely prepared in case of dire need.

The Vice-President is in no sense the second in command in a President's administration. In truth, he is entirely removed from any chain of command at all in the government. This guaranteed the independence of the Vice-President in the days of Aaron Burr, John C. Calhoun, Charles Dawes, and other free spirits who have occupied the office.

Today, the situation is quite different: it is much easier for high members of a President's administration to maintain independence from the Presidency. Top administrative officials can constitute a loyal opposition on government policy within the executive branch because their obligations run in at least three directions: upward to the President, downward to the agencies whose programs they supervise within the administration, and outward to the clientele their agencies serve.

Political executives serve the President best who serve their clients with devotion and promote the interests of their agencies with vigor. They know, moreover, that if in the process they conflict too much with Presidential plans or priorities the President can always fire them. If the President fails them in some serious way, they can resign.

The Vice-President can hardly fulfill his constitutional responsibilities by resigning, nor, in midterm, can he be dismissed. He has no anchor in the bureaucracy, no interest group constituency. Thus, uniquely in the executive branch, the modern Vice-President must discipline himself to loyalty to the President.

This sometimes has painful consequences for Vice-Presidents, especially when they attempt to emerge from the shadow of the President and run for the Presidency on their own. It is scarcely necessary to note Vice-President Humphrey's difficulty in persuading opponents of the Vietnam war that he and President Johnson were not Siamese twins.

Voters with longer memories may recall Vice-President Richard Nixon's similar problem in 1960, when Senator Kennedy wanted to get the country "moving again." Mr. Nixon somehow had to offer a new program of his own while defending the eight Eisenhower years, wrapping himself in the mantle of his popular predecessor, but taking no notice of the occasional pot-shots the general peevishly took at him. Neither Vice-President was fully able to run independently on his own record.

There seems, in short, to be no way for a Vice-President to avoid the dilemmas built into the office: unless he is scrupulously loyal to the President, he cannot get the access to the President that he needs to discharge his constitutional function; when he is loyal to the President, he is saddled, at least in the short run, with whatever characteristics of the President or his program the President's enemies or his own care to fasten on him. He sits there in the limelight, visible, vulnerable and, for the most part, powerless.

Nevertheless, as long as Vice-Presidents have some chance eventually to run for the Presidency, as they presently do, and are not arbitrarily excluded from further consideration as independent political leaders in their own right, there will be plenty of takers for the Vice-Presidential nominations. This contributes to the strength of political parties.

Vice-Presidential nominees can balance tickets, help to unite a warring party, and campaign effectively with party workers and before the public—as, for example Senator Lyndon Johnson did with conspicuous success in the election of 1960. Thus, Vice-Presidential nominees can help a great deal to elect a President. It is after the campaign is over that the Vice-President's problems begin.

Unless, of course, by a stroke of good fortune, he and his running-mate lose.

CONVERTIBILITY OF RESOURCES

Clearly, the social framework within which Presidential election strategies must be pursued distributes advantages and disadvantages rather importantly between the parties.

We have attempted to explain why the unequal distribution of key resources such as money and control over information do not necessarily lead to election victories for the parties and candidates which possess and use most of these resources. Might there not, however, be a cumulative effect which would greatly assist those who possessed both more money and more control over information? This effect may exist but it could obviously not be of overwhelming importance since the Democrats, who are usually disadvantaged in these respects, have won most of the recent elections. We can suggest three reasons for Democratic strength despite these disadvantages. First, the Democrats are able to convert other resources into money and control over information thereby narrowing the gap during campaigns. Second, the Democrats have superior access to other important resources which may overwhelm the Republican superiority in money and control over the media of information. Third, the Democrats are better able in general to convert some resources into others than are their opponents.

Once the Democratic party assumed the Presidency in 1933 and held it for twenty years, it was able to use the resource of official position to collect more campaign funds because contributors want access to the winner. The party could also get greater news coverage because the President's activities are newsworthy no matter what his party. The alliance of the Democrats with the large industrial unions has, at times, meant that the party received contributions in the coin of personal electioneering for which the Republicans had to lay out cash or do without. The superiority (perhaps the mere existence) of Democratic organizations in cities of large population with strategic impact on the Electoral College has sometimes led to the availability of election workers who did not have to be paid in cash—at least not during the campaign and not at all if the party lost the election. The appeals of the Democrats to ethnic, racial, and religious groups has meant that publications of these specialized groups might serve to offset the preponderant Republican orientation of the daily press.

The fact that the Democrats have approximately a three to two lead over Republicans in party identification is perhaps the most effective resource in the Democratic arsenal, so effective, indeed, that it is apparently more than enough to compensate for whatever advantages the Republicans gain through wealth and the mass media. For unless the Republicans manage to do something special, or the Democrats oblige, as they did in 1968, by falling into spectacular disarray, the voters will elect a Democrat by following their usual partisan dispositions. To be sure, other things such as turnout, for example, are not always equal; otherwise the Republicans would never win. But in the sheer numbers of nominal supporters the Democrats are ahead at the start.

Implicit in these remarks is the proposition that the Democrats in our era are better able to convert their resources into success at the polls than are the Republicans. That is, the party identification of a significant majority of the electorate can more easily be turned into electoral victory than money or control over information can be turned to winning the allegiance of citizens to a different party. Party identifications change but slowly and change significantly only under the impact of events in the society which profoundly affect the mass of citizens. No one really knows short of that how to go about changing the party identifications of masses of people in the same partisan direction.

The Republicans can use their advantage in turnout to overcome the Democratic advantage in party identification. They can try to make party identification seem less relevant at election time by putting up an attractive candidate who is "above" partisanship. They can capitalize on errors by Democrats or on dissatisfaction with a Democratic administration. No one can claim to predict the outcomes of elections yet to come; certainly we cannot. Nothing that has been said here means that a Republican might not win handily, as Eisenhower did in two elections and Nixon did in 1968 after the Vietnam issue decimated the Democratic party leadership. Speaking in terms of probabilities over several elections, however, it seems to us that the Democrats are likely to win more often than they lose.

SUMMARY

As politicians develop their strategies for winning nomination and election to the Presidency, they will have to keep in mind numerous facts that are given in their political environment, and probably not subject to change by anything they may do. Among these are the facts that:

1) Most voters are not sufficiently concerned with specific policies to change their votes in response to policy appeals.

2) Rather, they vote the way they do out of party habit.

3) They may or may not *turn out* in great numbers, however, and therefore it is necessary to activate intermediary organizations and party activists in order to help turn out one's own voters.

4) Parties seek to win elections as their major goal.

5) Either party has a reasonably good chance to win the election: the Democrats because they are in the majority; the Republicans because they are much more likely to turn out, and because they have better access to money and greater sympathy in the press.

6) Intermediary organizations such as interest groups and party organizations can be activated by policy commitments and reaffirmations and promises of access to governmental decision-making.

7) Each of the parties consists of a loose coalition of interest groups and state and local parties.

8) The Electoral College puts a premium on votes from large two-party states.

Most or all of these basic facts are well understood by Presidential candidates and their managers. They understand that getting nominated and getting elected present two separate, though interrelated, problems. Let us now see what sorts of political strategies they devise to master these problems.

NOTES

1. In a major work on public opinion, V. O. Key, Jr. states, "For most Americans issues of politics are not of central concern. . . ." At another point Key summarizes the literature as follows: "In analysis after analysis of opinions on specific issues, sizable proportions of persons have been shown to lack an opinion." *Public Opinion and American Democracy* (New York, 1961), pp. 47, 185. When asked "What things are you most concerned with these days?" two out of three people in a representative sample of registered voters in New Haven, Connecticut, spoke of personal matters like jobs, health, and children. Only one out of five cited local, state, national, or international affairs. Robert A. Dahl, *Who Governs?* (New Haven, 1961), p. 279. A similar survey conducted in Oberlin, Ohio, shows that only 17% of a random (but representative) sample say that they are concerned with public affairs. Aaron B. Wildavsky, *Leadership in a Small Town* (Totowa, N. J., 1964). Further supporting evidence may be found in Julian L. Woodward and Elmo Roper, "Political Activity of American Citizens," *American Political Science Review* 44 (December 1950), 872–875, and Samuel Stouffer, *Communism, Conformity and Civil Liberties* (Garden City, 1955), Chapter 3. Using data from the Survey Research Center, Philip E. Converse estimates that those

who are strongly ideological number about 3.5% of the voting population, and those who have some ideological capacities number no more than 12%. He finds that 17.5% of the population have attitudes with no issue content whatsoever, that 45% concentrate on matters of some immediate group interest, and that 22% are concerned largely with something in the nature of the times. See his article "The Nature of Belief Systems in Mass Politics," in *Ideology and Discontent*, ed. David E. Apter (New York, 1964), pp. 206–261. See especially the table and commentary on p. 218.

2. See Angus Campbell, Philip E. Converse, Warren E. Miller, and Donald E. Stokes, *The American Voter* (New York, 1960), pp. 89–115. Writing of the 1956 Presidential election, for example, the authors say that "the rate of turnout among persons of high interest exceeded that among persons of low interest by nearly 30 per cent . . ." (p. 102). See also Gordon M. Connelly and Harry M. Field, "The Non-Voter—Who He Is, What He Thinks," *Public Opinion Quarterly* 8 (Summer 1944), 175–187. The work of Angus Campbell and his associates at the University of Michigan's Survey Research Center, to which we will refer again, is based on numerous sample surveys of the entire American voting population. These studies, which have been going on since 1948, have through the years increased in breadth and sophistication and at the moment represent the largest pool of data we have on the political habits of Americans. The work of Paul Lazarsfeld, Bernard Berelson, and their associates at the Columbia Bureau of Applied Social Research has been going on since 1940. Rather than national sample surveys, the BASR group has collected data of a more focused kind, often limited to a single community. The BASR group pioneered in the use of panel surveys, which consist of series of re-interviews with a sample of respondents. For a description and critique of these and other materials we shall be using, see Peter H. Rossi, "Four Landmarks in Voting Research," in *American Voting Behavior*, eds. Eugene Burdick and Arthur J. Brodbeck (Glencoe, 1959), Chapter 1. Another interesting discussion of the SRC work is contained in Peter B. Natchez, "Images of Voting: The Social Psychologists," *Public Policy* 17 (Summer 1970), pp. 553–588.

3. Bernard Berelson, Paul F. Lazarsfeld, and William N. McPhee, *Voting* (Chicago, 1954), p. 25; Campbell *et al.*, *The American Voter*, pp. 475–483; Key, *Public Opinion and American Democracy*, pp. 195–199.

4. Campbell *et al.*, *The American Voter*, pp. 120–145. Robert E. Lane concludes, "Over the long run party identification has more influence over a person's vote decision than any other single factor. . . ." *Political Life* (Glencoe, 1959), p. 300.

5. The authors of *The American Voter* write that in comparison
to habitual party identifiers, ". . . Independents tend as a group to
be somewhat less involved in politics. They have somewhat poorer
knowledge of the issues, their image of the candidates is fainter,
their interest in the campaign is less, their concern over the outcome is relatively slight, and their choice between competing candidates . . . seems much less to spring from discoverable evalua-
tions of the elements of national politics." (Campbell *et al.*, p. 143.)
See also Berelson *et al.*, *Voting*, pp. 25–27, and, for a somewhat
different treatment, Robert Agger, "Independents and Party Identifiers," in *American Voting Behavior*, eds. Burdick and Brodbeck,
Chapter 17.

6. Berelson *et al.*, *Voting*, pp. 215–233. George Belknap and
Angus Campbell state that "for many people Democratic or Republican attitudes regarding foreign policy result from conscious
or unconscious adherence to a perceived party line rather than
from influences independent of party identification." "Political
Party Identification and Attitudes Toward Foreign Policy," *Public
Opinion Quarterly* 15 (Winter 1951–52), 623. Campbell and his
associates speak of "the electorate's profound loyalty to the existing parties. Our [Survey Research Center] studies regularly have
shown that three-quarters of the adult population grants outright
its allegiance to the Republican or Democratic Party and that
most of those who call themselves Independents acknowledge some
degree of attachment to one of the parties. These partisan identifications . . . appear highly resistant to change." (Campbell *et al.*,
The American Voter, pp. 552–553.)

7. The various voting studies previously cited all contain substantial discussions of this subject. See, especially, Robert E. Lane,
"Fathers and Sons: Foundations of Political Belief," *American
Sociological Review* 24 (August 1959), 502–511; Campbell *et al.*,
The American Voter, pp. 146–147. H. H. Remmers, "Early Sociali-
zation of Attitudes," in *American Voting Behavior*, eds. Burdick
and Brodbeck, pp. 55–67. Key, *Public Opinion and American
Democracy*, pp. 293–314, sums up in these words: "Children acquire
early in life a feeling of party identification; they have sensitive
antennae and since they are imitative animals, soon take on the
political color of their family . . ." (p. 294); see, especially, Fred
I. Greenstein, *Children and Politics* (New Haven, 1965), Chapter 4.

8. ". . . People are more likely to associate with people like themselves—alike in political complexion as well as social position."
(Berelson *et al.*, Voting, p. 83.)

9. Paul Lazarsfeld, Bernard Berelson, and Hazel Gaudet, *The
People's Choice* (New York, 1944), pp. 16–28.

10. *Ibid.*; Angus Campbell and Homer C. Cooper, *Group Differences in Attitudes and Votes* (Ann Arbor, 1956); Woodward and Roper, "Political Activity of American Citizens," 872–875; Key, *Public Opinion and American Democracy,* pp. 99–120, 121–181; Berelson *et al., Voting,* pp. 54–76. Unfortunately, Moses Rischin, *Our Own Kind* (Santa Barbara, 1960), has Presidential data only from the unusual Eisenhower elections.

11. V. O. Key, Jr., *Southern Politics* (New York, 1950) pp. 75–81, 223–228, 280–285. The South is becoming more evenly divided in its political loyalties because two trends have outweighed the effects of a third—the influx of Republicans into the South and the conversion of conservative Southerners to Republicanism have not been made up by the increasingly heavy turnout of black people who vote overwhelmingly Democratic in Presidential elections.

12. V. O. Key, Jr., "A Theory of Critical Elections," *The Journal of Politics* 17 (February 1955), 3–18; Campbell *et al., The American Voter,* p. 160. See, more generally, James Q. Wilson, *Negro Politics* (Glencoe, 1960). Barry Goldwater's 1964 candidacy intensified the Democratic loyalties of black voters, as we show on pp. 13–14, 47–48.

13. See Duane Lockard, *New England State Politics* (Princeton, 1959); Dahl, *Who Governs?* pp. 33–51, 216–217; Elmer E. Cornwell, "Party Absorption of Ethnic Groups: The Case of Providence, R. I.," *Social Forces* 38 (March 1960), 205–210; J. Joseph Huthmacher, *Massachusetts People and Politics* (Cambridge, Mass., 1959), pp. 118–126.

14. Samuel Lubell, *The Future of American Politics* (New York, 1951), pp. 129–157.

15. Campbell *et al., The American Voter,* pp. 55–57, 525–528, 537; Herbert H. Hyman and Paul B. Sheatsley, "The Political Appeal of President Eisenhower," *Public Opinion Quarterly* 19 (Winter 1955–56), 26–39.

16. The portions of this analysis which deal with voters and issues are taken from Chapter 8, "Public Policy and Political Preference," in Campbell *et al., The American Voter,* pp. 168–187.

17. In a methodologically excellent national sample survey conducted in 1954 which was designed to discover the concerns of the American people on subjects then agitating American political elites relating to Communism and civil liberties, Samuel Stouffer found: "The number of people who said that they were worried either about the threat of Communists in the U. S. or about civil liberties was, even by the most generous interpretation of occa-

sionally ambiguous responses, *less than 1 per cent.* Even world problems, including the shadow of war, did not evoke a spontaneous answer from more than 8 per cent." (Stouffer, *Communism, Conformity and Civil Liberties,* p. 59.) See Hazel Gaudet Erskine, "The Polls: The Informed Public," *Public Opinion Quarterly* 26 (Winter 1962), 669–677. This article summarizes questions asked since 1947 of national samples of Americans designed to ascertain their information on current news topics. Similar data for 1935–46 are contained in Hadley Cantrill and Mildred Strunk, *Public Opinion, 1935–1946* (Princeton, 1951).

18.   The data on which this conclusion is based refer to issues in rather general categories such as "economic aid to foreign countries," "influence of big business in government," and "aid to education." (Campbell *et al., The American Voter,* p. 182.) It is highly probable that the proportion of people meeting the three requirements would be substantially reduced if precise and specific policies within these general issue categories formed the basis of questions in a survey.

19.   The authors of *The American Voter* tentatively conclude that in the Eisenhower years, covered by their study, "people who paid little attention to politics were contributing very disproportionately to partisan change." (Campbell *et al.,* p. 264.)

20.   Philip E. Converse, "Information Flow and the Stability of Partisan Attitudes," *Public Opinion Quarterly* 26 (Winter 1962), 578–599.

21.   V. O. Key, Jr., with the assistance of Milton C. Cummings, Jr., *The Responsible Electorate: Rationality in Presidential Voting, 1936–1960* (Cambridge, Mass., 1966).

22.   Campbell *et al., The American Voter,* pp. 153–160; Key, "A Theory of Critical Elections," 3–18. Stouffer, *Communism, Conformity and Civil Liberties,* p. 87, says that Americans are concerned not with world problems, but with personal problems. He adds, "a 'business recession' finds a path into almost every home— whether it is that of a factory worker or that of a butcher who finds his sales of meat declining. It becomes a threat that is immediate and personal."

23.   Key asserts that "as has been demonstrated, the citizen's identification with party tends to produce a tie consistent with his policy preferences." (*Public Opinion and American Democracy,* p. 460.) See also Lazarsfeld *et al., The People's Choice,* Chapter 9.

24.   Richard A. Brody, Benjamin I. Page, *et al.,* "Vietnam, the Urban Crisis and the 1968 Presidential Election: A Preliminary Analysis," prepared for delivery at the 1969 meeting of the Amer-

ican Sociological Association, September 1969. The authors polled four national samples of the electorate during the campaign and asked numerous questions (rather than only a few) about each issue.

25. This notion is developed by Anthony Downs, *An Economic Theory of Democracy* (New York, 1957).

26. See Raymond A. Bauer, Ithiel de Sola Pool, and Lewis Anthony Dexter, *American Business and Public Policy* (New York, 1963), pp. 323–399, especially p. 373.

27. See Seymour M. Lipset, Paul F. Lazarsfeld, Allen H. Barton, and Juan Linz, "The Psychology of Voting: An Analysis of Political Behavior," in *Handbook of Social Psychology*, ed. Gardner Lindzey (Cambridge, Mass., 1954).

28. "Where the Vote Comes From: An Analysis of Electoral Coalitions from 1952–1968, *American Political Science Review* 66 (March 1972).

29. This discussion is drawn largely from Aaron Wildavsky, "The Intelligent Citizen's Guide to the Abuses of Statistics: The Kennedy Document and the Catholic Vote," *Politics and Social Life*, eds. Nelson W. Polsby, Robert A. Dentler, and Paul A. Smith (Boston, 1963), pp. 825–844. See also Thomas Flinn, "How Nixon Took Ohio," *Western Political Quarterly* 15 (June 1962), 276–279; Philip E. Converse, Angus Campbell, Warren E. Miller, and Donald E. Stokes, "Stability and Change in 1960: A Reinstating Election," *American Political Science Review* 55 (June 1961), 269–280; Andrew R. Baggaley, "Religious Influence on Wisconsin Voting, 1928–1960," *American Political Science Review* 56 (March 1962), 66–70; Rischin, *Our Own Kind;* and Angus Campbell, Philip E. Converse, Warren E. Miller and Donald E. Stokes, *Elections and the Political Order* (New York, 1966) pp. 96–124, an essay by Converse, "Religion and Politics: The 1960 Election."

30. See Ithiel de Sola Pool, Robert P. Abelson, and Samuel L. Popkin, *Candidates, Issues, and Strategies* (Cambridge, Mass., 1964), pp. 117–118.

31. See Converse in *Elections and the Political Order*, especially pp. 117 ff.

32. Pool, Abelson, and Popkin, *op. cit.*, pp. 68, 117–118.

33. Baggaley, "Religious Influence on Wisconsin Voting, 1928–1960," 66–70.

34. Converse, Campbell, Miller, and Stokes, "Stability and Change in 1960: A Reinstating Election," 269–280.

35. See Wildavsky, in Polsby *et al.*, *Politics and Social Life*, pp. 825–844.

36. The conclusion is far from implausible. In 1960, at least a quarter of a million Jews and over a million black citizens lived in Illinois. Over a million black people lived in Texas, and 174,387 of them were registered to vote, according to the U.S. Civil Rights Commission. ("Voting," *1961 U.S. Commision on Civil Rights Report*, 301.)

37. "Access" is the opportunity to press claims upon decision-makers. This does not imply that those who have more access are more successful in pressing their claims, but it is generally supposed that claims have a better chance of realization when they are presented repeatedly and auspiciously to decision-makers, and by "known" rather than "unknown" claimants. See David B. Truman, *The Governmental Process* (New York, 1951), pp. 264-270.

38. Our interpretation of parties is based largely on Pendleton Herring, *The Politics of Democracy* (New York, 1940); V. O. Key, Jr., *Politics, Parties and Pressure Groups*, 4th ed. (New York, 1958); David B. Truman, "Federalism and the Party System," in *Federalism Mature and Emergent*, ed. Arthur Macmahon (New York, 1955), Chapter 8; Anthony Downs, *An Economic Theory of Democracy;* and a burgeoning literature (some of it already cited) on state and local political party organizations. See, especially, Truman, *The Governmental Process*, pp. 262-287.

39. Herring, *The Politics of Democracy*, especially pp. 272-287. See also, Edward C. Banfield, *Political Influence* (New York, 1961).

40. The structure of American political parties is treated, among other places, in Key, *Politics, Parties and Pressure Groups;* Hugh A. Bone, *American Politics and the Party System* (New York, 1955); and William Goodman, *The Two-Party System in the United States* (New York, 1956).

41. See Warren E. Miller, "Presidential Coattails: a Study in Political Myth and Methodology," *Public Opinion Quarterly* 19 (Winter 1955-56), 26-39.

42. William S. Livingston, "A Note on the Nature of Federalism," *Political Science Quarterly* 67 (March 1952), 81-95.

43. See Robert R. Alford, *Party and Society* (Chicago, 1963), Chapter 6, "The United States: The Politics of Diversity." This reanalysis of a variety of surveys suggests that class-oriented voting in the United States, while it exists, does not polarize voters to the extent that can be found in Great Britain or Australia.

44. Herbert McClosky, Paul J. Hoffman, and Rosemary O'Hara, "Issue Conflict and Consensus Among Party Leaders and Followers," *American Political Science Review* 54 (June 1960), 406-427. The authors, who compared large samples of Democratic and Re-

publican leaders on twenty-four major public issues, conclude that "the belief that the two American parties are identical in principle and doctrine has little foundation in fact. Examination of the opinions of Democratic and Republican leaders shows them to be distinct communities of co-believers who diverge sharply on many important issues." They add, "Little support was found for the belief that deep cleavages exist among the electorate but are ignored by the leaders. One might, indeed, more accurately assert the contrary, to wit: that the natural cleavages between the leaders are largely ignored by the voters" (pp. 425–426).

45. Key, *Public Opinion and American Democracy*, p. 439, observes, "Of Democratic high participators . . . only 34 per cent fall into white-collar occupations; of the Republican group comparable in political activity, 48 per cent are from white-collar occupations. Substantially more Democratic than Republican high participators are blue-collar workers. Occupational differences between the party identifiers become more marked as level of political participation increases."

46. The 1964 interviews were conducted in the lobby of the Fairmont Hotel in San Francisco—where the California, Illinois, and New Jersey delegations were housed—by Aaron Wildavsky, Judy Gordon, Maralyn Millman, James Payne, and Joseph Paff. While these unstructured interviews in no way represent a systematic sample of the delegates, they were undertaken because they have one great advantage over the usual mail questionnaire: they can elicit spontaneous information about respondents' attitudes that a more structured method might well miss. The 1968 interviews were conducted at the Democratic Convention in Chicago by Aaron Wildavsky and associates, including Frank Levy, Andrew McFarland, Bill Cavala, Robert Nakamura, Jeffrey Pressman, Philip Auerbach, Jo Freeman, Laura Martin, Wallet Rogers and Theodore Totman. We wish to thank Dean Sanford Elberg of the Graduate Division of the University of California for providing the funds that made this research possible. It consists of approximately 500 interviews lasting from a few minutes to an hour. All the major delegations—California, New York, Illinois, Texas, Ohio, Pennsylvania—were covered, as were smaller delegations from every section of the nation. We placed ourselves in the hotels where the delegates stayed and were able to interview them easily from early in the morning until the late afternoon when the buses left for the convention hall. The violence that marked the convention week took place largely outside the hotels and did not inhibit our activities. We were never denied access to any hotel. A sample survey conducted at the convention by John W. Soule and James Clark of Florida State University ("Amateurs and Pro-

fessionals: A Study of Delegates to the 1968 Democratic Convention," *American Political Science Review* 64, September 1970, pp. 888–899) agrees with the main contention that the major difference among the delegates was stylistic rather than substantive. The material that follows is taken in revised form from Aaron Wildavsky, "The Goldwater Phenomenon: Purists, Politicians, and the Two-Party System," *The Review of Politics* 27, No. 3 (July 1965), 386–413, and "The Meaning of 'Youth' in the Struggle for Control of the Democratic Party," *The Revolt Against the Masses and Other Essays on Politics and Public Policy* (New York, 1971).

47. This is borne out by findings of the Michigan Survey Research Center. Integrity was the personal quality most admired in him by his supporters. See Angus Campbell, "Interpreting the Presidential Victory," in *The National Election of 1964*, ed. Milton C. Cummings, Jr. (Washington, 1966), p. 261.

48. See James Q. Wilson, *The Amateur Democrat* (Chicago, 1962).

49. See Jeremy Larner, *Nobody Knows: Reflections on the McCarthy Campaign of 1968* (New York, 1970).

50. Philip E. Converse, Warren E. Miller, Jerrold G. Rusk, and Arthur C. Wolfe, "Continuity and Change in American Politics: Parties and Issues in the 1968 Election," *American Political Science Review* 63 (December 1969), 1083–1105.

51. The unit rule is not prescribed in the Constitution or by Federal law. Rather, it is the result of individual state action which provides, in all states, that Electors for party nominees are grouped together and elected *en bloc*, on a "general ticket" such that a vote for one Elector is a vote for all the Electors on that ticket, with the majority vote electing all Electors for the state. Senator Thomas Hart Benton said in 1824, "The general ticket system . . . was the offspring of policy. . . . It was adopted by the leading men of [ten states] to enable them to consolidate the vote of the state. . . ."

Thomas Jefferson had earlier pointed out that ". . . while ten states choose either by legislatures or by a general ticket it is folly and worse than folly for the other states not to do it." In short, once a few states maximized their impact by using the unit rule, the others followed suit. See *Motion for Leave to File Complaint, Complaint and Brief, Delaware* v. *New York*, No. 28 Original, U.S. Supreme Court, October term, 1966; and Neal R. Peirce, "The Electoral College Goes to Court," *The Reporter*, October 6, 1966.

52. For 1960 figures, see Herbert E. Alexander, *Financing the 1960 Election* (Princeton, 1962), p. 10. Figures for 1964 are con-

tained in Herbert E. Alexander and Harold B. Meyers, "The Switch in Campaign Giving," *Fortune* (November 1965), 103–108. Figures for 1968 are contained in Herbert Alexander, "Financing Parties and Campaigns in 1968: A Preliminary Report" (mimeo, Citizens Research Foundation, Princeton, 1969).

53. Alexander Heard, *The Costs of Democracy* (Chapel Hill, 1960), pp. 7–8; Herbert E. Alexander, "Financing the Parties and Campaigns," in *The Presidential Election and Transition, 1960–61*, ed. Paul T. David (Washington, 1961), pp. 116–118; Alexander and Meyers, "The Switch in Campaign Giving." Alexander, "Financing Parties and Campaigns in 1968," p. 2.

54. Heard, *The Costs of Democracy*, pp. 18–22, 39; Alexander, "Financing the Parties and Campaigns," p. 118; Alexander and Meyers, "The Switch in Campaign Giving."

55. Alexander and Meyers, "The Switch in Campaign Giving."

56. Alexander, "Financing the Parties and Campaigns," p. 117.

57. Heard, *The Costs of Democracy*, p. 6.

58. *Ibid.*, p. 41; Herbert E. Alexander, *Financing the 1964 Election* (Princeton, 1966), pp. 68–69.

59. Heard, *The Costs of Democracy*, pp. 49–53.

60. For expenditure figures, see *ibid.*, pp. 17–24 and, for 1960, see Alexander, *Financing the 1960 Election*, pp. 9–13. The following table is adapted from figures in both these books.

	Democratic Percentage of Two-Party Vote	Democratic Percentage of Two-Party Expenditures
1932	59	49
1936	62	41
1940	55	35
1944	52	42
1948	52	39
1952	44	45
1956	42	38
1960	50	45
1964	61	41
1968	49	31

On the state level, our conclusion may not be correct, however. See Murray Levin and George Blackwood, *The Compleat Politician* (Indianapolis, 1962), pp. 227–243.

61. Alexander, "1968," p. 68.

62. Alexander, "Financing the Parties and Campaigns," p. 119.

63. Alexander, "1968," p. 9.

64. See Theodore H. White, *The Making of the President, 1960* (New York, 1961), pp. 71–74.

65. See *ibid.*, pp. 92–110, and Harry Ernst, *The Primary That Made a President: West Virginia, 1960* (New York, 1962), especially pp. 16–17, 29–31. Several factors appear to have contributed to Humphrey's difficulty in raising money. First and probably foremost, he had very little of his own to draw upon. Second, Adlai Stevenson was being indecisive. By refusing to withdraw himself, his backers were encouraged to wait and see rather than switch monetary support to Humphrey. Had Stevenson not been in contention, Humphrey might have gotten more money. And third, Humphrey apparently was unwilling to do things which would severely alienate the other candidates or otherwise jeopardize his future associations in the party. He may, therefore, have been restrained from actions which would have aided him. A revealing passage in White (pp. 109–110) indicates what may have been involved.

In New York, from which so much Stevenson money had originally come to Humphrey's coffers, Governor Abraham Ribicoff, acting on Kennedy's instructions, warned all Stevensonians that if they continued to finance the hopeless campaign of Hubert Humphrey, Adlai Stevenson would not even be considered for Secretary of State. Where necessary, Kennedy lieutenants were even rougher; in Connecticut, Boss John Bailey informed former Connecticut Senator William Benton . . . that if he continued to finance Humphrey (Benton had already given Humphrey $5,000 earlier in the spring), he would never hold another elective or appointive job in Connecticut. . . .

Benton disputes this story. "It was wholly out of character for John Bailey to say anything like the words Teddy White ascribed to him . . . John Bailey did get in touch with me, but what he said was this: 'Since you gave $5000 to Hubert's campaign I want you to even the account by giving $5000 to Jack Kennedy's campaign.' I told John that if Jack was nominated for the presidency, I would give him $10,000, which I later did." Quoted in Sidney Hyman, *The Lives of William Benton* (Chicago, 1969), p. 529.

66. In October 1968, for example, a multimillionaire named Stewart Mott offered to raise a million dollars for Hubert Humphrey, then in desperate need of cash. Mott "made it clear that the Presidential candidate would have to modify his views on

Vietnam." Humphrey refused Mott's offer. Herbert Alexander and
H. B. Meyers, "A Financial Landslide for the GOP," *Fortune*
(March 1970), p. 187.

67. Jasper B. Shannon, *Money and Politics* (New York, 1959),
p. 35.

68. Heard, *The Costs of Democracy*, pp. 212–232.

69. *Ibid.*, pp. 249–258.

70. See *ibid.*, and Shannon, *Money and Politics*, p. 59. On pages
13–65, Shannon presents a colorful history of American experience
in raising money for Presidential campaigns.

71. Alexander and Meyers, "The Switch in Campaign Giving,"
103–108. In 1968, the pattern of small giving continued, augmented
by the return to the Republican fold of many large contributors who
had defected to President Johnson in 1964. See Alexander, "1968."

72. Alexander, "1968," p. 64.

73. Alexander and Meyers, *op. cit.*, pp. 105, 186. Maurice Stans
started an analogous "R.N. Associates" for candidate Nixon in
1968. Jules Witcover, *The Resurrection of Richard Nixon* (New
York, 1970), p. 239.

74. Television stations have few programs of news commentary
and these are not usually overtly partisan. (To be sure, the
wealthier party may buy more TV time for its candidate, but we
have already discussed the limitations of this resource.) Radio
news commentary is more ubiquitous, but only those who initially
agree with commentators are likely to tune in regularly. Consider, however, the impact of television coverage of the 1968 convention in Chicago. One incident will suffice to give a sense of
the options open to television news directors under special circumstances: "Alioto rose on screen to nominate [Humphrey];
back and forth the cameras swung from Alioto to pudgy, cigar-
smoking politicians, to Daley, with his undershot, angry jaw, painting visually without words the nomination of the Warrior of Joy
as a puppet of the old machines. Carl Stokes, the black mayor of
Cleveland, was next—to second Humphrey's nomination—and then,
at 9:55, NBC's film of the bloodshed had finally been edited, and
Stokes was wiped from the nation's vision to show the violence
in living color.

The Humphrey staff is furious—Stokes is their signature on
the Humphrey civil-rights commitment; and Stokes' dark face is
being wiped from the nation's view to show blood—Hubert Humphrey being nominated in a sea of blood." Theodore H. White,
The Making of the President, 1968 (New York, 1969), pp. 300–302.

75. See Nathan B. Blumberg, *One-Party Press? Coverage of the 1952 Presidential Campaign in 35 Daily Newspapers* (Lincoln, Neb., 1954); Edwin Emery and Henry L. Smith, *The Press in America* (Englewood Cliffs, 1954), pp. 714 ff. Arthur Edward Rowse, *Slanted News: A Case Study of the Nixon and Stevenson Fund Stories* (Boston, 1957).

76. "634 For Nixon, 146 For Humphrey (and 12 For Wallace)," *Editor and Publisher*, November 2, 1968, pp. 9–10.

77. A. J. Liebling, with characteristic pungency, puts the proposition this way: "With the years, the quantity of news in newspapers is bound to diminish from its present low. The proprietor, as Chairman of the Board, will increasingly often say that he would *like* to spend 75 cents now and then on news coverage, but that he must be fair to his shareholders." *The Press* (New York, 1961), p. 5.

78. Bernard C. Cohen, in *The Press and Foreign Policy* (Princeton, 1963) presents figures from a variety of sources on foreign affairs news (Chapter 4). His conclusion: "The volume of coverage is low."

79. Following is an example, atypical but illuminating, of this aimlessness at work. Former House Speaker Joseph Martin in his memoirs describes the appearance of an editorial mildly critical of Presidential candidate Thomas E. Dewey in Martin's own newspaper (Martin was editor and publisher) on the day of Dewey's arrival in Martin's hometown during the 1948 campaign. "Behind all this fuss was a very simple explanation. Having a small staff, the *Evening Chronicle* bought 'boilerplate' editorials prepared by a syndicate. The day of Dewey's visit, the editorial in question happened to be on top of the pile, and a man in the composing room slapped it into the paper. Ironically, he was one of the most ardent Dewey supporters in North Attleboro. As for myself, I never read the editorial until it was well on its way to fame." Joseph W. Martin, Jr., *My First Fifty Years in Politics*, as told to Robert J. Donovan (New York, 1960), pp. 196–197.

80. See Richard Rovere, *Senator Joe McCarthy* (New York, 1959), pp. 137, 162–169.

81. See Frank Luther Mott, *The News in America* (Cambridge, Mass., 1952), p. 110, and Emery and Smith, *The Press in America*, pp. 541 ff.

82. See William L. Rivers, "The Correspondents After 25 Years," *Columbia Journalism Review* 1 (Spring 1962). On p. 5, he says, "In 1960, 57 per cent of the daily newspapers reporting to the *Editor and Publisher* poll supported Nixon, and 16 per cent sup-

ported Kennedy. In contrast, there are more than three times as many Democrats as there are Republicans among the Washington newspaper correspondents; slightly more than 32 per cent are Democrats, and fewer than 10 per cent are Republicans. . . . More than 55 per cent of the correspondents for newspapers consider themselves liberals; 26.9 per cent consider themselves conservatives."

83. See White, *The Making of the President, 1960,* pp. 333–338. On Barry Goldwater's press relations, see Charles Mohr, "Requiem For a Lightweight," *Esquire* (August 1965), 67–71, 121–122.

84. Witcover, *op. cit.,* p. 173. See also pp. 188–192.

85. Elmo Roper has observed that "On the civil rights issue [in 1948], Mr. Dewey draws the support of voters favoring exactly opposite things, and more than that, each side thinks Dewey agrees with them." Bone, *American Politics and the Party System,* p. 447.

86. This paragraph summarizes the major findings of researchers on what has come to be called the "two-step flow" of information. See Elihu Katz and Paul F. Lazarsfeld, *Personal Influence* (Glencoe, 1955).

87. Key, *Public Opinion and American Democracy,* p. 453.

88. An example would be in instances where candidates were not known to voters before the campaign, and where they ran without benefit of party labels, as in local nonpartisan elections. See Charles R. Adrian, "Some General Characteristics of Nonpartisan Elections," *American Political Science Review* 46 (September 1952), 766–776, Charles E. Gilbert and Christopher Clague, "Electoral Competition and Electoral Systems in Large Cities," *Journal of Politics* 24 (May 1962), 323–349, especially p. 344. See also Raymond E. Wolfinger and Fred I. Greenstein, "Regional Political Differences in California," *American Political Science Review* 63 (March 1969), pp. 74–86.

89. Campbell, *et al., The American Voter,* pp. 58, 530.

90. American Institute of Public Opinion Survey, released October 18, 1964. For other examples, see Nelson W. Polsby, *Congress and the Presidency* (Englewood Cliffs, 1971), p. 45.

91. Witcover, *op cit.,* pp. 462–463.

92. Kevin Phillips, *The Emerging Republican Majority* (New Rochelle, 1969).

93. *Ibid.,* p. 88.

94. *Ibid.,* pp. 21–22.

95. *Ibid.,* pp. 437–438.

96. *Ibid.*, p. 57.

97. *Ibid.*, pp. 72–77.

98. *Ibid.*, p. 294.

99. *Ibid.*, p. 206.

100. *Ibid.*, p. 286.

101. *Ibid.*, p. 186.

102. *Ibid.*, p. 441.

103. The material in this section is reprinted from Nelson W. Polsby, "Any Vice President is in Dilemma," Topical Comment, Los Angeles *Times*, August 28, 1968.

chapter two

the nominating process

National party conventions are notoriously puzzling to casual observers, both foreign and domestic. The tumult and the shouting, the threats and bargains, the claims and counter-claims seem so confusing that it is tempting to say the events make little sense. It is, therefore, worthwhile to show that a great many convention practices and events can be related to basic rules and circumstances of American politics.[1] The observer who understands, for example, that parties generally look for a winner and that primaries, platforms, and demonstrations may perform important functions in communicating the strength of the various candidates is in a much better position to appreciate what is happening than the person who attends only to the surface noise.

In our view the patterns of events at national conventions are largely a product of three factors: the goals of the politicians who do business there; the disparity between the information these politicians need in order to pursue their goals and the information at their disposal; and their power relationships. After a brief exposition of these factors, it will be possible for us to account for the strategies of the participants as they go about making the crucial choices which help determine the final outcome.

STRATEGIC CONSIDERATIONS

Goals

The delegates to national party conventions are selected state by state, in conventions or primaries, or by a combination of the two methods.[2] They represent the outcomes of processes that are slightly different in their legal requirements and political overtones in each of the states, the District of Columbia, and the territories—all of which send delegations to both party conventions. But when delegates arrive at the convention, they enter into a social system in which their roles are reasonably regularized. Not surprisingly, they try to behave in a way that will maximize their political power. The rational dice player will place his bets in accordance with his chances of winning under the rules of the game he is playing. Similarly, the "rational" delegate will be expected to be reasonably well informed about how his behavior effects his chances of achieving his goals, and he will behave in accordance with his information, his position in the game, and the goals he intends to achieve.

Since American national parties are such loose federations of independent state parties representing somewhat different combinations of interests, the great search at most conventions is for "The Man Who Can Win," for without hope of victory, over the years there would be little reason for a heterogeneous party to stay together. Even if the parties were far more cohesive than they are today, they still could not disregard the need to get into office now and then by nominating a popular candidate.

The desire to nominate a winner is widespread, but it is not equally distributed among delegates. It is weaker among delegates with deep and intense policy commitments and stronger among those who are not so fiercely committed to specific policies. Since state parties represent various interests and live somewhat diverse lives, we find that they differ in the nature and intensity of their policy preferences. Within the Democratic party outside of the South, for example, "Those states in which a powerful Democratic party organization predated Franklin Roosevelt tend to be moderate; those states in which the local Democratic party is a creation of the New Deal and of organized labor in politics tend to be the liberals." [3] Ideological divisions are also pronounced within the Republican party. Certain states consistently vote for conservative candidates. "Of the 23 states that supported Taft in 1952 only one, North Dakota, failed to cast a majority of its votes for Goldwater twelve years later." [4] Along another dimension, the desire to nominate a winner is strongest among delegates from states with a high degree of party competition or where the party is weak. Both of these groups of delegates need a popular candidate, in close states to increase their vote, and in states where the party is weak to bring them some patronage. On the other hand, winners are least needed in areas where the party is overwhelmingly dominant, where local fortunes will continue to be good regardless of what happens in the national election. But the one-party areas have long since ceased to control the conventions and competition is growing in many formerly one-party areas. [5]

Capitalizing on the understandable desire to nominate a winner, candidates seek to demonstrate that they can win and others cannot. They cite polls and make complicated electoral analyses in order to convince delegates on this point. Frequently, there appear to be several strong candidates and disagreements about which one is the most probable winner often take place because the delegates have private preferences and lack enough information about what the voters are likely to do. [6]

Politicians seek to maintain or increase their own political power. In order to do so, most of them feel that they must, in general, increase the potential vote for candidates whom they sponsor. The more leaders who agree on a candidate and the more interest groups and state party organizations that are working for his election, the greater are the chances that he will win office and provide those politicians who supported him with access to political power. Party unity, therefore, is perceived by politicians as an important prerequisite to the

achievement of victory. Unless party leaders achieve a consensus among themselves, the chances are diminished that they
will be able to elect a President. As a result, parties tend to
nominate candidates who at the least are not obnoxious to, and
ideally are attractive to, as many interest groups and state
party leaders as possible.[7] If winning becomes less important,
or ideology more important, or both, the incentive to find a
candidate with broad appeal will decline.

The members of each party may love their party on a senti-
mental basis. But do they love one another? The convention
tests party unity by determining whether the disparate elements which make up each party can agree on one man to
represent them—a man who cannot possibly be equally attractive to all of them. Party unity may aid in securing victory and
this provides an incentive for keeping all the factions under
the same party umbrella. But the differences among delegates
may be so great that no one is quite sure whether they can
agree. The much maligned party platform is exceedingly important in this regard not so much for what it makes explicit
but for the fact that it is written at all. The platform tests and
communicates the ability of the many party factions to agree
on something, even if on some crucial points major differences
have to be papered over.[8] Nixon in 1960 wanted a reasonably
strong platform on civil rights which would reflect his views
and not alienate Negro voters. As a result, he had a staff member draw up a lengthy statement of his own views. During the
course of the discussions on the platform subcommittee dealing
with civil rights, Nixon's spokesmen actively participated in
the discussion and bargaining. When it began to look as if the
subcommittee report would be most unsuitable, the Nixon staff
contacted the leaders of state delegations from which the members came. Nevertheless, Nixon's views became the minority
report of the subcommittee by an eight to seven vote. Finally,
Nixon himself was called in. He spoke to members of the full
platform committee, and his staff followed up seeking pledges
of support. The Nixon draft won by a vote of 55 to 45.[9]

One of the important estimates which rival party leaders

must make is how far they can go in attaining their preferences without completely alienating some faction, resulting in its withdrawal from the convention or refusal to support the party nominee in the election. This information may not be available until party factions begin to bargain at the convention.

While Hubert Humphrey in 1968 might have been willing to write a plank acceptable to opponents of the Vietnam war, President Johnson was not. Consequently, Humphrey never got the enthusiastic support of key Democratic activists who disagreed vehemently with Johnson's conduct of the Vietnam war. Where they did not damn Humphrey outright, they simply failed to show any enthusiasm. By the time they realized he still might be preferable to Nixon, it was too late; Humphrey never recovered from the demoralization of the early days of his campaign.

Delegates not only want to unify the party around a probable winner; they also want to make certain that they have a claim on him so that he will consider their requests favorably. Thus, they seek either a candidate who is known to be friendly to them, whose policy views tend to coincide with theirs, or who will be indebted to them because they have provided support toward his nomination. Jim Farley's famous list establishing priorities for distributing patronage—FRBC (For Roosevelt Before Chicago)—illustrates this point. It helps to explain the rush to get on the bandwagon by delegates who wish access to the winning candidate.

But it must never be forgotten that delegates come from state parties with internal lives of their own. The delegates spend over 1400 days every four years as members of their state parties and less than a week at the national convention. It would be unwise to commit acts at the convention—such as supporting a candidate unpopular in that state, or compromising at the wrong point in a fight over the platform—which would lead to years of bitter internal rivalry. Yet it is not always possible to avoid mistakes. Delegates may misjudge who will run well in their state and provide a "coattail effect."

Sometimes nominees run better in states which opposed them at the convention than in those which gave them support.[10] In any event, it is clear that in order to interpret or predict a state's behavior a Presidential aspirant must acquire information on internal party affairs which may prove indispensable to planning his strategy and may enable him to take advantage of or to avoid dangerous party splits.

We have seen that some delegates have strong policy preferences. Negroes and Southerners may care deeply about racial questions. Union officials and industrial executives may be unwilling to support candidates presumed to be hostile to the interests they represent. Delegates from the District of Columbia may consider crime and home rule to be of paramount importance while the men from Tennessee may be adamant about public power. There are consistent liberal and conservative blocs in both major parties. To some extent, therefore, intense policy preferences may restrict the actions of delegates who share them; delegates may seek the man who has the best chance of winning among those candidates who meet their specifications on crucial policies.

The major goal of the Presidential aspirant in the convention is to win the nomination; but in addition the nominating convention must be regarded as the first part of the election campaign. This is all the more reason why prospective candidates, even while belaboring one another in an attempt to get the nomination, must give due consideration to the necessity for party unity in case they win. There are several ways in which this party unity is achieved. One device available to the winner of a contested nomination is to select the disappointed Presidential aspirant with the second most votes in the convention as a Vice-Presidential nominee, as Kennedy selected Lyndon Johnson in 1960.

"My most critical problem," Richard Nixon wrote of the 1960 convention, "was to see that our Convention ended with all Republicans united behind the ticket. If this were to be accomplished, I knew I had to take some decisive action with regard to Nelson Rockefeller. . . . My goal was to beat Kennedy—not

Rockefeller. . . . I felt it was essential that he be an enthusiastic rather than a reluctant supporter of my candidacy after the Convention. His differences with [Eisenhower] Administration policies had to be ironed out." So Nixon took the initiative in meeting Rockefeller and from ten o'clock one evening until 4:30 the next morning they hammered out a joint statement.[11] Afterwards, Nixon was inevitably (and as it happens quite wrongly) accused of "selling out" to Rockefeller but this did not deter him in his search for party unity.

In 1968, Nixon's problem was to bring the South into his electoral coalition, and so he made a special effort in that direction in the convention, promising southern delegates that he would select no Vice-Presidential nominee who would "tear the party apart." [12]

Johnson's moves to insure unity at the 1964 Democratic Convention included naming Senator Hubert Humphrey to the Vice-Presidency in order to appease the liberals and compromising on the Mississippi Freedom Democratic Party challenge to the Mississippi delegation by seating the latter but allowing the former the status of observers.[13]

Incumbent Presidents and other obvious choices, such as Richard Nixon in 1968, are in a better position to treat the convention as the opening gun of their campaign. They can participate wholeheartedly in the party rituals, the speech-making, informal social gatherings, and the self-congratulation that give the party faithful at the convention a sense of identity and mission, and project over television an image of unity, purpose, and togetherness. Such nominees also can manipulate the party platform to offset their real or imagined weaknesses with the electorate and to capitalize on their strengths. In contested conventions, the platform must be negotiated among representatives of the leading contenders and major segments of the party, and so it is less easy to write a platform that the eventual winner can call his own and comfortably campaign on.

Thus, we can describe quickly the major goals of most delegates to national conventions. They want to gain power, to nominate a man who can win the election, to unify the party, to obtain some claim on the nominee, to protect their central core of policy preferences, and to strengthen their state party organizations.

Uncertainty

It is far easier to describe goals than to attain them. The attainment of each participant's goal requires a great deal of information about the future. What will the electorate do at the polls months after the convention? Who will other delegates to the convention support and for how long? What will be the effect of initial declarations and switches of support on other delegates? What bargains can a particular candidate make? What will be the consequences of the nomination for one's state party?

Answers to these and other questions about pre-convention and convention events are characteristically difficult to obtain and uncertain at best. There are good reasons for this. The answers depend, first, on national and world conditions, which we have not learned how to predict—war, depression, inflation, urban unrest. To pick an extreme example, the candidate who appears likely to win in peacetime may not be able to command the support of the electorate during open warfare unless he happens to be the incumbent President. Second, the answers depend on a complex series of events involving the actions, reactions, and intentions of others. To obtain a claim on the winner, a delegate (or delegation) often must contribute to his support at the convention by guessing who will win in time to "get on the bandwagon." But more than one bandwagon may appear to be in the making, and delegates and their political leaders may have difficulty deciding when the best time is to make the jump and gain great bargaining advantages for themselves. Then, too, a delegation's estimate of who will win may be determined, in part at least, by the estimate it makes about what other delegations are going to do. And their behavior, in turn, may be influenced by what still others do or say they are going to do. This situation may result in a self-fulfilling prophecy where a delegation's estimate of who is most likely to win leads to actions which influence others in the same direction and confirms its original expectation. A third difficulty in acquiring the necessary information results because delegates are required not merely to predict an isolated set of occurrences (although this would be difficult enough) but to gauge the outcome of complex chains of events. If nominee A receives support from delegation B and wins decisively in primary C, then he will be in a position to bargain with delegation D and to use this leverage to gain support from party leader E, which in turn, will lead to the possibility of heading off rival nominee F, and so on.

There are some potentially reliable sources of information—primaries, polls, balloting on procedural motions or on the platform, successive nominating ballots, shifts by key delegations —which are avidly observed. But these publicly available indicators of what might happen in the future do not necessarily have meaning in themselves; they are given meaning by interested observers. Unless the significance attributed to the indicators is widely shared and clear beyond any doubt, so that one overwhelming favorite emerges, the delegate is still left with the troublesome problem of interpretation.

Many of the standard indicators may be perceived to be ambiguous. Did Senator John F. Kennedy emerge from the 1960 Wisconsin primary with a margin of *only* 100,000 votes, or did he win by *the substantial margin* of 100,000?[14] Did Robert Kennedy win a "smashing victory" over Eugene McCarthy in the 1968 California primary by receiving 46% of the vote to McCarthy's 42%, or did he fall short? [15] Perceptions (and hence interpretations) of identical indicators may vary widely depending on the delegate's predispositions, or on the amount of reinforcement or counter-interpretation to which he is subjected. Unless a delegate's interpretation of events coincides with those made by others, his predictions and the actions based on them may be invalidated. At best, the delegates swim in a sea of uncertainty.

What delegates believe about what is happening determines the premises of many decisions. One report on this subject was made by Colonel Jack Arvey who led the forces in Illinois which wanted to draft Adlai Stevenson in the 1952 Democratic Convention.

> Cook County Chairman Joe Gill and I were having dinner . . . when one of our ward committeemen came running over to tell us an important roll call vote was under way on the seating of Virginia. . . . Gill and I hurried back into the hall. Illinois had already been recorded 45–15 against seating Virginia. It suddenly dawned on us what was happening. The strategy of the Kefauver backers and the Northern liberal bloc was to try and make impossible demands on the Southern delegates so that they would walk out of the Convention. If the total Convention vote was thus cut down by the walkout of delegates who would never vote for Kefauver, then the Tennessee Senator would have a better chance of winning the nomination. Our Illinois delegation quickly huddled and then changed our vote to 52–8 in favor of seating Virginia.
>
> The eight opposed included Senator Douglas and other backers of Kefauver.[16]

Now, whether or not Arvey correctly guessed the strategy of the Kefauver forces, this anecdote provides a vivid picture of the premises on which the action of the Stevenson group was based.

Power

In the past, a relatively few party leaders controlled the decisions of a large proportion of the delegates to conventions. Delegates to national conventions are chosen, after all, as representatives of the several state party organizations, apportioned according to a formula laid down by action of previous national conventions. While it is true that official decisions are made by a majority vote of delegates, American party organizations are often centralized at state and local levels. This means that such hierarchical controls as actually exist on the state and local levels will assert themselves in the national convention. Until recently the probabilities were fairly good that both major parties at any given time would have succeeded in electing a substantial number of Governors and Mayors of important cities; the chances were also fairly good, therefore, that a substantial number of delegates would be controlled hierarchically. Some states, of course, may be badly split with no one holding the lever to much more than his own vote.[17]

Normally, state party organizations are unified by incumbent Governors. Without the centralizing forces of state patronage and coherent party leadership embodied by a man in the Governor's chair, state parties tend to fragment into local satrapies or territorial jurisdictions which can be played off one against another by astute aspirants for the Presidential nomination. The lack of strong leadership at the state level also means that a set of Presidential preferences and strategies for pursuing them is less likely to be worked out in advance and agreed upon by all elements of the state party. Decentralized state parties thus become happy hunting grounds for early starters in the Presidential sweepstakes. They can move into a vacuum, make alliances and receive commitments, and build delegate strength from the ground up.

The importance of Governors at national conventions (and along with them hierarchical control of state delegations) has diminished over the last quarter century. There has been a little noticed but important secular decline in the number of Governorships that are up for election in years during which Presidents are also running for office, as the table on page 126 indicates. From the thirty-three Governorships that were open to election in 1944, the number has declined to twenty-one in 1972. Many states are changing the two-year gubernatorial term to a four-year term and are providing for the gubernatorial election in the middle of the President's term of office. This is intended to isolate gubernatorial elections from national electoral currents. But it may also mean that the number of state delegations to national party conventions controlled by Governors will decrease as the motivation of Governors to protect their own fortunes by finding popular Presidential candidates also decreases. This trend thus far has had its most pronounced effect upon the Republican party, where the number of Republican Governors up for election in Presidential years declined from twenty in 1944 to eight in 1968.

Decline in the Number of Gubernatorial Elections in Presidential Election Years (Excluding Hawaii and Alaska)

YEAR	NUMBER OF ELECTIONS
1944	33
1948	31
1952	31
1956	31
1960	27
1964	26
1968	25
1972	21

Source: *World Almanac*, 1944, 1948, 1952, 1956, 1960, 1964, 1968.

Decline in the Number of Republican Governors up for Election in Presidential Election Years (Excluding Alaska and Hawaii)

YEAR	NUMBER OF REPUBLICAN GOVERNORS UP FOR ELECTION
1944	20
1948	19
1952	15
1956	16
1960	11
1964	7
1968	8

Source: *World Almanac*, 1944, 1948, 1952, 1956, 1960, 1964, 1968.

This fact helps account for the willingness of Republican delegates to nominate Barry Goldwater even though he could reasonably have been expected to hurt the party's chances in many states. There were Republican state leaders in 1964 who winced at the thought of a disastrous defeat in November, but there were fewer such leaders than there might have been because there were only sixteen Republican Governors at the Republican Convention. The advantages to Goldwater's early candidacy under these circumstances are obvious. Governors might have had sufficiently hierarchical control over their delegations to keep them from precipitously joining the Goldwater bandwagon. The absence of central leadership on a state-by-state basis meant that delegates were freer to follow their personal preferences and also free to weigh ideological considerations more heavily than they could have if they had been responsible to a leader who would suffer badly if Republicans were defeated for state offices.

There are also cases when effective leadership is exercised by men who are not the highest elected officials. In 1956, for example, it was quite clear that party leader Carmine DeSapio had more to say about what the New York delegation did than did Governor Averell Harriman. Leadership in the state organization may belong to a national committeeman, a Congressman, a coalition of county officials, or an elder statesman.

The power of elected leaders over their state party organizations varies as well. Governor Dewey was able to wield virtually absolute control over the New York Republican delegation when he was in office.[18] Other Governors may be able to throw their votes to certain candidates but not to others because the delegates would not permit it. The delegation may agree to stick with its leader for a specified number of ballots and no further. Then internal bargaining may take place with the Governor acting as first among equals, but no more than that. The desire to maximize the delegation's bargaining power by maintaining a united position may cause a Governor to make concessions to some of his delegates.

Barring catastrophic events—depression, war, scandal—the President's power is most certainly strong enough to assure him of renomination within the limits imposed by the anti-third-term (the 22nd) amendment to the Constitution. This is not merely because his is the greatest, most visible, office in the land with all sorts of patronage and other controls over potential delegates. There is, in addition, the fact that his party can hardly hope to win by repudiating him. To refuse him the nomination would, most politicians feel, be tantamount to confessing political bankruptcy or ineptitude.

This rule was not broken in 1968. President Johnson had scheduled the convention of the Democratic Party to coincide with his birthday in anticipation of his renomination. The fact that his birthday fell in late August left his successor, Hubert Humphrey, with little time to heal the wounds and raise the money needed for victory in November. The challenges of McCarthy and Kennedy in that year demonstrated, however, that the costs of party insurgency are high: not only do insurgents rarely win their party's nomination, their party usually loses the election in such years.

The Presidential power over national conventions has historically extended to (1) the right to renomination, or to designate the party nominee, effectively exercised in eighteen of the twenty conventions since the Civil War in which the President interested himself in the outcome; (2) the power to dictate the party platform; (3) the power to designate the officers of the convention; (4) the power to select many delegates—especially potent historically in the case of Republican delegations during the days of the one-party Democratic South, when Republican Presidents, until the passage of the Hatch Act, drew upon a corporal's guard of Federal patronage appointees to man this sizable convention bloc.

The constitutional amendment limiting Presidents to two terms may eventually change the power of a two-term incumbent radically, but we doubt it. The party still must run on the Presidential record, and the outgoing President still seems likely to control the management of the convention. Before President Roosevelt broke the two-term tradition, outgoing Presidents controlled conventions even when no one expected them to run again. Presidents Truman and Johnson were also very influential in 1952 and 1968 when they were not candidates for re-election.[19]

In the absence of hierarchical control by an incumbent President, decision-making at conventions is ordinarily coordinated by a process of bargaining among party leaders. We think of bargaining as a method by which activities are coordinated in situations where controls between individuals approach equality, where no leader by himself can fully dominate another. Each leader represents a state party or faction within a state which is independently organized and not subject to control by outsiders. In the presence of disagreement and the absence of coercion, leaders must persuade one another, compromise, and form coalitions if they are to gain sufficient support to carry the day. Although the leaders may differ in their preferences among possible candidates, they believe that participating in the bargaining process will aid them in achieving their goals and inform them of the goals and tactics of others, which in turn may help them in attaining their goals.

Prerequisites to bargaining may be summarized as (1) no hierarchical controls; (2) interdependence of bargainers; (3) disagreement among bargainers; and (4) expectation of gain. When the President is of the opposite party, or chooses not to intervene, the convention becomes a bargaining system because no political leader beside the President is in a position to control the national convention by himself. The interdependence of party leaders may be established by reference to the custom of American democracy which allows the voters to replace the elected officials of one party with those of another at general elections. In order to mobilize enough nationwide support to elect a President, party leaders from a large number of constituencies must be satisfied with the nominee. Without agreement on a nominee, none of them is likely to enjoy access to the eventual President; hence, party leaders are interdependent and expect to gain from the outcome of the bargain. Because of the different amounts of access to different aspirants which delegates carry with them into the convention, the preferences of delegates are likely initially to disagree.[20] Most politicians believe that bargaining is necessary and not dishonorable, although Senator Goldwater in 1964 and Senator McCarthy in 1968 took the position that the gains to be expected by bargaining were greatly outweighed by the loss of ideological purity and commitment.[21]

PRE-CONVENTION STRATEGIES

The selection of a Presidential nominee is the business which dominates the convention. From this it follows that decisions preceding the Presidential nomination are important or unimportant largely depending upon their implications for the Presidential nomination. Decisions not taken unanimously which precede the Presidential nomination in the convention are almost always tests of strength between party factions divided as to the Presidential nomination. These decisions are usually more important for the information they communicate on the strength of the candidates than for their actual content.[22]

Perhaps the first strategic decision facing an avowed candidate is whether to attempt to become a front-runner by entering primaries, barnstorming the country, and publicly seeking support at state conventions. The advantage of this strategy is that a candidate may build up such a commanding lead (or appear to do so) that no one will be able (or will try) to stop him at the national convention. The disadvantage is that an open campaign may reveal his inability to acquire support or may lead other candidates to band together in order to stop him. Adoption of this position depends for its success, then, upon the front-runner's ability to predict accurately both how he will fare compared to others in open competition, and what others will be able to do when they discover his lead. He may, for example, try to anticipate whether his activity will stimulate a coalition of opponents who are otherwise unlikely to get together. If such a coalition seems likely, the candidate may issue communications playing down the extent of his support. But this tactic may discourage new supporters who would have been attracted by a display of strength. Candidates can never be entirely certain that they are striking the right balance between reticence and aggressiveness, which may explain why unabashed attempts to use bandwagon *or* dark horse strategies in relatively undiluted form are quite common.

The dark horse is an avowed candidate who avoids primaries and much open campaigning. Like Stuart Symington in 1960, or Richard Nixon in 1964, he is content to be everyone's friend and no one's enemy.[23] As Abraham Lincoln wrote to a supporter in 1860 describing his dark horse strategy: "My name is new in the field, and I suppose I am not the first choice of a very great many. Our policy, then, is to give no offense to others—leave them in a mood to come to us if they shall be compelled to give up their first love."[24] The strategy of the dark horse is to combine with others to oppose every front-runner. His hope is that when no front-runner is left he will appear as the man who can unify the party by being acceptable to all and obnoxious to none. The dangers the dark horse faces are that he will enter the convention with too little support to make a strong bid or that some other dark horse will prove preferable. How much support is enough to make a serious bid but not enough to be shot at as a front-runner? How far behind the front-runner can a candidate permit himself to get without becoming entirely lost from sight? Either an intuitive ability to guess or an exceedingly accurate apparatus for collecting information on the present strength of candidates, as well as on the likely effect of different levels of strength on other delegates, must be part of the serious dark horse's equipment.

Primaries

Primaries are important largely because the results represent an ostensibly objective indication of whether a candidate can win the election. The contestants stand to gain or lose far more than the growing number of delegate votes which may be at stake. Thus a man situated as Richard Nixon was in 1960 would be ill-advised to enter a primary unless the information at his disposal led him to believe that he was quite certain to win. This stricture applies with special force to any candidate who is well ahead in delegate support. All he can gain is a few additional votes, while he can lose his existing support by a bad showing in the primary since this would be interpreted as meaning that he could not win in the election. The candidate who is far behind, or who has to overcome severe handicaps, however, has little or nothing to lose by entering a risky primary. If he wins, he has demonstrated his popularity; if he loses, he is hardly worse off than if he had not entered the primary at all. Such was the case when John F. Kennedy quieted the apprehensions of Democratic politicians about the religious issue by winning in Protestant West Virginia.[25] In 1964 Goldwater needed a primary victory in California to show uncommitted delegates that he had voter appeal, even though at the start of the primary campaigns he had been a prominent candidate. He accepted the risk of losing the nomination if he lost the primary because he needed proof of popularity to get the votes necessary for nomination.[26] Nixon, who had lost the Presidency in 1960 and the Governorship of California in 1962, had a similar problem in 1968. He had to enter the primaries in order to dispel his "loser" image.[27]

The man who is behind in securing convention support or whose ability to win is in doubt engages in strategies of entice-ment in which he issues siren calls inviting the leading con-tenders into a primary. He suggests that they are cowardly, lacking in fighting spirit, afraid to face the public. By luring them into a primary, he hopes to deal a severe blow to their chances and thereby boost his own. In order to avoid this trap, it may be necessary for candidates to publicize their disdain for primaries, to specify in advance all the reasons why such a contest would be unnecessary, unfair, and a waste of time. The candidate who finds himself in a primary (and wishes to live and fight again another day) does well to have alibis ready to explain away seemingly disadvantageous results.

In a primary in which there are many contenders a defeated candidate may attempt to gain advantage from what may be re-garded as an ambiguous result by claiming that the man who actually won was allied to him ideologically. The results may then be viewed as a victory for the ideology rather than defeat for the candidate. After La Follette had won an overwhelming victory in the 1912 Republican primary in North Dakota, Theo-dore Roosevelt issued a statement "claiming an immense progressive victory." He even went beyond this to count the La Follette delegation as part of the Roosevelt camp once it had cast "a complimentary vote for La Follette."[28] In the same way, Rockefeller supporters in 1964 hailed the New Hampshire

Republican primary, which was won by Henry Cabot Lodge, as a defeat for Goldwater and a victory for the moderate wing of the Republican party. Something similar went on in 1968; supporters of both Eugene McCarthy and Robert Kennedy claimed that all those who had voted for either man in the primaries had voted against Hubert Humphrey.[29]

One strategy for primaries, the write-in, offers the maximum possibility of gain with the minimum possibility of loss. If a candidate gets virtually no votes, he can easily explain this by saying that he did not campaign and that it is difficult for people to write in names. If he receives over 10 per cent of the vote, he can hail this as a tremendous victory under the circumstances. In Nebraska in 1964 Nixon received 35% of the vote as a write-in in the primary and it was "claimed that 'Nebraskans have nominated the next Republican candidate for President . . .' a claim that was forgotten after the Nixon debacle in Oregon just three days later."[30]

If a candidate should win, he can build it up to the sky, stressing the extraordinary popularity required to get people to go to all the trouble of writing in a name.[31] But the man who is behind cannot rest content with being able to explain away a poor showing; he must win to establish himself as a contender. The strategy of the write-in, consequently, is most accessible to the man who is ahead and hopes to solidify his position while minimizing his risks.

The foregoing discussion should help us to understand why those who win primaries sometimes do not win the nomination. Part of the reason is that not all primaries actually commit delegates to vote for a candidate. Of greater significance, however, is the fact that primary activity is often (though by no means always) a sign that a candidate has great obstacles to overcome and must win many primaries in order to be considered for the nomination at all. The image communicated to political professionals by a few primary victories, unless they are overwhelming, may be less that of the conquering hero than that of the drowning man clutching at the last straw.

Thus, entering and winning primaries may be of little value unless the results are widely interpreted in such a way as to improve a candidate's chances. The contestant who "loses" but does better than expected may reap greater advantage from a primary than the one who wins but falls below expectations. It is, therefore, manifestly to the advantage of a candidate to hold his claims down to minimum proportions. Kennedy tried in 1960 to follow this advice in Wisconsin—he claimed Humphrey had been Wisconsin's third Senator—but the press, radio, and TV took note of his extensive organization and of favorable polls, and in advance pinned the winner-by-a-landslide label on the Senator from Massachusetts.[32] Early predictions in the 1968 New Hampshire primary were that Eugene McCarthy would receive somewhere around 10% of the vote. When he eventually polled 42%—against Lyndon Johnson's 48% write-in vote—it was widely interpreted as a victory, in part because it was so unexpected.[33] The public media have taken some of the control over "expectations" from the candidates.

Yet there is more to the strategy of primaries than mere calculation of chances on the candidate's part. The desires of the existing state organizations may also have to be taken into account. The state organization may be sponsoring a favorite son who, it hopes, may be nominated in case of deadlock. It may wish to remain uncommitted in order to increase its bargaining power by making a claim on the winner in return for throwing last minute support to him. The party may be divided and fear internecine warfare over rival candidates which would leave it in a shattered condition. For all of these reasons, the state leadership may request candidates to stay out and may threaten to work against them in the primary and at the convention if they disobey. Presidential aspirants may have to rest content with second or third choice support unless their position is so desperate that they have little to lose by antagonizing the state party.

Paradoxically, the candidate who can show that he has no choice but to enter a primary may gain a bargaining advantage.[34] The state leaders may then decide that it is worth making concessions to him to avoid the internal strife that would be caused by a primary contest. This is more or less what happened in 1960, when John Kennedy, fortified by a poll claiming that he would win, insisted that he absolutely had to have Ohio's votes to have a chance at the national convention. Ohio Governor Michael DiSalle, who wanted to run as a favorite son, had to back down in order to avoid a primary fight that could have been extremely embarrassing to him, and he ran on a slate pledged to Kennedy. The Governor's decision was prompted by the knowledge that the Cuyahoga County (Cleveland) party faction, which was hostile to him, would run a slate pledged to Kennedy and use this as a weapon to reduce the Governor's stature within the state. The struggle for power within a state may have much to do with its action before and at the convention.[35]

State and District Conventions

Most of the delegates are still chosen, not by primaries, but by state and district conventions. This process has historically provided relatively few contests over the selection of delegates, although these may be important. Taking over the state and district conventions that chose the Republican delegations to the 1964 convention was the heart of Barry Goldwater's strategy, and under the direction of Clifton White it was a brilliant success. The belated realization of anti-Johnson forces in 1968 that this was where so much of the action was prompted them to demand, and get, substantial changes in the rules governing the selection of delegates for the next convention in 1972. These included abolition of unit rule voting in state and district conventions and a rule that delegates to the national convention had to be chosen in the year of the convention itself rather than at some earlier time as had been the case in some states.[36]

Most attempts to influence delegates chosen outside of primaries are made after they are selected. The first strategic requirement for the candidate seeking to influence these delegations is an intelligence service, a network of informants who will tell him which delegations are firmly committed, which are wavering, and which may be persuaded to provide second or third choice support. Advance reports on the opportunities offered by internal divisions in the state parties, the type of appeal likely to be effective in each state, and the kinds of bargains to which leaders are most susceptible, may also be helpful. The costs of this information may come high in terms of time, money, and effort, but it will be worth it to the serious candidate who needs to know where to move to increase his support and block his opponents.

Aspirants for nomination vary greatly in the degree to which they know other politicians throughout the country. Men like Richard Nixon, Hubert Humphrey, and Barry Goldwater, who have travelled extensively and given assistance to members of their party may simply need to keep their files up to date in order to have a nationwide list of contacts. When the time comes they know whom they can call upon for assistance in gathering information, persuading delegates, and generally furthering their cause. Candidates who lack this advantage, however, have to take special steps in order to build up their political apparatus. In paving the way for Franklin D. Roosevelt's nomination in 1932, James A. Farley began early by sending invitations to Roosevelt's inauguration as Governor of New York to party leaders throughout the country. Most invitations were refused but a valuable correspondence grew out of this approach. Farley next sent a small manual containing a few facts about the New York Democratic party organization to people throughout the country. The response encouraged a follow-up pamphlet which presented, without comment, the New York gubernatorial vote in every county since 1916. It was intended to be impressive testimony of FDR's vote-getting ability. When many people wrote back expressing an interest in FDR's candidacy, offering suggestions, or just saying "thanks," Farley replied with a personal message and endeavored to keep up the contact through further letters, phone calls, and even a phonograph record. Later, in 1931, Farley took a trip through the West, ostensibly to visit the Elks Convention in Seattle, but actually to contact over 1,000 party leaders in all but three states west of the Mississippi. Upon his return, every one of Farley's contacts received a personal letter.[37]

The well-organized candidates contact the delegates personally or through close associates. They may show a winning personality, make implied promises of good things to come, discuss or avoid controversial issues of special importance to the locality, as seems best calculated to increase their support. If a favorable public opinion poll is handy or can be arranged, this will often be cited to substantiate the claims of victory which must be made to convey the impression that it would be a good idea to climb on the bandwagon. More than one can play at this game, however, and "pollsmanship" is becoming a common art whose practitioners know how to secure the desired impression and blunt harmful ones. There are good reasons to suppose that the number of polls taken exceeds the number made public since sometimes the news they disclose disappoints the candidate who paid for them.

AT THE CONVENTION

While the selection of a site for the convention is often interpreted as one of the pre-ballot indicators of various candidates' strength, it is in fact usually the rather routine outcome of the weighing of one major and several very minor factors. The major factor is the size of the convention city's preferred contribution to the national party committee; this money comes partly from the city government (sometimes in the form of cash, usually in much larger contributions in kind, such as special travel arrangements, security and housekeeping services, etc.), but mostly from various business groups which stand to profit from a week-long visit of 6,500 delegates and alternates, their families and friends, and thousands of media representatives, dignitaries and other convention personnel.

There are a variety of other factors, however, which may tip the balance between cities offering roughly equal contributions. One of these is the quality of facilities, the convention hall and hotel and entertainment accommodations. For example, Philadelphia's James Tate headed as large and as loyal a Democratic organization in 1968 as Chicago's Richard Daley, and his city was closer geographically to Lyndon Johnson in Washington, but Philadelphia simply could not provide 20,000 first-class hotel rooms.[38] All things being equal, an incumbent President is likely to prefer a city near enough to Washington to allow him to keep close tabs on convention business and to travel easily back and forth to the convention while at the same time playing his role away from it as "President of all the people." And, naturally, the wishes of a sitting President will not be farthest from the minds of the site committee of the national committee, which does the choosing. In addition, they will have in mind some other marginal factors. There are areas where parties do not like to have conventions; Democrats do not hold them in the South, for the number of black delegates they will have is vastly greater than that of Republicans, and delegates might face untoward incidents there. Conversely, the Republicans in 1968, by selecting Miami Beach for the first Republican Convention ever held south of the Mason-Dixon line, may well have facilitated a "Southern strategy" if they intended to pursue one. Both parties prefer to bring their publicity and their business to cities and states where the mayor and the governor are members of the party, since this may give added access to and control of public facilities.

The timing of a convention varies between mid-July and late August. There are two general things which can be said about it. One is that the out party will normally hold its convention before the ins, on the theory that their man will need more of a publicity boost earlier; in 1960, this was Democrats before Republicans, in 1964 and 1968, it was Republicans before Democrats. Also, if there is an incumbent President, he will schedule the convention to fit his timetable. At its most momentous, this may coincide with an international peace offensive; in 1968, the date of the Democratic Convention seems to have been set with nothing more in mind than the President's birthday.

Once assembled, the national convention is a mass meeting in which the participants necessarily play widely varying and unequal roles. The candidates and their chief supporters are busily, perhaps frantically, perfecting their organization and trying to influence as many delegates as they can. The leaders of "bossed" or "pledged" delegations are either actively supporting their candidate or negotiating for the disposal of the votes they command within the limits of discretion which their delegation places on them. These are the men who conduct negotiations among the delegations when an impasse develops. There are also factional leaders and independent delegates within state delegations who play an important part in determining what their delegation or a part of their delegation will do. They bargain *within* their delegation rather than *among* the various state delegations. The ordinary delegate, however, whose vote may have been pledged in a primary or who is controlled by others may have little to do. He stands and waits, important only if the nomination becomes closely contested and circumstances operate to release him from prior commitments and the control of his state party organization. Only then will he be assiduously wooed, occupying a place in the scheme of things much like the independent delegates. In setting the stage for the balloting, therefore, we will deal first with candidates and their organizations, and then with the delegates—party "bosses" and leaders of large delegations, independent delegates, and state factional leaders, and finally the rank-and-file delegates.

Candidates and Their Organizations

There is an extraordinarily wide divergence among candidate organizations. They range from the comprehensive, integrated, and superbly effective to the fragmented, uncoordinated, and virtually nonexistent. We can only suggest the range of organizational accomplishment through some general comment and a few examples.

In 1960, Senator John F. Kennedy wanted a communications network which would provide him with a continuing and accurate stream of vital information.[39] He wanted detailed personal information about as many delegates as possible in order to know how they were likely to vote and how they might best be persuaded to stay in line or to change their minds. More than a year before the convention the Kennedy-for-President organization started a card file containing information on people throughout the nation who might be delegates and who might influence delegates. Included on each card was the prospective delegate's name, occupation, religion, party position, relation (if any) to the Kennedy family or its leading supporters, ambitions, policy preferences if strongly held, and likely vote. This was brought up-to-date prior to convention time and entries were made in a central register as new information developed. Thus when it appeared that a delegate needed to be reinforced or might not vote for Kennedy, his card was pulled, and the information was used in order to determine the best way to convince him.

At the national convention, before the balloting for the Presidential nomination starts, one or more days are consumed in a variety of party rituals: speech-making, the seating of delegates, the presentation of the platform, "ladies day," and so on. During that time delegates and their leaders mill about, exchange greetings and gossip. It is this set of circumstances that challenges even the most efficient candidate organization.

In order to keep an up-to-date, and when necessary, an hour-by-hour watch on developments within the state delegations, the Kennedy organization assigned an individual to each state. This person might be a delegate or an observer such as a Senator or a member of the candidate's staff. When it was deemed inadvisable to choose a delegate for fear that any choice would alienate one faction or another, a person outside the state was chosen. These liaison men kept tabs on individual delegates and maintained a running record of the likely distribution of votes. When necessary, the liaison men sent messages to the candidate's headquarters and reinforcements were sent to bolster the situation. At the Kennedy headquarters the seriousness of the report would be judged and a decision made on how to deal with it. Senator Kennedy himself might call the wavering delegate, one of his brothers might be dispatched, a state party leader might intervene, or some other such remedy applied.

In the hurly-burly, crush, and confusion of convention activity, it cannot be assumed that any messages which are sent are necessarily received, or that decisions which are made are communicated to those who must carry them out. The Kennedy organization took great care to prepare a message center which would receive messages and locate the people they were aimed at and which could send out instructions and receive feedback on the results. Each key staff person was required to phone his whereabouts to a central switchboard. This made it possible for the Kennedy forces at the convention to deploy and reassign their people on a minute-by-minute basis, as developments seemed to require.

A system set up only to deal with emergencies would have limited usefulness to a candidate who wanted regular reports so that he could appraise them in a consistent way. Every morning every liaison man assigned to the Kennedy headquarters attended a staff meeting at which he deposited with the secretary a report on his activities for the previous day. These reports were sent to what was called the "secret room" and the information was transferred to state briefing files. From these files, a daily secret report of delegate strength was written and given to the candidate and his top advisers.

At the morning staff meetings, Robert Kennedy would ask each liaison man for his estimate of the number of Kennedy votes. Keenly aware of the dangers of communicating an attitude which suggested that he wanted high estimates, Robert Kennedy challenged the liaison men if he felt that their estimates were too high, but not if they appeared too low. On occasion he would reprimand a liaison man for including a delegate as a certain Kennedy supporter when other information indicated that this was not true. The success of this procedure was indicated by the fact that by the time the alphabetical order of balloting had reached Wyoming on the first (and last) ballot, the Kennedy organization's estimate of their delegate strength was proven correct within a one vote margin.[40]

The danger of confusion and mishap is multiplied during the balloting because the convention floor is filled and it is difficult

to move about freely. The Kennedy organization arranged for
telephones on the convention floor. Six telephones were set up
beneath the seats of chairmen of friendly delegations who were
seated around the gigantic convention hall. These phones were
connected to the Kennedy headquarters outside the hall. Inside
the headquarters, staff members sat near the telephone and
simultaneously scanned several television sets to look for possible defections. Had the telephones failed to work (they were
pretested), walkie-talkie radios were available to take their
place.[41]

By comparison with the Kennedy efforts, most of the organizations which have successfully nominated Presidential
candidates in American history have been uncoordinated, diffuse affairs. For example, in 1952 none of the various factions
in the Democratic party that favored the nomination of Adlai
Stevenson had the wholehearted cooperation of their candidate, information gathering was casual, tactical maneuvers
were in some cases hit upon accidentally or as afterthoughts.
The factions working for the Stevenson nomination did not
cooperate with one another to a significant degree and in fact
squabbled among themselves on occasion. Yet Stevenson was
nominated, his success came about because he was the second
choice of an overwhelming number of delegates who could not
agree on any of their first choices, and the first choice of a
significant number of leaders in spite of his disinclination to
pursue the nomination in an organized fashion.[42]

Delegates
There are two identifiable categories of delegation activists:
(1) party bosses and state leaders who control many votes
other than their own and who participate in high level negotiations on the disposition of these votes and (2) delegates of
independent standing who may control only their own votes or
those of a faction within their home state, but who, because
of their special skills at negotiation and maneuver, or because
of their high personal prestige, or simply because of the open
and unbossed character of their state delegation, play signifi-

cant roles at the convention. From this latter group are drawn the delegates who man the key subcommittees and committees on the platform and on credentials, and they often have a real voice in determining the vote of their delegation.

The roles of these activists may be contrasted with the activities of rank-and-file members of bossed delegations— delegations pledged by primary law, or in the hands of local and state party leaders. It is not uncommon for large state delegations to split their votes into halves or thirds, so as to enable a large number of the party faithful to make the trip to the convention city; but these votes are not often independently cast. Essentially, party leaders of the large delegations determine the disposition of these votes. The delegates who, in a formal sense, hold the votes are thus left with little or no political decision-making to participate in. They spend their time milling around and conversing with one another. Some delegates may sample the recreational facilities of the convention city. Others may visit the campaign headquarters of the candidates. The more fortunate ones return home at least with something to talk about—perhaps a word from a famous television newscaster who could be counted a celebrity. But for the most part these delegates find themselves crushed by the masses of people, uncertain of whom to speak to (especially before delegates' badges are issued as identification), and subject to rebuff. Many of them are important people back home, but at the convention they often feel like "a little fish in a big pond" and worry about their status in the new environment.

As the convention provides an environment conducive to anxiety, so it also provides opportunities for adjustment. Anxiety induced by strangeness of place can sometimes be mitigated but not erased by familiarizing oneself with the surroundings. There is not enough time for that. Instead, the delegates immediately seek out familiar connections with the past. The cry goes out: "Are there Rotarians to make up a meeting?" and soon a quorum is found and a convivial group goes through the old ritual. Mayors breakfast together; black delegates converse and go off to a convention-wide meeting of their fellows. Congressmen meet their associates from the Capitol; union members converse about their special policy interests; and delegates from the large counties seek each other's company. Still, some are left out.

In view of the preceding comments, the functions for delegates include personal attentions like handshakes from the leading candidates and pictures taken with prominent persons. Richard Nixon's practice in 1960 of having a separate photograph taken of himself with every delegate, however exhausting and perfunctory this may appear, demonstrates a real appreciation of what this gesture means to many delegates.

Straws in the Wind

When an incumbent President desires renomination, his influence is normally great, his party can hardly hope to win by repudiating him, and his nomination is virtually assured.[43] Sometimes, the titular leader of the party or some other candidate is so far ahead, as Nixon was in 1960 and 1968, that there is nothing left for the delegates to do but ratify the decision that has already been negotiated by leaders of the state parties.

But here we are mainly concerned with those nominating conventions where there is uncertainty at the time of the convention about who will be the nominee. In an uncertain convention, delegates crave information on what is going to happen and when. For most of them, of course, the convention is a spectator sport, since they will be acting under instructions from the voters in their state primary or from their state party leaders. But even so, they want to know who is ahead and who is behind and what the chances are of majority agreement on one of the leading candidates. Rumors are rife because no one has been able to establish an unshakable claim of victory, because it is to the advantage of more than one aspirant to be thought to be winning, and because people like to speculate. In the grip of uncertainty, the delegates grasp for any objective information that may be gleaned from the events of the convention itself.[44]

Before the balloting on the candidates begins at the convention, there often are votes on contested delegations, on a plank in the platform, on some rule governing convention life such as a loyalty pledge, or on the person who is to be permanent chairman. If some of the candidates become identified with one or the other side on these preliminary votes, the results may be considered a test of who is likely to win the nomination. Thus, candidates who identify themselves with one side or another may prejudice their chances of nomination. They must calculate the effects of the loss of such a vote. In 1932, Franklin Roosevelt nearly lost his bid for the nomination by coming out against the two-thirds rule then required for nomination. Fortunately for his chances, FDR's supporters at the convention discovered that the opposition to the change in rules was greater than the opposition to him and he beat a hasty retreat from his previous position.[45]

Many of the same strategic considerations hold in relation to any conflict that may develop over the permanent chairman. This struggle may be important because the chairman has significant procedural powers at the convention. He can speed up adjournment to give a particular candidate time to make bargains, or he can harm another's chances by refusing to recognize a state delegation about to go over to that candidate at a crucial moment. The importance of being chairman was demonstrated at the 1920 Republican Convention when Senator Henry Cabot Lodge wanted to permit the party leaders to find a way out of an impasse that had developed. Shortly after the fourth ballot, Senator Reed Smoot of Utah moved to adjourn the proceedings. A resounding "no" echoed throughout the auditorium as Lodge put the motion to a vote and immediately declared the convention adjourned.[46] Twenty years later, at another Republican Convention, Senator John Bricker of Ohio asked Chairman Joseph Martin for a recess before the sixth ballot. This would have given the Taft and Dewey forces time to make a deal. Partial to the Willkie cause, however, Martin refused the request and the balloting continued, to be ended by victory for Willkie.[47]

Unless victory appears assured it may be unwise for a can-

didate to challenge a popular chairman. An alternate strategy
is to accept an unfavorable chairman but to put forth a stream
of publicity stressing the chairman's partiality, so that he
feels under continuous scrutiny and may bend over backward
to avoid charges of favoritism. Nowadays, however, the usual
practice is for representatives of the leading candidates to
agree upon major personnel of the convention—keynoter, permanent chairman, platform committee chairman—by negotiation well ahead of the convention itself.

Virtually any action can take on added significance if it reveals information hitherto unavailable to all. In the 1932 Democratic Convention a vote on seating a contested delegation was
taken under conditions which freed many of the delegates from
the unit rule. This revealed which delegations were closely
divided, information that imposition of the unit rule had
helped to hide.[48]

Such apparently trivial matters as the date or the place in
which the convention meets may take on special meaning if
those decisions are believed to affect the fortunes of candidates. The fact that the 1844 Democratic Convention was delayed while Van Buren's letter opposing the annexation of
Texas was having its effects was known at that time to be
prejudicial to his chances. Locating the 1928 Democratic Convention in Houston, Texas, was widely interpreted as a move
to mollify people in the South and led to the conclusion that
this was necessary because party leaders intended to nominate
Al Smith.

While candidates are being nominated, and during the balloting, demonstrations—partly spontaneous, largely prearranged
—take place on the floor. This raucous display is meant to let
everyone know that a candidate has many loyal supporters.
Hopefully, a demonstration at a crucial moment might succeed
in igniting the spark of enthusiasm among the multitude of
uncertain delegates. But, as supporters of Adlai Stevenson
learned in 1960, this has the possibility of working only when
delegates are really uncertain and uncommitted.

Despite the fact that everyone seems aware of what is going
on, the same old tricks are played at every convention. Part of

the reason is that once this practice has begun, unanimous consent is necessary to eliminate it; otherwise, the candidate who received no ovation would be deemed to have no support or not enough sense to stimulate it artificially. Another part of the rationale behind demonstrations should be clear from our argument: reliable information may be so scarce that, despite all warnings, delegates may be swayed (as was the Republican Convention of 1940 that nominated Wendell Will-kie) by the most immediate, tangible evidence before them— the roar of the crowd.[49]

The Balloting

The one route to political power open to all delegates in the convention is to contribute to the majority essential for the nomination of the man they believe will be the winner. This explains the so-called "bandwagon" behavior which can be seen in operation at many conventions. When delegates believe that one Presidential aspirant is certain of nomination, they will attempt to record themselves as voting for that aspirant as quickly as possible. Delegates committed to a favorite son candidate will trade their votes for access (or what they hope will be access) to the candidate they think most likely to win nomination. Note the differences in these two statements. In the first, delegates know which candidate will win, and hope to earn his gratitude by voting for him. In the corollary, dele-gates are less certain of the outcome, hence their commitment to an aspirant is more costly for him. The prospective candi-date, in these circumstances, often makes promises of access to delegates in return for their support.

An aspirant who leads in votes for the nomination must actually win the nomination by a certain point in time, or else his chances of eventually winning decline precipitously, even though he remains temporarily in the lead. This is true when delegate support is given candidates because of the expectation of victory. When this victory falls short of quick materializa-tion, delegates may question their initial judgment. Thus, the longer a candidate remains in the lead without starting a bandwagon, the greater the chance that his supporters will reassess his chances of victory and vote for someone else. In order to maximize access, delegates prefer to support the eventual winner before he achieves a majority. They are therefore guided by what they expect other delegates to do, and are constantly on the alert to change their expectations to conform to the latest information. This information may be nothing more substantial than a rumor, which quickly takes on the status of a self-fulfilling prophecy, as delegates stampede in response to expectations, quickly realized, about how other delegates will respond. The strategies which a candidate adopts depend, therefore, not only on showing that he can win but also on his position in the convention. So long as he keeps gaining support, no matter how slightly, he is still in contention because it is assumed that he may have more strength in reserve. But the front-runner who begins to manifest any decline, or even in some cases a leveling-off in votes on successive ballots, can expect to see uncommitted delegates conclude that he has shot his bolt and begin to shift their support to more hopeful prospects.

Considered as a source of information, the balloting indicates whether a candidate is gaining or falling behind. One strategy sometimes used in this connection is to "hide" a few votes on early ballots by giving them to others and reclaiming them little by little so as to show a steady increase.[50] Or a candidate may decide to bide his time and delay making his bid. In that case a weak initial total of votes is not likely to be commented upon because the front-runner occupies the center of attention. Later, a dark horse may occasion surprise by his rapid climb and hope that most delegates will decide to hitch their wagons to a rising star.

Aspirants sometimes combine their voting strength in the convention in order to prevent a front-running candidate from gaining a majority. They will then negotiate the nomination among themselves. If the front-runner's victory promises other aspirants insufficient access, they may defeat him by preventing a bandwagon in his favor. An apparently successful case of combining against the front-runner occurred in

1920 when Harry Daugherty, Harding's manager, realizing that General Leonard Wood had to be defeated to give Harding a chance, offered to lend Governor Lowden every vote he could spare until the Governor passed Wood in the balloting. Then the alliance would be terminated. "Certainly you couldn't make a fairer proposition," Lowden responded, and the agreement was consummated.[51]

The rational aspirant who leads but lacks a majority will bargain and promise access to leaders representing the requisite number of votes, if he believes that no bandwagon will appear unstimulated. He may offer the Vice-Presidential nomination to one or more leaders of important states; he may hint at cabinet posts, patronage, or preferred treatment; he may explore concessions on policy. But this account is too simple. Before he can bargain, the candidate must know with whom to bargain. And among those delegations which might be swayed must be found the ones amenable to what he can offer. The necessity of maintaining an apparatus for obtaining this information is evident.

The front-runner may reasonably expect to win without cost (that is, without making promises) unless leaders of opposing factions reach agreement on a ticket, and appear likely to combine against him. Early front-runners often win nominations precisely because they face a divided opposition.

The case of the Democrats in 1960 is a perfect example of this. In the pre-convention maneuvering, Adlai Stevenson might have cut into John Kennedy's liberal and labor support, had he made himself available as a candidate. Many party regulars from the urban political machines, and, in particular, ex-President Truman, had no special liking for Kennedy, and Senator Johnson could draw on a rather substantial reservoir of strength from Southern delegations determined not to walk out even though they knew they would not approve of the civil rights plank of the platform.

These groups could not get together and settle on a candidate who was more satisfactory to *all* of them than the front-runner, Senator Kennedy. Labor clearly would accept no one to the right of Kennedy, the Southerners could abide nobody to

the left of him. Adlai Stevenson was perhaps the leading candidate whose ideological location, prominence in the party, and
public record could pass muster with these groups, but he had
alienated Truman and in any case refused to go to work on his
own behalf. And so, Kennedy's opposition stayed divided.

If a candidate thinks he can win on his own, he may be reluctant to risk sacrificing his ambition by "making a deal" to
combine against a front-runner. Yet if he hesitates too long, he
may lose all. This is apparently what happened to Thomas E.
Dewey in the 1940 Republican Convention. As Senator Arthur
Vandenberg recorded it in his diary, "I offered to flip a coin
with Dewey to see which side of the ticket each would take.
Dewey never saw me again until the final voting. But it was
too late. He missed the boat when he clung to his own first
place ambitions. Between us we could have controlled the convention if it had been done in the first instance.[52]

The candidate who wishes to get support must show that he
already has some to begin with. This is particularly the case
when one contender is considering throwing his support to
another in order to assure the latter's nomination. There would
be no point in sacrificing one's chances in favor of another
candidate who would then not have enough votes to win. This
kind of situation occurred around the time of the fiftieth ballot
at the 1924 Democratic Convention. Al Smith informed Senator Oscar Underwood of Alabama that if two more Southern
states would give Underwood their support, Smith would also
give the Senator his support. The Underwood forces accepted
the offer but they were unable to find other Southern states
who would support their candidate, and so the scheme fell
through.[53]

The bargaining process itself may be an excellent source of
information on what important delegates are likely to do under
a variety of circumstances. A series of probing actions may be
carried out to discover what these delegates want, what they
will take, what they will give in return. Out of the negotiations
which are carried on among leaders may emerge the begin-
nings of a commonly held picture of the shape of events to
come.

Bargains may be tacit rather than explicit, made through intermediaries rather than by principals. Exactly what was promised may not be entirely clear or may be distorted later on, if this is deemed advantageous. The man who wishes to collect what he believes to be his due may have trouble securing effective guarantees. Thomas Dewey never quite manifested the same understanding that Charles Halleck did about an offer of the Vice Presidency in return for support in the Republican Convention of 1948.[54] One delegate to the 1960 Democratic Convention told reporters that he was the nineteenth person to be offered the Vice-Presidency by the Kennedy forces. Under the circumstances, he allowed as how he would take cash.[55]

It is possible that much less comes out of the convention in terms of reward for support than is commonly supposed. An incoming President, for example, may well decide to handle patronage through the dominant party faction in a state rather than suffer the disabilities of supporting a weak dissident faction that helped him at a convention. Nevertheless, if delegates believe that rewards are likely to follow support, as many apparently do, their actions will conform to this belief.

One by one the leading candidates try their luck. Timing is of the essence. Each candidate seeks the strategic moment to push his candidacy. A miscalculation, a decision, perhaps, to move ahead before sufficient support is available for the final push, may prove fatal to a candidate's chances. In a closely contested convention the prize may go to the candidate who possesses sufficient information about the intentions of others to make the successful move.

Whispering campaigns are begun, saying "Candidate X is certain to win; get on the bandwagon while you still have a chance." Rumors appear that a crucial delegation will swing to a particular candidate. The balloting may remain substantially unchanged and reveal no secrets. It is difficult to know what to believe. No mass meeting of thousands of delegates can hope to find out who is acceptable to most of them. It is up to the leaders to assert control.

In the absence of quick agreement at the convention, the

demonstrations and adjournments give party leaders time to meet and see if a candidate can be found who can receive a majority of votes. Generally, the most important leaders are Governors who exercise considerable influence in their state and may be able to control the votes of its delegates. National committeemen, state chairmen, elder statesmen, and Congressmen may be among those who attend. This is the "smoke-filled room" of convention lore. Its participants try to work out an agreement which will meet their desires. But they are severely limited in choice by their estimate of what the people will accept at the polls and what the other delegates will stand for. The leaders are men of independent influence and different interests and there may be only a limited range of agreement among them.

Little is known about negotiations among party leaders at conventions. But what we do know suggests that the essential trick is to convince others that one's preferred view of what will happen, or must happen, is the correct one. This is apparently what took place in the 1920 Republican Convention when Harry Daugherty succeeded in convincing party leaders that a deadlock was inevitable and that only Harding could break it. Much the same kind of thing occurred in 1844 when Gideon Pillow and George Bancroft spread the word that Cass, Calhoun, or Van Buren could not possibly win but that Polk would carry the day.[56]

In order to break a deadlock, it is necessary to convince some delegates that the candidate they prefer cannot win and that they would be well advised to switch to a man who can. The leaders at the 1920 Republican Convention decided to communicate this point convincingly by calling for several additional ballots during which nothing changed.[57] This also helped to assure losing party factions that their candidates had had a fair chance. At the 1924 Democratic Convention, however, which went to 103 ballots, the lengthy voting apparently did not communicate the hopelessness of their cause to the leading candidates. Not only did incompatibility and intransigence block bargaining, but short-lived booms kept arising, an indication that the delegates shared no common view of future events.[58] The shock to loyal party members was so great that many years later John Nance Garner chose to submerge his own chances and throw the 1932 convention to Franklin Roosevelt, rather than risk another agonizing stalemate.[59]

The Vice-Presidential Nominee

When the convention finally selects its Presidential candidate, it turns to the anticlimactic task of finding a running mate. Vice-Presidential nominees are chosen to help the party achieve the Presidency. Party nominees for President and Vice-President always appear on the ballot together and are elected together. Since 1804, a vote for one has always been a vote for the other.

The Vice-President occupies a post in the legislative branch of the government which is mostly honorific, and his powers and activities in the executive branch are determined by the President.[60] The electoral interdependence of the two offices gives politicians an opportunity to gather votes for the Presidency. Therefore, the prescription for an "ideal" Vice-Presidential nominee is the same as for a Presidential nominee, with two additions: he must possess those desirable qualities the Presidential nominee lacks, and he must be acceptable to the Presidential nominee.

The Vice-Presidency is the most frequent position from which Presidents of the United States are drawn. One-third of our thirty-six Presidents have been Vice-Presidents. (Three were first elected in their own right; eight first took office upon the death of a President.) American history has given us eleven good reasons—one for each man who succeeded to the Presidency—for inquiring into the qualifications of Vice-Presidents and for examining the criteria by which they are chosen.

The Presidential candidate who has firm control over his nomination is in a position to use the Vice-Presidential slot to help win the election. This is what Abraham Lincoln did in 1864 when he chose a "War Democrat," Andrew Johnson, who he hoped would add strength to the ticket.

In the same way, John F. Kennedy chose Lyndon Johnson

to help gather Southern votes, especially in Texas, and Richard Nixon chose Henry Cabot Lodge in 1960 to help offset the Democratic party advantage in the Northeast. In 1964 President Johnson chose a man who was helpful in unifying the party and maintaining its good electoral prospects. Johnson's own credentials as a liberal Democrat down through the years were not strong; when Kennedy picked him as Vice-President he was opposed on these grounds by many labor leaders and by leaders from several of the most important urban Democratic strongholds. Thus, in choosing Senator Hubert Humphrey, a long-time liberal leader, President Johnson adhered to the familiar strategy of ticket balancing.

Recent Vice-Presidential candidates have often been distinguished men who had a great deal to recommend them. But the help they could offer their parties was undoubtedly an important consideration. Spiro Agnew was chosen in 1968 because with the Democrats badly divided and Nixon assured of the nomination, it was important to find a running-mate who was not hated by anyone. Nixon had seen the results of a poll indicating that all of the leading candidates for the Vice-Presidency would hurt his chances of election more than they would help him. Agnew was little known outside his home state of Maryland, had been a Rockefeller supporter and had defeated a Democratic segregationist in his gubernatorial race, was a member of one of the "newer" ethnic groups (Greek-Americans), and impressed Nixon with his personal qualities. At the time of his selection, he was, as he himself said, not exactly a household word. No one suspected that he would later become one.[61]

Sometimes a Presidential candidate will try to help heal a breach in the party by offering the Vice-Presidential nomination to a defeated party faction. Or the Presidential candidate may try to improve his relationships with Congress by finding a running mate who has friends there. Harry Truman was chosen by Franklin Roosevelt for both these reasons.

Humphrey balanced his ticket in 1968 by choosing Senator Edmund Muskie, a taciturn, moderate man, a member of an ethnic group (Polish-Americans) concentrated in the cities of the Eastern seaboard, to balance off his own Midwest populist background and fast-talking style.

A Republican Presidential candidate from the East will try to pick a Vice-President from the Mid or Far West, though both will probably reside in large, two-party "swing" states. A liberal Democrat running for President will try to find a more conservative running mate. And so on. If it is impossible to find one man who combines within his heritage, personality, and experience all the virtues allegedly cherished by American voters, the parties console themselves by attempting to confect out of two running mates a composite father-son image of forward-looking-conservative, rural-urban, energetic-wise leadership which evokes hometown, ethnic, and party loyalties among a maximum number of voters. That, at least, is the theory behind the balanced ticket.

There have been times when a President has insisted on having his personal choice selected as Vice-President. Andrew Jackson was adamant about running with Martin Van Buren, and Franklin Roosevelt went so far as to write out a refusal to accept the Democratic nomination in 1940 when party leaders balked at the thought of Henry Wallace.

The Presidential nominee clearly is expected to have a lot to say about whom he will run with on the party ticket. More and more in recent years the expectation has been that the Presidential candidate would make the choice himself after due consultation with party leaders. Indeed, failure to act decisively may well be regarded now as a sign of weakness. Yet there have been times when Presidential candidates have not wished to become involved in internal party battles and have let the convention decide. William Jennings Bryan would not even allow his own Nebraska delegation to vote on the Vice-Presidential nomination at the 1896 Democratic Convention, and Adlai Stevenson preferred to let Estes Kefauver and John F. Kennedy fight it out for the prize in 1956.

When especially able men have appeared in the office from time to time, this may have been due more to the blessings of Providence than to wise actions on anyone's part. If good results require noble intentions, then the criteria for choosing Vice-

Presidents may leave much to be desired. Why should the great parties, we might ask, not set out deliberately to choose the man best able to act as President in case of need? Should ticket balancing and similar considerations be condemned as political chicanery?

In a speech to the Harvard Law School Forum in 1956, former Vice-President Henry A. Wallace declared: "The greatest danger is that the man just nominated for President will try desperately to heal the wounds and placate the dissidents in his party. . . . My battle cry would be—no more deals—no more balancing of the ticket." In 1964, the Republican party evidently also endorsed this view. The selection of the 1964 Republican nominee, William Miller, was intended to violate criteria used in the past for balancing the ticket. Although he came from a region different from Barry Goldwater and is a Catholic, he was chosen primarily because of his ideological affinity with the Presidential candidate. The special style of Goldwater and his supporters required that consistency of views, opposition to the other party on as many issues as possible, and refusal to bargain prevail over the traditional political demands for compromise, flexibility, and popularity.[62]

From the standpoint of the electoral success of candidates, balancing the ticket seems only prudent. But there are reasons as well for ordinary citizens to prefer that candidates make an effort in this direction. One of the chief assets of the American party system in the past has been its ability (with the exception of the Civil War period) to reduce conflict by enforcing compromise within the major factions of each party. A refusal to heal the wounds and placate dissidents is nothing less than a declaration of internal war. It can only lead to increased conflict within the party. Willingness to bargain and make concessions to opponents is part of the price for maintaining unity in a party sufficiently large and varied to be able to appeal successfully to a population divided on economic, sectional, racial, religious, ethnic, and perhaps also ideological grounds. To refuse entirely to balance the ticket would be to risk changing our large, heterogeneous parties into a multiplicity of small sects of "true believers" who care more about maintaining their internal purity than about winning public office.

This is not to suggest that the President and Vice-President must be worlds apart in their policy preferences in order to please everyone (or no one). There is obvious good sense in providing for a basic continuity in policy in case a President should die or be disabled. But this need not mean that the two men should be identical in every respect, even if that were possible. Within the broad outlines of agreement on the basic principles of the nation's foreign policy and of the government's role in the economy, for example, a President would have no great difficulty in finding a variety of men who were somewhat more or less liberal than himself, who appealed to somewhat different groups, or who differed in other salient ways. To go this far to promote party unity, factional conciliation, and popular preference should not discomfort anyone who realizes the costs of failing to balance the ticket in some important way.

Actually there is no evidence whatsoever to suggest that Vice-Presidents add or detract from the popularity of Presidential candidates with the voters. By helping unite the party, however, and by giving diverse party leaders another focus of identification with the ticket, a Vice-Presidential nominee with the right characteristics can help assure greater effort by party workers and this may bring results at election time.

Even if balancing the ticket does not help the party at the polls, it may indirectly help the people. The act of balancing the ticket may aid our political parties in maintaining unity within diversity and thereby in performing their historic function of bringing our varied population closer together rather than pulling it further apart.

THE FUTURE OF NATIONAL CONVENTIONS

One of the lessons of recent Presidential elections may be that national conventions are declining in importance as decision-making bodies.[63] They are not now taken seriously as decision-making instruments of the party of an incumbent President. The turnover of delegates from convention to convention is very high, averaging about 60%. This suggests the introduction of large numbers of delegates who are recruited by national candidates rather than by local parties. The success of Senator Kennedy in 1960, Senator Goldwater in 1964, and Richard Nixon in 1968 make it plausible to argue that increasingly commitments are being made earlier and earlier in the nomination process, even when the nomination of the out-party is being contested among several factions.

The large number of first-ballot nominations in recent years suggests that important things are happening in the out-party before the convention meets. Nationwide television coverage of the primaries gives early-bird candidates a head start on the free publicity of the election year.[64] Private polls (as well as those published in the newspapers) put more in-

Number of Presidential Ballots in National Party Conventions
1928-1968*

Year	Democrats	Republicans
1928	1	1
1932	4	①
1936	①	1
1940	①	⑥
1944	①	1
1948	①	3
1952	3	1
1956	1	①
1960	1	1
1964	①	1
1968	1	1

First Ballot Total 9/11 (5 incumbents) 9/11 (2 incumbents)

Combined (Democrats and Republicans) First Ballot Nominations:
Nonincumbents: 11/15
Incumbents: 7/7

* Nominations won by incumbents are circled

formation about the comparative popularity of candidates in the hands of party leaders earlier than before. Thus the pressures upon state party leaders to decide what they want to do seem to be urging them to make decisions earlier in the election year—before national publicity creates a rush of sentiment in one direction or another that takes matters wholly out of their hands. When one or a few party leaders come to feel the need for early decisions, soon the others must follow suit, or lose their own room for maneuvering. These early decisions must, perforce, take place at widely separate places on the map, thus enhancing the bargaining power of candidates who can deal with party leaders piecemeal under these circumstances, rather than having to face them *en masse* at a convention where they can wheel and deal with one another.

If this tendency is correctly identified—and we should argue that it is a tendency for which only scattered and inconclusive evidence can presently be assembled—it leads to the further conclusion that over the long run, as mass communications media continue or possibly increase their saturation coverage of early events in the election year, successful candidates (at least of the out-party) increasingly will have to have access to large sums of money apart from the resources generally available to the party, a large personal organization, and an extra measure of skill and attractiveness on the hustings and over television. In these circumstances, other resources—such as the high regard of party leaders—would come to be less important. Thus, early candidacy, opulent private financing, and strong personal organizations such as characterized both the Kennedy and Goldwater preconvention campaigns can overcome strong misgivings on the part of party leaders whose main concern is winning elections. If out-party candidates in the future follow similar strategies, the national convention as a decision-making body may go into eclipse.

APPENDIX: SELECTION OF DELEGATES TO NATIONAL CONVENTIONS

Not all states have primary elections, and different primaries provide for the expression of different kinds of preferences. These differences have rather substantial consequences for the behavior of state delegations at the national conventions. Primaries can vary in the following ways:

1) with regard to voters. In some states in order to vote in a primary, one must have been registered as a voter with the party whose primary one votes in. This is the "closed" primary. In the "open" primary, the voter is allowed to appear at the polls and ask for the primary ballot of the party whose delegates he wishes to help choose, and no questions are asked.

2) with regard to the way in which alternatives are presented. In some states, delegates run under their own names. In others, they run as pledged to one Presidential aspirant or another. In still others, delegates are run on a candidate's slate, and are identified only in terms of the Presidential hopeful they support.

3) with regard to the number of alternatives. Some states provide for the entering of Presidential candidates on the ballot without their consent; in others, the candidate himself must take the initiative in placing his name on the ballot.

4) with regard to the existence of a preference primary. In some states, in addition to the election of delegates, voters are given the opportunity to express a direct Presidential preference. Furthermore, in some states there is a preference primary without election of delegates to the national convention—the delegates being chosen by state party conventions. And in some states the delegates to *state* conventions are chosen by means of the preference primary.

5) with regard to the legal standing of the preferences expressed in the primary. In some states, the Presidential preferences of voters in the primary are regarded as advisory on the state delegation. In others, the delegation is legally bound to support the candidate designated until released, or as long as the candidate has a chance to win.

SOURCES: a. *Nomination and Election of the President and Vice-President of the United States*, 86th Congress, 2nd Session, House Document No. 332 (Washington, 1960). b. *Compilation of the 48 Direct Primary Systems*, 2nd ed., comp. League of Women Voters of New York (National Municipal League, N.Y.: March 1957). c. *Preferential Presidential Primaries*, Library of Congress, Legislative Reference Service (Washington, 1961).

States	Method of Selecting Delegates to National Conventions	Candidate's Consent Needed to be on Ballot	Preferential Primary— Advisory or Binding	Open or Closed Primary
Alabama	primary, if contest[1]	no	optional[2]	closed
Alaska	state conventions	no	no	
Arizona	state executive committees	no	no	
Arkansas	state committee	yes	optional[3]	closed
California	primary	yes	yes—advisory	closed
Colorado	district delegates by district conventions; delegates-at-large by state convention	no	no	
Connecticut	state conventions	no	no	
Delaware	state conventions	no	no	
District of Columbia	primary	no	yes—binding	closed
Florida	primary	no	yes—advisory	closed
Georgia	Republicans — state convention; Democrats—state committee	no	no	
Hawaii	state conventions	no	no	
Idaho	state conventions	no	no	
Illinois	district delegates by primary; delegates-at-large by state convention	yes	yes—advisory	closed
Indiana	state conventions	yes	yes—binding	closed
Iowa	state conventions	no	no	
Kansas	state conventions	no	no	
Kentucky	state conventions	no	no	
Louisiana	district delegates by district conventions; delegates-at-large by state convention	no	no	
Maine	Republicans—district conventions; Democrats—state convention	no	no	
Maryland	primary	no	yes—binding	closed
Massachusetts	primary	no	yes—binding	closed
Michigan	state delegate convention	no	yes—binding	closed

States	Method of Selecting Delegates to National Conventions	Candidate's Consent Needed to be on Ballot	Preferential Primary— Advisory or Binding	Open or Closed Primary
Minnesota	district delegates by district conventions; delegates-at-large by state convention	no	no	
Mississippi	state conventions	no	no	
Missouri	state conventions	no	no	
Montana	state conventions	no	no	
Nebraska	primary	no	yes—advisory	closed
Nevada	state conventions	no	no	
New Hampshire	primary	no	yes—advisory[4]	closed
New Jersey	primary	no	yes—advisory	closed[5]
New Mexico	primary	yes	yes—binding	closed[6]
New York	delegates-at-large by state conventions; others—primary	no	no	closed
North Carolina	Republicans—district & state conventions; Democrats — state convention	no	no	
North Dakota	state conventions	no	no	
Ohio	primary	no	yes—advisory[4]	closed
Oklahoma	state conventions	no	no	
Oregon	primary	no	yes—binding	closed
Pennsylvania	primary	no	yes—advisory[4]	closed
Rhode Island	primary	yes	yes—advisory[4]	closed
South Carolina	state conventions	no	no	
South Dakota	primary	no	yes—advisory	closed
Tennessee	state conventions	no	no	
Texas	state conventions	no	no	
Utah	Republican — district & state conventions; Democrats — state convention	no	no	
Vermont	state conventions	no	no	
Virginia	state conventions	no	no	
Washington	state conventions	yes	no	
West Virginia	primary	no	yes—advisory	closed
Wisconsin	primary	no	yes—advisory[4]	open
Wyoming	state conventions	no	no	

1 In practice, this means that Democrats use primaries; Republicans use state and district conventions.
2 If held, advisory.
3 A preferential primary must be held by a Presidential candidate's party if such candidate so petitions the state committee six months prior to the national conventions. If a preferential primary is held, it is binding on delegates.
4 Binding if, and only if, the delegate has pledged himself to a Presidential candidate on the ballot.
5 Voters must be registered with a party, but can ask for either party's ballot.
6 A state convention held after the primary will divide delegates between the top two candidates in proportion to their share of the primary votes.

NOTES

1. Much of the discussion in this chapter is drawn from our own observations of the nomination process over the mass media, for one of us in person at the Democratic National Conventions of 1960 and 1968, and the Republican National Convention of 1964, and from a set of basic texts on American parties and elections, including Moisei Ostrogorski, *Democracy and the Party System in the United States* (New York, 1910); C. E. Merriam and H. Gosnell, *The American Party System* (New York, 1929); Peter H. Odegard and E. A. Helms, *American Politics* (New York, 1938); Pendleton Herring, *The Politics of Democracy* (New York, 1940); E. E. Schattschneider, *Party Government* (New York, 1942); D. D. McKean, *Party and Pressure Politics* (Boston, 1949); V. O. Key, Jr., *Politics, Parties and Pressure Groups*, 4th ed. (New York, 1958); H. R. Penniman, *Sait's Parties and Elections* (New York, 1952); Hugh A. Bone, *American Politics and the Party System* (New York, 1955); Austin Ranney and Willmoore Kendall, *Democracy and the American Party System* (New York, 1956); William Goodman, *The Two-Party System in the United States* (Princeton, 1960); and Gerald Pomper, *Nominating the President: The Politics of Convention Choice*, 2nd ed. (New York, 1966).

We also found quite useful a more specialized literature on nominations, including Paul T. David, Malcolm C. Moos, and Ralph M. Goldman, *Presidential Nominating Politics in 1952*, Vols. I-V (Baltimore, 1954); Paul T. David, Ralph M. Goldman, and Richard C. Bain, *The Politics of National Party Conventions* (Washington, 1960); and Richard C. Bain, *Convention Decisions and Voting Records* (Washington, 1960).

2. See *Nomination and Election of the President and Vice-President of the United States including the Manner of Selecting Delegates to National Political Conventions*, 86th Congress, 2nd Session, House Document No. 332 (February 15, 1960) for an exhaustive description of the selection process, state by state, summarized in

the table on pp. 112–114. This is updated in *Nomination and Election of the President and Vice-President of the United States including the Manner of Selecting Delegates to National Political Conventions* compiled under the direction of Felton M. Johnson by Richard D. Hupman and Eiler C. Ravnholt with Robert L. Tienken, Senate Item 998 (January 1964), 43–46.

3. Frank Munger and James Blackhurst, "Factionalism in the National Conventions, 1940–1964; An Analysis of Ideological Consistency in State Delegation Voting," *The Journal of Politics* 27 (May 1965), 384. This article is a welcome corrective to the older view that delegates held no strong personal views and fits in well with recent research on party activists.

4. *Ibid.*, 378–379.

5. See, for example, Donald S. Strong, *Urban Republicanism in the South* (University, Ala., 1960); E. E. Schattschneider, *The Semi-sovereign People* (New York, 1960), Chapter V, "The Nationalization of Politics"; John C. Donovan, *Congressional Campaign: Maine Elects a Democrat*, Eagleton Series, Number 16 (New York, 1958); and Research Division, Republican National Committee, *The 1962 Elections* (mimeo., Washington, 1963).

6. See Paul Tillet, ed., *Inside Politics: The National Conventions, 1960* (Dobbs Ferry, N.Y., 1962) and Aaron B. Wildavsky, "The Intelligent Citizen's Guide to the Abuses of Statistics," in *Politics and Social Life*, eds. Nelson W. Polsby, Robert A. Dentler, and Paul A. Smith (Boston, 1963), pp. 825–844.

7. Key in *Politics, Parties and Pressure Groups*, p. 443, states succinctly the qualities of the ideally "available" Presidential candidate. He includes such factors as residence in a large politically uncertain state. He also says ". . . a man must be a Protestant [This was published in 1958] of good American stock and name to be 'available.' He should not be too closely affiliated with any particular interest or group nor should he have committed himself on a great and contentious issue before the time is ripe. Yet he must stand for something or a complex of things—a general point of view—in public life." Other factors listed are appearance, personal vigor, the possession of an attractive wife and children, and the luck to be in the right place, age group and so on, at the right time.

8. See Herring, *The Politics of Democracy*, pp. 203–224; Edward F. Cooke, "Drafting the 1952 Platforms," *Western Political Quarterly* 8 (September 1955), 465–480, and Part III of Tillett, *Inside Politics: The National Conventions, 1960*.

9. Karl A. Lamb, "Civil Rights and the Republican Platform: Nixon Achieves Control," in *Inside Politics: The National Conventions, 1960,* ed. Paul Tillett, pp. 55–84. Nixon was also concerned to see that his party made a good impression on television. Nixon, *Six Crises* (New York, 1962), pp. 313–320.

10. This is a point made by David, Goldman, and Bain, *The Politics of National Party Conventions,* pp. 398–404.

11. Richard M. Nixon, *Six Crises,* pp. 313–314.

12. See Jules Witcover, *The Resurrection of Richard Nixon* (New York, 1970), p. 343.

13. See Theodore H. White, *The Making of the President,* 1964 (New York, 1965), Chapter 9.

14. See Harry W. Ernst, *The Primary That Made a President: West Virginia, 1960* (New York, 1962), p. 5 and Theodore H. White, *The Making of the President, 1960* (New York, 1961), pp. 94–95 for indications that participants were not at all clear at the time how to interpret these results.

15. See Richard Scammon and Ben J. Wattenberg, *The Real Majority* (New York, 1970), pp. 135–140; David Halberstam, *The Unfinished Odyssey of Robert Kennedy* (New York, 1969), p. 214; Arthur Herzog, *McCarthy for President* (New York, 1969), p. 173; White, p. 89; Bruce Page, Godfrey Hodgson, and Lewis Chester, *An American Melodrama* (New York, 1969), p. 357, for alternative interpretations. Note also the reaction of one McCarthy worker to McCarthy's loss (by 49% to 42%) of the 1968 New Hampshire primary to Lyndon Johnson, running as a write-in candidate: "Nor did anyone know what would be considered a good vote. We had to rely on the press after the vote was in to tell us whether it was respectable or not. If the press called 25% a good showing for McCarthy, then it would be so. If the press called 40% a decisive loss for McCarthy, it would be that. . . .

"When the votes were tallied, I was somewhat surprised that a full 48% of the voters liked LBJ enough to write in his name. But since all the newscasters said that our 42% was a great victory for McCarthy, we were ecstatic." Ben Stavis, *We Were the Campaign* (Boston, 1969), p. 25.

16. Jack Arvey, as told to John Madigan, "The Reluctant Candidate," *The Reporter* (November 24, 1953).

17. In 1960, for example, Minnesota Democrats split among delegates friendly to Senator Humphrey and Governor Freeman— and to both of them. Freeman nominated John F. Kennedy for President. Senator Eugene McCarthy nominated Adlai Stevenson. And most of the delegation ended up voting for Humphrey.

18. David, Moos, and Goldman, *Presidential Nominating Politics in 1952*, II, pp. 155–166.

19. For Truman, see Harry S. Truman, *Years of Trial and Hope* (Garden City, 1956), pp. 499–503 and Alben Barkley, *That Reminds Me* (Garden City, 1954), pp. 225–232. For Johnson, see Theodore H. White, *op. cit., passim.*

20. For a general discussion of bargaining, see Robert A. Dahl and Charles E. Lindblom, *Politics, Economics and Welfare* (New York, 1953) *passim* and several works by Charles E.. Lindblom that have been written since then, especially his *Bargaining: The Hidden Hand in Government* (Santa Monica, 1955) and *The Intelligence of Democracy* (New York, 1965).

21. For Goldwater, see Nelson W. Polsby, "Strategic Considerations" in *The National Election of 1964*, ed. Milton C. Cummings, Jr. (Washington, 1966), pp. 82–110, and Aaron Wildavsky, "The Goldwater Phenomenon: Purists, Politicians, and the Two-Party System, *Review of Politics* 27 (July 1965), pp. 386–413. For McCarthy, see Eugene McCarthy, *The Year of the People* (Garden City, 1969), pp. 228–229.

22. One famous example has already been cited: The seating of Virginia in the 1952 Democratic Convention. See Allan P. Sindler, "The Unsolid South," in *The Uses of Power*, ed. Alan Westin (New York, 1962), pp. 230–283. See also Abraham Holtzman, *The Loyalty Pledge Controversy in the Democratic Party*, Eagleton Series, Number 21 (New York, 1960). Another example is, of course, the seating of Texas delegates at the 1952 Republican Convention. See Malcolm C. Moos, *The Republicans* (New York, 1956), pp. 468–479; William S. White, *The Taft Story* (New York, 1954), pp. 176–183; and David, Moos, and Goldman, *Presidential Nominating Politics in 1952*, pp. 69–85.

23. See the articles on Symington in Eric Sevareid, ed., *Candidates, 1960* (New York, 1959) and Ralph G. Martin and Edward Plaut, *Front Runner, Dark Horse* (Garden City, 1960). See also Nixon, *Six Crises*.

24. Carl Sandburg, *Abraham Lincoln: The Prairie Years* (New York, 1926), II, p. 330. To an Indiana leader, Lincoln wrote that Republicans should "Look beyond our noses and say nothing on points where we should disagree."

25. See Ernst, *The Primary That Made a President;* White, *The Making of the President, 1960.*

26. James Reston, "The Organized Disorder in California," *New York Times*, June 3, 1964, p. 30.

27. See Witcover, *op. cit.*, Chapter 10.

28. Elting E. Morison, *The Letters of Theodore Roosevelt* (Cambridge, Mass., 1954), p. 525. See also George E. Mowry, *Theodore Roosevelt and the Progressive Movement* (Madison, 1946).

29. Cf., for example, Jack Newfield, *Robert Kennedy: A Memoir* (New York, 1969), p. 293. For a different view, cf. Scammon and Wattenberg, *op. cit.*, Chapters 7–8.

30. Robert D. Novak, *The Agony of the G.O.P. 1964* (New York, 1965), p. 368. In the 1964 Nebraska Republican primary the results were:

Goldwater	67,369	49%
Nixon (write-in)	42,811	35%
Lodge (write-in)	22,113	16%

31. General Eisenhower's write-in vote of over 100,000 in Minnesota in 1952 is, of course, an example of what we have in mind. See David, Moos, and Goldman, *Presidential Nominating Politics in 1952*, I, p. 32.

32. Ernst, *op. cit.*, Theodore White, *op. cit.*

33. See Theodore White, *op. cit.*, p. 89; *Melodrama*, pp. 79–99; Herzog, *op. cit.*, p. 97; Newfield, *op. cit.*, p. 218.

34. Cf. Thomas Schelling, *The Strategy of Conflict* (Cambridge, Mass, 1960), pp. 19–23.

35. See Aaron B. Wildavsky, "What Can I Do? Ohio Delegates View the Democratic Convention," in *Inside Politics: The National Conventions, 1960*, ed. Paul Tillett, pp. 112–130 (Dobbs Ferry, 1962).

36. The Report of the McGovern Commission of the Democratic National Committee said: "A minority of the Rules Committee of the 1968 Democratic National Convention brought to the floor a proposal to further 'democratize' the selection of delegates to future conventions. They proposed that the 1972 Convention shall require, in order to give all Democratic voters . . . full and timely opportunity to participate in nominating candidates, that (1) the unit rules be eliminated in all stages of the delegate selection process and (2) all feasible efforts [be] made to assure that delegates are selected through party primary, convention, or committee procedures open to public participation within the calendar year of the national convention. This minority report of the Rules Committee, subsequently passed by the delegates assembled in Chicago, carried an unquestionably stern mandate for procedural reform." *A Mandate for Reform*, A report of the Commission on Party Structure and Delegate Selection to the Democratic National Com-

mittee. Chairman. Democratic National Committee, April 1970, p. 15. In early 1971 Senator McGovern announced his candidacy for the Presidency and resigned from the Commission. His successor as chairman was Representative Donald Fraser of Minnesota.

37. James A. Farley, *Jim Farley's Story* (New York, 1948), pp. 11–13 and his *Behind the Ballots* (New York, 1938), p. 70; see also John F. Carter, *The New Dealers* (New York, 1934), p. 34.

38. Theodore H. White, *The Making of the President, 1968* (New York, 1969), p. 259, estimates that the Democrats need 20,000 good hotel rooms for their convention.

39. Material on the Kennedy organization in 1960 is drawn from Fred G. Burke, "Senator Kennedy's Convention Organization," in *Inside Politics: The National Conventions, 1960*, ed. Paul Tillet (Dobbs Ferry, 1962), pp. 25–39.

40. *Ibid.*, p. 39.

41. Recognizing the importance of communication at the Republican Convention of 1860, a supporter of Abraham Lincoln carefully seated all the solid Seward states close together and as far as possible from the states whose delegates were in some doubt about whom to support. Glyndon G. Van Deusen, *Thurlow Weed: Wizard of the Lobby* (Boston, 1947), p. 253. Mayor Daley arranged for something similar at the Democratic National Convention in 1968, but the level of protest about excessive security procedures and the lack of communications facilities reached such a pitch that whatever strategic advantages Daley might have hoped for evaporated.

42. See David, Moos, and Goldman, *Presidential Nominating Politics in 1952*, I; Robert Elson, "A Question for Democrats: If Not Truman, Who?" *Life* (March 24, 1952); Albert Votaw, "The Pros Put Adlai Over," *New Leader* (August 4, 1952); Douglass Cater, "How the Democrats Got Together," *The Reporter* (August 19, 1952); Arvey and Madigan, "The Reluctant Candidate: An Inside Story," *op. cit.*; and Walter Johnson, *How We Drafted Adlai Stevenson* (New York, 1955).

43. Presidents Andrew Johnson and Arthur are the only clear exceptions since the Civil War, Coolidge and Wilson may also have had vague hopes of renomination.

44. See Ostrogorski, *Democracy and the Party System in the United States*, pp. 145–160, for excellent descriptions of convention confusion. Tillett, *Inside Politics: The National Conventions, 1960* contains more up-to-date material in the same vein. White,

The Making of the President, 1964, in contrast, describes the order and efficiency of conventions, like those in 1964, when there was no real contest for the nomination (see especially pp. 201–202). See also Ralph G. Martin, *Ballots and Bandwagons* (Chicago, 1964).

45. See Roy V. Peel and Thomas C. Donnelly, *The 1932 Campaign: An Analysis* (New York, 1935), pp. 92–93. Arthur Schlesinger, Jr., writes that strategist James Farley opposed the attempt to attack the two-thirds rule, "knowing well that not all delegates who were for Roosevelt were against the rule, and fearing that a defeat on this issue might set back the whole Roosevelt drive." Roosevelt backed down just in time. *The Crisis of the Old Order, 1919–1933* (Boston, 1957), pp. 299–300. See also Robert Morss Lovett, "Big Wind at Chicago," *The New Republic* (July 13, 1932), p. 228.

46. Wesley Bagby, "The 'Smoke-Filled Room' and the Nomination of Warren G. Harding," *Mississippi Valley Historical Review* 41 (March 1955), 657-674.

47. Caroline T. Harnsberger, *A Man of Courage—Robert A. Taft* (Chicago, 1952), p. 146. See also Joseph Martin's memoirs, *My First 50 Years in Politics* (New York, 1960).

48. Peel and Donnelly, *The 1932 Campaign: An Analysis,* pp. 95–96.

49. Crowd sentiments, of course, are largely determined by the distribution of the tickets. Normally, these are apportioned by the national committee among state party organizations, big financial contributors, and supporters of the various prominent candidates for President on as equitable and neutral a basis as party leaders can arrange. Thus, a gallery overwhelmingly in favor of a particular candidate is a rare phenomenon and suggests a rather more organized behind-the-scenes movement than meets the eye.

50. For instance, on the Roosevelt election of 1932: "Farley had held a few votes in reserve for the second ballot, knowing the importance of showing an increase each time round." Schlesinger, *The Crisis of the Old Order, 1919–1933,* p. 306.

51. Harry Daugherty, *The Inside Story of the Harding Tragedy* (New York, 1932), pp. 36, 46; and Mark Sullivan, *Our Times* (New York, 1926–1935), II, 54. See also, Wesley Bagby, "The 'Smoke-Filled Room' and the Nomination of Warren G. Harding," pp. 657–674.

52. Arthur Vandenberg, Jr., ed., *The Private Papers of Senator Vandenberg* (Boston, 1952), p. 6.

53.   Frank R. Kent, *The Democratic Party* (New York, 1928), p. 493.

54.   See Jules Abels, *Out of the Jaws of Victory* (New York, 1959), pp. 65–68.

55.   See Aaron Wildavsky, "What Can I Do? Ohio Delegates View the Democratic Convention," *op. cit*, pp. 112–130.

56.   See Edward Stanwood, *A History of the Presidency from 1788 to 1897* (Boston, 1898), pp. 206–225.

57.   Mark Sullivan, *Our Times, VI*, 35–67. See also Daugherty, *The Inside Story of the Harding Tragedy*, pp. 41–55.

58.   See Kent, *The Democratic Party*, pp. 483–505.

59.   Ferdinand Lundberg, *Imperial Hearst* (New York, 1936), pp. 273–275 and Schlesigner, *The Crisis of the Old Order, 1919–1933*, pp. 304–308.

60.   See Irving G. Williams, *The American Vice-Presidency: New Look* (New York, 1954).

61.   The best accounts of the selection of Spiro Agnew are in T. White, *The Making of the President, 1968*, pp. 244–253, and Witcover, *The Resurrection of Richard Nixon* (New York, 1970), pp. 349–355.

62.   Most of the one hundred and thirty-odd Goldwater delegates we interviewed at the Republican Convention were prepared to sacrifice victory if victory meant becoming a "me-too" party or "going against principles" by adopting what they termed the "devious and corrupt" balanced tickets of the past.

63.   William Carleton, "The Revolution in the Presidential Nominating Convention," *Political Science Quarterly* 72 (June 1957), pp. 224–240.

64.   Obviously this entails risks as well as opportunities. George Romney was the first serious Republican candidate in the field in 1968, and the early exposure before he could put together a fully coherent position on the Vietnam issue almost certainly caused his downfall. See White, *op. cit.*, pp. 54–61, and Witcover, *op. cit.*, pp. 171–191.

chapter three

the campaign

Once the conventions are over, the two Presidential candidates "relax" for a few weeks until Labor Day when they ordinarily begin their official campaigning. From that date onward they confront the voters directly, each carrying the banner of his political party. How do the candidates behave? Why do they act the way they do? And what kind of impact do their activities have on the electorate?

For the small minority of party workers, campaigns serve as a signal to get to work. How hard they work depends in part on whether the candidates' political opinions, slogans, personalities, and visits spark their enthusiasm. The workers may "sit on their hands," or may pursue their generally unrewarding jobs—checking voting lists, mailing campaign flyers, ringing doorbells—with something approaching fervor. They cannot be taken for granted; activating them and imbuing them with purpose and ardor is perhaps the first task of the candidate.

For the population at large, much of which is normally uninterested in politics, campaigns call attention to the advent of an election. Some excitement may be generated and some diversion provided for those who were not aware, until they turned on the TV, that their favorite program had been preempted by a political speech. The campaign is a great spectacle. Talk about politics increases, and a small percentage of citizens may even become intensely involved as they get caught up in campaign oratory.

For the vast majority of citizens in America, campaigns do not function so much to change their minds as to reinforce their previous convictions. As the campaign wears on, the underlying party identification of most people rises ever more powerfully to the surface. Republican and Democratic identifiers are split further apart (polarized) as their increased awareness of party strife emphasizes the things that divide them.[1]

The Survey Research Center at the University of Michigan has found repeatedly that about three-quarters of those in its samples eligible to vote claimed a party identification; of these, three-fifths were Democrats.[2] Thus, the outstanding strategic problem for Democratic politicians is to get their adherents to turn out and to vote for Democratic candidates. No need to worry about Republicans or Independents if Democrats can do their basic job. Thus Democrats stress appeals to the faithful. They try to raise in their supporters the old party spirit. One of their major problems, as we have seen, is that most citizens who identify with them are found at the lower end of the socio-economic scale and are less likely to turn out to vote than those with Republican leanings. So the Democrats put on mobilization drives and seek in every way to get as large a turnout as possible. If they are well-organized, they scour the lower income areas. They try to provide cars for the elderly and infirm, baby sitters for mothers, and, occasionally, inducements of a less savory kind to reinforce the party loyalty of the faithful. The seemingly neutral campaigns put on by radio, TV, and newspapers to stress the civic obligation to vote, if they have any effect at all, probably help the Democrats more than the Republicans.[3]

For Republicans involved in Presidential nominating politics, the most important fact of life is that their party is without question the minority party in the United States. What is more, the Republicans can claim the allegiance of what seems to be a minority of citizens that has shrunk somewhat over the last twenty-five years.

In Presidential elections in which considerations of party are foremost and allowing for the greater propensity of Repub-

Percentage of adults identifying themselves as:

	Republican	Democratic	Other
1940	38	42	20
1950	33	45	22
1960	30	47	23
1964	25	53	22
1968	27	46	27

Sources: AIPO News Release, November 8, 1964; Gallup Monthly Index, August, 1968.

licans to turn out and vote, it has been plausibly argued that the Democrats could expect to win with around 53% or 54% of the vote.[4]

This is close enough to kindle hope justifiably in Republican breasts; despite the clear Democratic majority in this country, it must be assumed that either major party can win a Presidential election. But over the last thirty years it has generally been necessary for the Republicans to devise a strategy that could not only win, but win from behind.

THREE UNDERDOG STRATEGIES

With the handwriting so plainly on the wall, the strategic alternatives available to Republicans can hardly be regarded as secret. They can be boiled down to three possibilities. First, Republicans can attempt to deemphasize the impact of party habit as a component of electoral choice by capitalizing upon a more compelling cue to action. The nomination of General Eisenhower, the most popular hero of the Second World War,. overrode party considerations and is a clear example of the efficacy of this strategy.[5] Efforts to play upon popular dissatisfaction in a variety of issue areas also exemplify this strategy, but these dissatisfactions must preexist in the population and must be widespread and intense before they will produce the desired effect. When issues do come to the fore in a compelling way, the payoff to the advantaged party is sometimes enormous, because these are the circumstances under which new party loyalties can be created.

Another possible Republican strategy, similar in some ways to the first, also seeks to depress the saliency of party in the minds of voters by blurring the differences between the parties, by seeking to efface certain of the stigmata that have been attached to the party over the years as stereotypes having general currency (e.g., "party of the rich").[6] This strategy gives full recognition to the arithmetic of Democratic superiority and also to the unit rule of the Electoral College, which weighs disproportionately votes cast in the large states that so often contain the heaviest concentrations of traditional allies of the Democratic party.[7] It has been used by Republican nominees such as Willkie, Dewey, and Nixon, with results that often fell short—sometimes barely short—of victory; in consequence this "me-too" strategy has over the years become increasingly controversial among Republicans. The fact that no Republican candidate has actually been able to gain a majority vote with it has created doubts about its efficacy.[8] The "me-too" strategy may entail the advocacy of policies generally favored by most American voters, but this approach apparently does not correctly mirror the political sentiments of Republican activists.[9] Critics of the "me-too" approach have argued that this strategy merely alienates potential Republican voters while failing to attract sufficient Democrats. Alienated Republicans, so goes this argument, seeing no difference between the policies espoused by the major parties, withdraw from politics into apathy.[10]

Thus, a third strategy, whose claim of victory is based upon the presupposition of a hidden Republican vote, can be identified. This was the strategy pursued by the Goldwater forces in 1964. It has as its main characteristic the attempt to sharpen rather than blur party lines on matters of substantive policy. Goldwater supporters argued that he could win, basing their case upon the possibility that he could put together a coalition in the Electoral College of Southern and Western states, and, in particular, upon the notion of a hidden vote. But did this hidden vote exist—or was this argument an instance of misperception on the part of those who believed it and supported Goldwater thinking he could win?

The resulting disastrous consequences for the Republican party at the congressional and state levels[11] invite the exercise of hindsight on the question of the hidden Republican vote. But, for once, hindsight merely confirms foresight. It was apparent before the election as well as afterward that there are only very weak factual grounds supporting the notion of a hidden Republican vote, waiting to be tapped by an unequivocally conservative candidate.

In examining the evidence we must first ask where the Republican vote could be hidden that this strategy seeks to tap. Presumably not among Democrats, at least outside the South, since this approach relies so heavily upon sharpening the cleavage between the two parties. Nor can there be much of a hidden vote among disaffected conservative Republicans who fail to turn out, since the best knowledge we have of Republicans is that they do turn out and vote Republican.[12]

The only other possible location for the hidden vote is among those who profess to no regular party affiliation—roughly 25% of the potential electorate. What do we know about these people that might lead us to conclude that they can be moved to vote Republican by a highly ideological appeal based on conservative and right-wing doctrines?

There is, in fact, no reason at all to suspect that these people can be reached in this way. All the information we have on party neutrals indicates that they are much less interested, less informed, less likely to seek information about politics, and less likely to vote than are regular partisans. Non-affiliates are relatively unconcerned about issues and are only dimly aware of political events.[13] Efforts to reach this population, to attract their attention, are likely to fail. Attempts to outline issue positions to them, to engage their support in behalf of any self-consistent philosophical and political position, seem on a par with the famous campaign to sell refrigerators to Eskimos.

There is a well-known suspicion, voiced from time to time by imaginative writers, that conservative elements of the population are in fact alienated from politics and sit in the wings, frustrated, immobilized and without party loyalties, until someone pursuing a Goldwater-like strategy gives them the "choice" they are looking for. This is probably a canard. What fragments of evidence we have point to the probability that the dedicated conservatives and right-wing ideologues who are sufficiently interested in politics to hold strong opinions about public policy do in fact belong to political parties and participate actively in them. Outside the South, it seems certain, these people are almost all Republicans. Thus, the hidden vote that Goldwater hoped to attract was probably hidden inside the vote Richard Nixon received in 1960.[14]

Another assumption underlying the hidden vote theory is that in 1964 it would have been possible to attract this mythical vote in substantial numbers without losing the allegiance of large numbers of more moderate people who supported the almost-successful candidacy of Richard Nixon in 1960.

In fact, this proved impossible to accomplish. An enormous number—probably around 20%—of Nixon's 1960 supporters voted for Lyndon Johnson in 1964.[15] But this outcome might have been extrapolated from poll and primary election data in the pre-convention period which showed that, even among Republican voters, Goldwater enjoyed far from overwhelming support.[16]

In addition, he aroused great antipathy among the general population. According to the Gallup poll in mid-September, 38.3% of respondents expressed definite hostility to Goldwater (including 14.7% expressing the most extreme hostility on an 11-point scale) while only 8.1% expressed any antipathy at all toward President Johnson.[17] Likewise, on a number of issues, Louis Harris surveys found that sizable majorities in the general population defined themselves as opposed to positions that they believed Senator Goldwater held.[18]

The election of 1964, as a result of the Goldwater nomination, and the campaign strategy he pursued, was an extremely good test of the hidden vote hypothesis, and also, by indirection, of the "me-too" Republican strategy, which was closer to the strategy of Richard Nixon in 1968. Nixon's main tactic was to avoid antagonizing voters, avoid direct confrontations with the opposition or with the press, and avoid saying anything controversial about Vietnam.[19]

Because of Nixon's hair-breadth plurality over Humphrey, a conclusive explanation for his victory cannot be given. It is clear, though, that he won back almost all of the Republicans who had deserted their party in the Goldwater election four years before. He also won over many Democrats who had voted for Johnson. Indeed, "a full 40 percent of Nixon's vote came from citizens who had supported Lyndon Johnson in 1964!"[20] Votes received by the Democratic party dropped from 61% in 1964 to something less than 43% in 1968, a total loss of 19%. The vote for the Republican presidential candidate rose a comparatively small 4% from 39 to 43. Naturally, the third party candidacy of George Wallace made up the difference. Insofar as the matter can be determined at all, almost all of Wallace's votes came from people who nominally consider themselves Democrats but who, in his absence, would have given more of their votes to Nixon than to Humphrey. The primary effect of the Wallace candidacy therefore was to decrease slightly Nixon's margin of victory.[21]

Despite the unusually severe defections from the Democratic Party at the Presidential level, the party label continued to exert its customary force at state and local levels. The House of Representatives was virtually a stand-off. The *Congressional Quarterly* shows that where the Democrats had occupied 57.7% of the legislative seats in the state capitols throughout the nation before the election, afterwards they retained virtually the same proportion despite the fact that there were contests of some kind in 43 states.[22] While there is ample evidence that people defected from the Democratic candidate in large numbers, it is premature—and in fact probably incorrect—to say that they have abandoned their party for good.

The strong Democratic recovery in the 1970 election bears this out. In the Senate, the Democratic class of 1958—first elected in a Republican recession, reelected in the Goldwater landslide—finally faced a reasonably normal electoral situation. They sustained a net loss of only two seats. Meanwhile, in the House, the Democrats picked up nine seats. They might have done better, but Nixon's 1968 coattails were nonexistent and it is Presidential coattail victories every four years that more than any other factor produces the decline in House seats held by the President's party in the mid-term election. In 1970 Democrats also registered dramatic gains in state elections, gaining a net of eleven Governors. Thus from a perspective one election later than 1968, the Republicans look very much like the minority party the vast majority of polls and elections have indicated they are.

THEORY AND ACTION

The contents of election campaigns appear to be largely opportunistic. The swiftly changing nature of events makes it unwise for candidates to lay down all-embracing rules for campaigning which cannot meet special situations as they arise. A candidate may prepare for battle on one front and discover that the movement of events forces him to fight on another. Yet on closer examination, it is evident that the political strategist has to rely on some sort of theory about the probable behavior of large groups of voters under a few likely conditions. For there are too many millions of voters and too many thousands of possible events to deal with each as a separate category. Keynes pointed out years ago, quite rightly, that those among us, including politicians, who most loudly proclaim their avoidance of theory are generally the victims of some long dead economist or philosopher whose assumptions they have unknowingly assimilated. The candidates must simplify their picture of the political world, or its full complexity will paralyze them; the only question is whether or not their theories, both explicit and implicit, will prove helpful to them.

What kind of organization shall they use or construct? How shall they raise money? Where shall they campaign? How much time shall they allocate to the various regions and states? What kinds of appeals shall they make to what voting groups? What kind of personal impression shall they seek to create or reinforce? How far should they go in castigating the opposition? These are the kinds of strategic questions to which Presidential candidates need answers—answers which necessarily vary depending on their party affiliations, their personal attributes, whether they are in or out of office, and on targets of opportunity that come up in the course of current events. Let us take up each of these questions in turn, taking care to specify the different problems faced by "ins" and "outs" and by Democrats and Republicans. For purposes of illustration, we shall turn often to the last three elections.

INS AND OUTS

While the incumbent may have disadvantages to offset some of his advantages, as we saw Chapter 1, the challenger faces his own set of problems. He may not be well known and may find that much of his effort must be devoted to publicizing himself. All the while, the President is getting reams of free publicity and is in a position to create major news by the things he does—administrative actions to help black people in the North or to take pressure off segregationist school boards in the South, a march into Cambodia or a cease-fire in Vietnam.

The candidate aspiring to office may find that he lacks information, which puts him at a disadvantage in discussing foreign policy and defense issues. On the other hand, he may deliberately forbear from finding out too much for fear that he be restrained in his criticism by an implied pledge not to use information the President has furnished to him. Perhaps the major advantage the challenger possesses is his ability to criticize policies freely and sometimes in exaggerated terms, whereas the incumbent is often restrained by his current official responsibilities from talking too much about them. Obligations to other nations, for example, may restrain a President from talking about changes in foreign policy or from tipping his hand in a case like Vietnam.

FRIENDS, VOLUNTEERS, AND PROFESSIONALS

While the incumbent has a going organization, molded and tested through years in office, the challenger has to build one piecemeal as he goes along in the frantic days of the campaign when there is never enough time to do everything that has to be done. Should he have a man of his own run the show without much of a nod to the professionals? They may resist, if not sabotage, his efforts. Should he enlist the cooperation of the old party men knowing that he may thereby lose some control over his campaign? Should there be two centers of campaigning with the inevitable duplication and problems of coordination? There is apparently no costless solution to this problem. There always seems to be grumbling from party professionals and the candidate's own men about their relationship.

All candidates seek special volunteer organizations to help attract voters who prefer not to associate themselves with the party organizations. The distaste with which some middle and upper class people regard the rather earthy and predominantly lower class party organizations is difficult to overcome. It is easier to construct new organizations in which they can feel ennobled by attachment to an Eisenhower or Stevenson rather than (as they may feel) associating with a group of vulgar politicians. The danger here is that the volunteer organizations will take on lives of their own and attempt to dictate strategy and policy to the candidates. A few of the volunteers may transfer to the regular party and this may lead to serious internal dissension as happened in the successful move to oust Carmine DeSapio of Tammany Hall in New York City. The candidates need the volunteers, but it is advisable for them to follow the lead set by Kennedy and Nixon in keeping tight reins on volunteers, thus assuring reasonable coordination of efforts and avoiding the possibility of capture.

The mechanics of electioneering are no simple matter; they cannot be entrusted wholly to amateurs. Not only must the candidate get to his various speaking engagements on time, but he also needs to have some good idea of whom he is speaking to and what kind of approach to take. In the hurly-burly of the

campaign, where issues and plans may change from day t\
where yesterday's ideas may have to end up in the wasteba\
to make room for today's problems, where changes of sched\
are made in response to the opportunities and dangers suggested by private and public polls, a poor organization can be
severely damaging. The troubles of Adlai Stevenson present a
case in point. His apparent distaste for the niceties of organization in 1956 hurt him badly. He was excessively rushed going
from one place to another so that he lost the valuable assets of
composure and thoughtfulness which should have been his stock
in trade. If he continually made speeches which were inappro-
priate for his audiences, it may have been because he was badly
informed about who his audience would be, not because he was
talking "over people's heads." For instance, he once went to
New Haven during the 1956 campaign, and made a speech
redolent with allusions to Yale and Princeton, with punch lines
depending on knowledge of what the "subjunctive" was, to an
audience which happened to be composed largely of old-time
Democratic party workers from around Connecticut.[23] To be
sure, some mixups, if not a few outright fiascoes, are inevitable
given the frantic pace and the pressure of time. Resilience is
not the least qualification of a Presidential candidate.

WHERE TO CAMPAIGN?

In deciding where to campaign, the candidates are aided by
distinctive features of the national political structure which go
a long way toward giving them guidance. They know that it is
not votes as such that matter but rather electoral votes which
are counted on a state-by-state basis. The candidate who wins
by a small plurality in a state gains all the electoral votes there
are for that state. The candidates realize that a huge margin of
victory in a state with a handful of electoral votes will not do
them nearly as much good as a bare plurality in states like New
York and California with large numbers of electoral votes. So
their first guideline is evident: campaign in states with large
electoral votes. There is, however, not much point in campaign-

ing in states where a candidate is bound to win or to lose. Thus, states which almost always go for one party receive only perfunctory attention. Hence, the original guidelines may be modified to read: campaign in states with large electoral votes which are doubtful. In practice, a "doubtful" state is one where there is a good chance for both parties to capture the state, and politicians usually gauge this chance by the extent to which the state has delivered victories to both parties at some time in recent memory. Republicans and Democrats thus spend more time in the large doubtful states, such as New York, Ohio, Illinois, Pennsylvania, Texas, and California, than they do elsewhere. Even if one or two one-party states should change in one election, the likelihood of such an event is too slim and the payoff in terms of electoral votes too meager to justify extensive campaigning when time might better be spent elsewhere. As the campaign wears on, the candidates take soundings from the opinion polls and are likely to redouble their efforts in states where they believe a personal visit might turn the tide.

Here we once again come across the pervasive problem of uncertainty. No one really knows how much value in changed votes or turnout is gained by personal visits to a particular state. Most voters have made up their minds. Opponents of the candidate are unlikely to go to see him anyway and one wonders what a glimpse in a motorcade will do to influence a potential voter. Yet no one is certain that whistle-stop methods produce no useful result. Visiting localities may serve to increase publicity because many of the media of communication are geared to "local" events. It also provides an opportunity to stress issues like public power or race relations which may be of special significance to citizens in a given region. Party activists may be energized by a glimpse at, or a handshake with, the candidate. New alliances, such as the one that emerged in 1964 between Goldwater and many long-time Democratic sectors of the deep South, can be solidified. And so rather than let the opportunity pass, the candidates usually decide to take no chances and get out on the hustings. They hedge against uncertainty by doing all they can.

Consider the case of John Kennedy in Ohio. He traversed that pivotal state several times in the 1960 campaign and exerted great physical effort in getting himself seen traveling there. But when the votes were counted, he found himself on the short end. The future President professed to be annoyed and stumped at why this happened. An analysis of the voting returns showed that Kennedy's vote was correlated in a high and positive degree with the percentage of Catholic population in the various counties.[24] Kennedy made a considerable improvement over the Democratic showing in 1956, but that was not enough to win. Despite evidence of this kind, which suggests that personal appearances may well be overwhelmed by other factors, visits to localities will undoubtedly continue. Who can say, to take a contrary instance, that Kennedy's visit to Illinois did not provide the bare margin of a few thousand votes necessary for victory?

There was a time when Presidential nominees faced the serious choice of whether to conduct a front porch campaign or to get out and meet the people. A candidate like Warren Harding, who his sponsors felt would put his foot in his mouth every time he spoke, was well-advised to stay home. More hardy souls like William Jennings Bryan took off in all directions only to discover that to be seen was not necessarily to be loved. An underdog, like Harry Truman in 1948, went out to meet the people because he was so far behind. A favored candidate, like Thomas Dewey in 1948, went out to meet the people to avoid being accused of complacency. Everybody is doing it probably because it is the fashion, and the spectacle of seeing one's opponent run around the country at a furious pace without following suit is too nerve-wracking to contemplate. It is beside the point that no one knows whether all this does any good. Richard Nixon seems to have learned from his enervating experience in 1960, when he pledged to visit each and every state, and then had to follow through, despite a severe illness. In 1968, he ran a different kind of campaign, taking account of the fact that radio and television make it possible to reach millions, without leaving the big metropolitan areas. Nixon did a small amount of traditional campaigning, which was faithfully chronicled by the press corps that followed him around the country. But more basic to his strategy was the technique of fixing upon regional centers and making major appearances and speeches in these places, followed by elaborate, regionally oriented television commercials that reached the voters directly—"over the heads," so to speak, of the news media that were covering and interpreting only the part of the campaign they could see—which did not include Nixon's television programs.[25]

DOMESTIC ISSUES

On the broad range of domestic affairs and "pocketbook" issues, the Democrats are highly favored as the party most voters believe will best meet their needs. Statements like "The Democrats are best for the workingman" and "We have better times under the Democrats" abound when people are asked to state how they feel about the Democratic party. The Republicans, on the other hand, are viewed as the party of depression under which jobs are scarce and times are bad. A campaign in which the salient issues are economic, therefore, is more likely to aid the Democrats than the Republicans.[26]

Economic policy thus occasions little difficulty for the Democratic party. Its task is to be liberal in several senses of that word. It promises something for everyone. There are sizable extensions of social welfare programs financed by the Federal government, increased minimum wages for the underpaid, medical insurance for the aged, high price supports for the farmer, irrigation for arid areas, flood protection and power dams for the river basins, and so on. No one is left out, not even businessmen who are promised prosperity.

Republicans are clearly on the defensive in the realm of domestic policy, a situation stemming from the fact that they were in office when the Great Depression took place. They try to play down domestic issues. They do best when emphasizing foreign policy ("bring the boys back from Korea"), style issues ("mink coats and five percenters"); general management of government ("we can do it better") ; or an outstanding personality ("I like Ike"). When domestic issues are debated, a Republican candidate like Richard Nixon takes care to stress that he is in favor of the New Deal's social reforms whatever else he may say about it. And he adds that he is in favor of helping farmers, laborers, old people, pensioners, teachers, and other worthy folk extend their gains. That he will do this better and cheaper becomes his refrain and the major point of difference with his opponent. He is understandably upset at Democratic insinuations that he and his party have not become fully reconciled to Social Security. Over and over again Nixon insists that he and his opponent agree on goals of domestic policy, and that the only difference separating the two men is the minor matter of means.[27] For if the gulf between the parties is thought to be wide on "pocketbook" issues, a majority of voters would unhesitatingly choose the Democrats.

Both parties, of course, have some difficulty in reconciling their Presidential and Congressional wings, but in the realm of domestic policy the Democrats have an easier task. The crucial electoral votes come from large states where the labor union and minority group interests reinforce the Presidential aspirant's demand for liberal policies. Democratic conservatives, who are in any event in a minority even in Congress, can be and largely are increasingly ignored. A strong civil rights stand risks loss of Southern support, but black voters are strategically placed in states with the highest number of electoral votes. Since Franklin D. Roosevelt, all Democratic Presidential candidates have decided that they can win without the South but not without the large states in other sections of the country. Television and radio make the old practice of saying different things in different parts of the country rather more dangerous than it used to be. In fact, a kind of reversal has set in. Contemporary candidates are more likely to get favorable publicity if they attack segregation before Southern audiences. This not only comes immediately to the attention of admiring audiences in the Northern black strongholds, but also not incidentally demonstrates the courage and integrity of the candidate. Whether from conviction or calculation of advantage, Democratic candidates have no trouble coming out strongly for civil rights.

The Republicans face much more difficult problems of internal dissension. Their Congressional contingent is cohesive and generally conservative. The result is that Republican Presidential candidates more often than not repudiate their Congressional brethren. Party conservatives do not like the "me-too" implications of the stands taken by their Presidential candidates like Nixon. In the past they have felt he ought to hit harder at what they regard as Democratic statism and looseness with the public purse. But the numbers of strategically placed voters, or the groups from whom they take their cues, who disagree with this approach in domestic affairs is too great for a Republican candidate who wants to win to forget them. Though Nixon talked tough at times in remarks directed to selected Republican audiences, he understandably refused to alter the tenor of his remarks in general. Like all Republican candidates since 1936, with the exception of Barry Goldwater, he apparently concluded that there were not enough conservatives to elect him, that they had no place to go, and that he would get their votes anyhow as, indeed, he did. Nixon continued to send conservatives like Agnew and Senator Thurmond out on the hustings to mollify the right-wing. But he refused to commit political suicide by making wholesale attacks on the Democratic party and its domestic policies.

FOREIGN AFFAIRS

In the realm of foreign affairs, the Republicans have the advantage. The fact that the Democrats occupied the Presidency during World Wars I and II and the Korean War apparently convinced most voters that Democrats tend to lead the country to war. This belief may be reinforced by the first years of the war in Vietnam. Republicans have on the whole escaped this stigma and are known as the party of peace.[28] Whether they continue to maintain this reputation is no doubt partially contingent on President Nixon's success in concluding the country's Indo-Chinese involvement. Whether this impression of Democrats is any more useful or valid than that of Republicans as the party of depression is beside the point for present purposes. We are after the strategic implications, which are important. For if foreign affairs issues can be made sufficiently important to enough voters, the Republicans stand a better chance of winning. Republicans generally do best by building up foreign affairs and playing on the fear that Democrats are not competent in this field. Democrats have the choice of de-emphasizing foreign policy, something that has become increasingly difficult to do, or trying to show somehow that they are more peace-loving than Republicans, though also at least as tough on Communism.

How this used to work in practice can be seen in Richard Nixon's 1960 campaign, as the lamb of domestic controversy turned into the lion of foreign affairs. Nixon sought to differentiate himself as much as possible from Kennedy in the field of foreign affairs. He suggested that he was uniquely capable of securing peace without surrender, and that Kennedy was not. He tried to strengthen the prevailing impression of the Democratic party as the party of war. He implied alternatively that Kennedy would permit the Communists to make unwarranted advances (for example, in Matsu and Quemoy), and that the Democrats would make rash moves (Cuba). Even Nixon's espousal of an aggressive line, such as he took regarding Matsu and Quemoy, helped him because in foreign affairs voters trust the Republicans. On the other hand, Kennedy's equally aggressive stand toward Cuba in his speeches did not correspondingly help him.[29]

All this may appear paradoxical, but it is perfectly understandable in the light of our knowledge of voting behavior. Kennedy did not succeed in convincing most voters that issues of foreign policy were more important than domestic concerns. He won on his party affiliation, on domestic issues, and on his appeal to Catholics.[30] Had he accomplished his purpose of alerting voters to the importance of foreign affairs, there is every reason to believe he would have lost support, since voters, in line with their previous inclinations, would have decided that the perilous times called for a Republican in the White House.

The television debates reflected this. Those viewers of the debates who were especially attentive to foreign policy issues were more likely to be pro-Nixon than pro-Kennedy, just the reverse of the situation in domestic affairs. A summary of public opinion surveys on the debates concludes: "The evidence suggests that foreign affairs was the paramount issue during the entire campaign and . . . since Nixon was generally conceded to be the more expert and experienced in foreign affairs—he was far ahead of Kennedy in perceived ability at 'handling the Russians' and 'keeping the peace'—the focus on foreign affairs was clearly to Nixon's advantage." [31]

Foreign affairs was also an area that helped Nixon in the 1968 campaign. He managed to combine peace with toughness without saying exactly how he would bring peace or where he would get tough. Democratic dissension on the war issue did not hide the fact that Democratic Presidents were in office when the war expanded and were unable to end it. Nothing Nixon said could have added to that, and anything more specific would have gotten him into trouble with one side or the other in a campaign where his major strategy was to anger as few people as possible.

This discussion suggests a strategic dilemma for President Nixon in 1972. If the analysis is correct, it is not clear what electoral benefit he can achieve by making peace in Vietnam in time for the 1972 election. If making peace means depressing the saliency of foreign problems, and correspondingly inviting the attention of the electorate to domestic ones, then Republican success at terminating American involvement in the war may well count against Republicans in 1972.

LAW AND ORDER

If, on the whole, foreign affairs and war and peace are Republican issues, and domestic welfare and the economy are Democratic issues, what about the third great cluster of problems, variously labeled (and understood) as law and order, domestic violence, and race relations? As Scammon and Wattenberg point out, this issue has grown enormously in prominence to voters over the last few years:

Suddenly, some time in the 1960's, "crime" and "race" and "lawlessness" and "civil rights" became the most important domestic issues in America.[32]

It is too early to tell whether this cluster of issues works consistently for or against a particular political party. More likely, over the short run, it works against incumbents. Not all incumbents have suffered from it—as witness the reelection in 1970 (though by a sharply reduced majority) of Governor Ronald Reagan of California. There is evidence, however, that suggests that this issue has the potential to give President Nixon some difficulty. Here, for example, are the results of a Harris survey [33] asking about President Nixon's handling of his job in August, 1970, a year and a half after he assumed office:

	Positive	Negative	Not Sure
Working for peace in world	51%	45%	4%
Relations with Russia	47	40	13
TV Speeches, Press Conferences	42	48	10
Handling Cambodia	40	48	12
Handling Vietnam war	40	54	6
Handling Middle East Crisis	38	47	15
Approach to health legislation	37	50	13
Handling war in Laos	32	52	16
Keeping economy healthy	31	63	6
Handling race problems	30	62	8
Relations with Congress	29	57	14
Handling taxes and spending	28	64	8
Handling student protestors	27	65	8
Handling antiwar protestors	25	64	11
Keeping down cost of living	19	79	2

Whereas his overall rating was 35% positive, 51% negative, and 14% not sure, Nixon received much higher ratings, which we interpret as a normal Republican bonus, in the field of foreign affairs: 51% positive for "working for peace in the world," 47% positive in "handling relations with Russia," 42% positive for "handling Cambodia," 40% positive for "handling Vietnam war." These were, on the whole, the most favorable dimensions in the popular response to Nixon. On domestic economic issues, Nixon received unfavorable ratings: on "keeping economy healthy" 31% favorable, 63% unfavorable; on "handling taxes and spending" 28% favorable, 64% unfavorable; on "keeping down cost of living" 19% favorable, 79% unfavorable.

On the law, order, and race problems, responses to President Nixon were nearly as unfavorable: on "handling race problems" 30% favorable, 62% unfavorable; on "handling student protestors" 27% favorable, 65% unfavorable; on "handling antiwar protestors" 25% favorable, 64% unfavorable. This cluster of issues may well be so intractable over the short run that whoever has the responsibility of governing will suffer at the hands of public opinion no matter what he does or omits doing to deal with it. We can only say with confidence at this point that neither party seems to have captured a position with respect to these issues such that they can be sure that when it becomes salient, they know they stand to win or lose.

PRESENTATION OF SELF

Another set of strategic problems concerns the personal impression made by the candidates. A candidate is helped by being thought of as trustworthy, reliable, mature, kind but firm, a devoted family man and in every way normal and presentable. No amount of expostulation about the irrelevance of all this ordinariness as qualification for an extraordinary office wipes out the fact that candidates must try to conform to the public stereotype of goodness, a standard which is typically far more demanding of politicians than of ordinary mortals. It would be a rather excruciating process for a candidate to remodel his entire personality along the indicated lines. And, to be fair, the candidates are not so far from the mark as to make this drastic expedient necessary or they would not have been nominated in the first place. What the candidates actually try to do is to smooth off the rough edges, that is, to counter the most unfavorable impressions of specific aspects of their public image to which they believe they are susceptible. Kennedy, who was accused of being young and immature, hardly cracked a smile in his debates with Nixon, while the latter, who was said to be stiff and frightening, beamed with friendliness. Kennedy restyled his youthful shock of hair, and Nixon thinned his eyebrows to look less threatening.

The little things that some people don't like may be inter·· preted favorably by other people. Hubert Humphrey was alleged to be a man who could not stop talking; his garrulousness, however, is just another side of his encyclopedic and detailed knowledge of the widest variety of public policies. He might talk too much to suit some, but the fact that he knew a lot pleased others.

The political folklore of previous campaigns provides candidates with helpful homilies about how to conduct themselves. Typical bits of advice include the following: always carry the attack to your opponent; the best defense is offense; separate the other candidate from his party; when in doubt as to the course which will produce the most votes, do what you believe is ethically or morally right; guard against acts that can hurt you because they are more significant than acts that can help you; avoid making personal attacks which may gain sympathy for the opposition. Unfortunately for the politicians in search of a guide, these bits of folk wisdom do not contain detailed instructions about the conditions under which they may be applied.

The case of Adlai Stevenson suggests a familiar dilemma for candidates. Shall they write (or have written) new speeches for most occasions or shall they rest content to hammer home a few themes, embroidering just a little here and there? No one really knows which is better. Stevenson is famous for the care which he devoted to his speeches and the originality he sought to impart to his efforts. Had he won office he might have established a trend. As it is, most candidates are likely to follow Kennedy, Nixon, Johnson and Goldwater in using just a few set speeches. In view of the pervasive inattention to public affairs and political talk in our society, this approach may have the advantage of driving points home (as well as driving mad the newsmen who must listen to the same thing all the time).[34]

More important, perhaps, is the desirability of appearing comfortable in delivery. Televised speeches may establish the major opportunity for a candidate to be seen and evaluated by large numbers of people. Eisenhower's ability to project a radiant appearance helped him; Stevenson's obvious discomfort before the camera hurt him. On this point we have evidence that those who listened to Stevenson's delivery over radio were more favorably impressed with him than those who watched him on TV.[35] In 1968, Richard Nixon used regional television appearances as a means of reaching voters directly and making an end run around what he feared would be hostile press coverage of his campaign.[36] With television occupying an important place in American life, ability to make a good appearance is not a trivial matter. There is little reason to believe, however, that we are headed for a society in which TV performers can run for public office and expect to win—except, of course, in California, where party organizations traditionally have had little control over the selection of candidates to run for office.

The major difficulty with the strategic principles we have been discussing is not that they are too theoretical, but that they do not really tell the candidates what to do in case they are mutually incompatible. Like proverbs, one can often find principles to justify opposing courses of action. ("Look before you leap," but "he who hesitates is lost."). Nixon in 1960 could not take full advantage of international affairs without hitting so hard as to reinforce the unfavorable impression of himself as being harsh and unprincipled. Kennedy could hardly capitalize on the Rooseveltian image of the vigorous leader without attacking the foreign policy of a popular President.

The result is that the candidates must take calculated risks when existing knowledge about the consequences of alternative courses of action is inadequate. Here, hunch, intuition, and temperament necessarily play an important role in choosing among competing alternatives.

THE TELEVISION DEBATES

The famous TV debates of 1960 between Nixon and Kennedy provide an excellent illustration of the difficulty of choosing between competing considerations in the absence of knowledge as to the most likely results. With the benefit of hindsight, many observers now suggest that Nixon was obviously foolish to engage in the debates.

Let us try to look at the situation from the perspective of each of the Presidential aspirants at the time. Kennedy issued a challenge to debate on television. The possible advantages from his point of view were many. He could use a refusal to debate to accuse Nixon of running away and depriving the people of a unique opportunity to judge the candidates. Among Kennedy's greatest handicaps in the campaign were his youth and the inevitable charges of inexperience. Television debates could and did help to overcome these difficulties by showing the audience not so much that Kennedy was superior in knowledge but that there was not that much difference in the information, age, and general stature of the two men. Whatever administrative skills or inside information Nixon might have would not and did not show up on the screen as the candidates necessarily confined themselves to broad discussions of issues known to all politically literate people. Kennedy could only guess but he could not know that Nixon would not stump him in an embarrassing way in front of millions of viewers. But Kennedy was in a position to know that despite the reams of publicity he had received, he was unknown to many voters, much less known than the Vice-President. Here was a golden opportunity to increase his visibility in a sudden and dramatic way. And his good looks were not calculated to hurt him with those who like to judge the appearance of a man.[37]

Nixon was in a more difficult position. To say "no" would not have been a neutral decision, it would have subjected him to being called a man who was afraid to face his opposition. Saying "yes" had a number of possible advantages. One stemmed from the numerical disadvantage of the Republican party. Normally, most people do not pay very much attention to the opposition candidate, making it difficult to win them over. They avoid contact with his statements and screen out his messages. Televised debates would provide a unique instance in which huge numbers of people attracted to both parties could be expected to tune in attentively. Nixon had good reason for believing that if he made a favorable impression he would be in a position to convince more of the people (the Democratic identifiers) he needed to convince than would Kennedy. The risk that Kennedy might use the opportunity to solidify the support of those attracted to a Democrat simply had to be taken. Another potential advantage which might have accrued to Nixon arose from the heritage of his previous political life. He had been labeled by some people as "tricky Dick," an immoral and vindictive man. This picture might have been supplanted on television by the new Nixon of smiling visage and magnanimous gesture who had it all over his opponent in knowledge of public affairs. Nixon had to judge whether his handicap was serious or whether it was confined to convinced liberals whose numbers were insignificant and who would never have voted for him in any event. He also had to guess whether it would be worthwhile to overcome this handicap, even if it also meant giving Kennedy an opportunity to overcome his own disabilities.[38] Perhaps a record of success in debate situations going back to high school was not irrelevant in guiding Nixon to his eventual decision to go on television with his opponent.[39] Surveys taken after the event suggest that Nixon miscalculated.[40] But if he had won the election instead of losing it by a wafer-thin margin, he would hardly have been reminded of any error on his part, and there would probably have been discussions of what a brilliant move it was for him to go on TV.

The election of 1964 presented an entirely different set of circumstances. President Johnson, an incumbent enjoying enormous personal popularity at the head of the majority party, had nothing to gain and everything to lose by debating his rival. And so, despite strenuous efforts by Senator Goldwater and his allies to involve the President in debates, none were held.

By 1968, observers were beginning to question whether candidates would ever again seek an epic confrontation with one another on the 1960 model. What seems to be required before the likely occurrence of such a debate is two major candidates equally eager for such a battle. If one is an incumbent, or feels himself securely in the lead, there is little incentive to debate. Hubert Humphrey pursued Richard Nixon fiercely on this point in 1968, but Nixon prudently refrained from a debate that would needlessly have risked his chances of victory. Had John Kennedy lived to debate again, in 1964, he might have established a "tradition" that would have been difficult for future candidates to break.

GETTING A GOOD PRESS

Although we have seen that newspapers themselves—whether in editorials or stories—do not markedly influence reader opinion, it is still important for a candidate to get the most favorable coverage possible. It usually does not pay to try to line up support from publishers who have already made up their minds before the campaign has officially started. But the candidates can and do assiduously court the newspapermen assigned to them.[41]

The space a candidate gets and the slant of the story may depend to some extent on how the reporters regard him. If they find it difficult to get material, if they find the candidate suspicious and uncommunicative, this too may have its effect on how much and what gets published. Little things like phasing news to meet the requirements of both morning and afternoon newspapers or supplying reporters with human interest material is helpful to the candidate. Thus, the personality of the candidate, his ability to command the respect of the rather cynical men assigned to cover him may count heavily. Democratic candidates probably have to work a little harder at cultivating good relations in order to help counteract the editorial slant in most papers. They also must make the most of their opportunities in public appearances, radio and TV speeches to counteract the impression given in segments of the press. If what they say and do "makes news," and their press secretaries help promote the stories, they may get space through the desire of the newspapers to sell copies.

Thus far, we have spoken of the press as if it were a monolithic entity. So do the candidates for the most part. But they also recognize that there are all sorts of papers with differing biases, needs, and audiences. A great deal of a candidate's attention is devoted to stories destined for the Negro, religious, and ethnic interest group press. The circulations of these publications may not be huge but it is assumed that these papers have readers who are concerned with topics of special interest to smaller and more attentive constituencies. A story on religion in a Protestant journal may do more to convince people than much greater coverage in the daily press.

MUD-SLINGING AND HECKLING

In the closing days of what appears to be a close race, there may be a temptation for the parties, now thoroughly engrossed in the heat of battle, to unloose a stream of invective directly at the other side. How much of this they do and how often they do it is partially determined by the kind of people they are. In the long run, however, the standards of the voting population determine the standards of the candidates. Should it happen that vituperation is rewarded, we can expect to see it occur again. Should it prove to be the case, however, as in the Scandinavian countries, that departures from proper deportment are severely punished at the polls, candidates can be expected to take the hint.

In the United States we seem to be in a middle position in regard to mud-slinging. It is not everyday practice but neither is it a rarity. A history of Presidential campaigns suggests that vituperation is largely irrelevant to the outcomes of campaigns and that its benefits are problematical.

Thomas Jefferson was accused of seducing a highborn Virginia maiden, fathering a brood of mulattoes, and being an atheist. Andrew Jackson was called a murderer, gambler, and an adulterer. Lincoln was charged with being a vulgar village politician and fourth-rate lawyer. President Grover Cleveland was accused of fathering an illegitimate child and, though he was not certain of its paternity, he admitted responsibility. His opponents taunted him with the chant:

> *Ma, Ma, where's my Pa?*
> *Gone to the White House*
> *Ha! Ha! Ha!*[42]

The point is, however, that all these men won office as have many others who have been subject to similar aspersions.

Even more instructive is the case of William Henry Harrison whom Democratic politicians derogated with the remark that he would be content to spend the rest of his life in a log cabin drinking hard cider. His party seized on this to make him into a symbol of the common man and drowned out all attempts to discuss issues with cries about humble living in log cabins. Van Buren, the Democratic candidate, was crushed with doggerel like this:

> *Let Van from his coolers of silver drink wine*
> *And lounge on his cushioned settee*
> *Our man on his buckeye bench can recline*
> *Content with hard cider is he.*

The candidate faces the difficulty of deciding what kind of invective to ignore as potentially damaging and what kind to turn to his advantage. Franklin Roosevelt paid no attention to most accusations about him but seized on an attack involving his dog, Fala, to rib his opponents unmercifully for impugning a dog that could not reply.[43] If all else fails, it is always possible to take the advice attributed to a Chicago politician who said that in politics, as in poker, the way to meet scandalous charges was to "Call 'em and raise 'em. If you are denounced as a fool, call your opponent a damned fool; if he says you are a crook, call him a robber; if he intimates that you are careless with the truth, tell your audience that he is a pathological liar."

Why, we may wonder, are men supposed to behave in a more exalted fashion in politics and in the midst of a passionately fought contest than we would expect of them in other areas of life? Successful public officials, like successful businessmen and union leaders, deal with man as he is, not as they would wish him to be. Campaigning is concerned primarily with winning support; any secondary effects it may have, such as educating the public, are incidental. If we wonder at the level of appeals made to us in elections we need only look so far as our own qualities to get the answer. There are occasions when we might be thankful that our politicians do not fully reflect the ethical standards actually practiced (not preached) in society. Knowledge of our own character may explain the wish (and expose the fallacy) of expecting politicians to be better than we are.[44]

However, the standards of the voting population do not necessarily determine the actions of organized hecklers. Heckling has probably always been a part of any politics in which votes are publicly solicited, though Americans have never indulged in the practice to the degree that it exists in Great Britain.

The heckling in the 1968 campaign was different from that of recent American politics in its scope. Both Hubert Humphrey and George Wallace had to face frequent, deliberate, disruptive activities on the part of groups of young people whose aim was to prohibit them from speaking at all, rather than to "score points" on them through clever interruptions. If a rule of thumb were to be developed from this, it would seem to be that extreme conservatives and moderate liberals were most likely to face such activity, while moderate conservatives (e.g.,

Richard Nixon) and extreme liberals (e.g., various Peace-and-Freedom type candidates) would escape. To the degree that such heckling had any impact, it ultimately probably gained a little sympathy for the candidate under fire. Unlike mudslinging, however, where a campaign which boomerangs is usually quickly squelched by party leaders, the disruptive forms of heckling in 1968 were less easy to control. The hecklers had no candidate who might have lost votes by being identified with them and, in any event, their purpose was to show contempt for the electoral process rather than for any single candidate.

FEEDBACK

As the campaign progresses, the candidates attempt to take soundings from various sources and to modify their behavior as seems best suited to make the most of opportunities as they arise. But this process presents tremendous problems in the chaotic atmosphere of a campaign. Even under conditions of comparative tranquility, who knows what the world is like? In our everyday lives we make assumptions that simplify reality tremendously in order to make decisions. Consider, then, the poor candidate who must try to take hold of a complicated universe in which the actions and the reactions of millions of voters, his own staff, his opponents, party workers, the press, and other relevant publics have to be taken into account under widely varying conditions. There is, of course, hardly any time to think about these matters. The strategies adopted by the candidates surely depend on some notions about what the consequences of these strategies will be. In turn, it is necessary to make assumptions about how people are going to act in response to one's own actions. Yet, no one can be certain that the simple picture of the world in his mind corresponds to the complex reality.

The candidate evolves an organization and a staff whose purpose in part is to inform him of the state of the political world. But he comes to know soon enough that it is unwise to trust his closest associates completely. Their fortunes are identified with his, their future prospects may depend on his, and their very battles for him may warp their judgment. Will they come to think that bad news should be withheld lest it sap his will to win? Will their hopes and fears color their judgment? Will the fact that they, in turn, depend upon other "loyalties" mean that those they trust are also unreliable? It is clear that the candidate has to place some sort of discount on the reports of his advisers. But it is not clear how much of a discount should be taken.

In trying to get a more objective estimate of the political situation, a candidate has a number of devices available—polls, the mass media, audience reaction—which are better than nothing but which are ambiguous and difficult to interpret. The first question about a poll is whether or not to believe it. Perhaps the apparent findings are more an artifact of the way the questions are phrased and the kind of people who administer them than of any objective reality. When in doubt candidates may have two polls taken, though this is terribly expensive, and find that they do not correspond. Then the candidates, who have some reason to fancy themselves political experts, may cast the polls to the winds and rely on their own observations. Moreover, polls are static things and conditions may change more rapidly than a polling organization can find out. The questions asked may be the important ones in the mind of the pollster but not necessarily in that of the voter. And if the results seem intolerably pessimistic, the candidate may decide that there is no point in listening to the voice of doom anyhow. So he may turn next to the mass media. If newspapers happen to be on his side, he risks the distortions of favoritism; if they are against him, he risks the distortions of malice. If they are neutral he may wonder if they know any more about what is going on than he does. Yet he ignores what they say at his peril. The candidate cannot possibly read all the papers or listen to all the commentators, he requires summaries. Here again appears the risk of unconscious distortion by his eager staff.

Closest to the candidate's experience in the mad rush of the campaign are the audiences he addresses, and he may anxiously scan their response. At the beginning of the campaign, he is likely to try out different approaches on audiences composed of the party faithful. As a result, he may discover that what the "people" want are the kinds of traditional cries that rally those who are already disposed to vote for him; but this, at least for Republicans, may not reach the voters he needs to convince. The Republican candidate discovers that the people want an end to disastrous government spending, and the Democratic standard-bearer learns that they want more welfare programs. As the campaign progresses, candidates begin to believe that the crowds are no longer so one-sided, and their varying size and enthusiasm may be read as significant portents. There are, however, many different possible reasons to explain why crowds turn out: curiosity, desire to heckle, nothing else to do, a look at a glamorous figure, as well as the desire to support a particular candidate. A large crowd may mean many things. It may mean that the candidate's managers have picked their spot wisely (such as, market day at a farm distribution center) and have brought their man to a crowd rather than a crowd to him. Or a large crowd may mean that the candidate has succeeded in gaining intense support from the strongest party identifiers, but its enthusiasm may tell him nothing about his general prospects or the appeals he needs to make. The disparity between the roaring crowds and the vote in a state like Ohio may have brought home the reality of this kind of misperception to the Kennedy forces.[45]

The feedback a candidate gets can hurt him if it reinforces and amplifies negative soundings that lead to pessimistic interpretations of his chances. Consider the plight of Vice-President Humphrey in 1968. He emerged from the Democratic convention with his party in disarray, and his own image tarnished because he could neither condemn, condone, nor control events in the streets of Chicago or on the convention floor. Before he could pull his party together, he received indications that his campaign was falling apart. In the first few weeks the crowds (compared to those for Nixon) were poor wherever he went. Although a candidate normally rises in the estimation of the people after he has received exposure during his nomination, his public opinion poll rating dropped precipitously after the convention. All at once his chances seemed pitifully small. An immediate result was that financial contributions did not come in as expected. Consequently Humphrey did not have enough money to go on TV in the early days of his campaign when it might have helped him most, and he had to spend a considerable portion of his first month raising the necessary funds. In those days Humphrey was pyramiding his liabilities and discovering why it is hard to start on your way up when everyone tells you you are already too far down.

While the candidate is making his assessment as best he can, others in his organization are doing the same. The party organizer, for example, may gauge the trend of the campaign by the number of people who show up at party headquarters willing to do some work. This may be as good an index as any. Like the mass meeting, however, attendance at headquarters may be an unreliable indicator of success. Party headquarters may be attracting an influx of a special, limited segment of the public attracted to a man like Adlai Stevenson or lonely people who find this a good way to meet others. The reports of workers in the various states may or may not be more useful. Although they may be wholly accurate, they are subject to the usual biases and may be representative only of narrow portions of the public rather than a good sample of the electorate.

After an election it may be amusing to note that an activity like Les Biffle's nationwide tour masquerading as a chicken farmer proved more reliable for Harry Truman than the polls;[46] during the campaign, however, this was just one among a number of clues. The candidates are always in the dark because they can never be sure which clues to believe or whether to believe any of them. If they had lots of time, they might pore over the various clues, signals, and hints and arrive at a composite estimate which might make some sense. Time is in terribly short supply, however, and so the Presidential candidate is reduced to a haphazard savoring of some of the relevant signs. He may add some credence to one clue, subtract from another, and ultimately rely on his own intuition. The conduct of a campaign is far from being an established science; at best it is a shaky art.

One hears much about campaign blunders as if there really was objective assurance that another course of action would have turned out better for the unfortunate candidate. The most famous of these in recent years was Thomas E. Dewey's decision in 1948 to mute the issues, which was said to have snatched defeat from the jaws of victory.[47] A vigorous campaign on his part, it was said, would have taken steam out of Harry Truman's charges, and would thus have brought victory to Dewey. Perhaps. What we know of the 1948 election suggests that it provoked a higher degree of voting on the basis of economic class than any of the elections which have succeeded it.[48] A slashing attack by Dewey, therefore, might have polarized the voters even further. This would have increased Truman's margin since there are many more people with low than with high incomes. Had the election gone the other way—and a handful of votes in a few states would have done it—we would have heard much less about Dewey's blunder and much more about how unpopular Truman was supposed to have been in 1948.

A whole series of "mistakes" have been attributed to Richard Nixon. Here are two, culled from a best-selling book on the 1960 campaign. On the civil rights plank of the Republican platform: "The original draft plank prepared by the Platform Committee was a moderate one. . . . This plank, as written, would almost certainly have carried the Southern states for Nixon and, it seems in retrospect, might have given him victory. . . . On Monday, July 25th, it is almost certain, it lay in Nixon's power to reorient the Republican Party toward an axis of Northern-Southern conservatives. His alone was the choice. . . . Nixon insisted that the Platform Committee substitute for the moderate position on civil rights (which probably would have won him the election) the advanced Rockefeller position on civil rights. . . ."[49] On Nixon's failure to protest the imprisonment of Martin Luther King during the campaign: "He had made the political decision at Chicago to court the Negro vote in the North, only now, apparently, he felt it quite possible that Texas, South Carolina, and Louisiana might all be won to him by the white vote and he did not wish to offend that vote. So he did not act—there was no whole philosophy of politics to instruct him.[50]

Apparently, there are times when hindsight converts every act of a losing candidate into a blunder. Victory can have the same effect in reverse. Consider the situation of Richard Nixon, 1968 version, as he dealt with the same Southern white-Northern black dilemma—in the same way. Theodore White reports:

> Nixon had laid it down, at the Mission Bay gathering, that none of his people, North or South, were to out-Wallace Wallace. He insisted, as he was to insist to the end of the campaign, that he would not divide the country; he wanted a campaign that would unify a nation so he could govern it. To compete with Wallace in the South on any civilized level was impossible. . . . Instead, Nixon would challenge Wallace in the peripheral states—Florida, North Carolina, Virginia, Tennessee, South Carolina. . . . It was only later that the trap within this strategy became evident—for, to enlarge his base in the Northern industrial states, Nixon would have to reach across from the rock-solid Republican base there, across center, to the independents, the disenchanted Democrats, to the ghettos. But to do that would be to shake the peripheral strategy in the new South. And to hold to the course he had set for the peripheral strategy limited his call in the North.[51]

Nixon's strategy was aimed, in both years, at chipping off the "peripheral" Southern states while not taking such a strong anti-civil rights position as to bring Northern blacks to the polls in great numbers and to turn Northern suburban whites against him.

In 1968, of course, he won; his margin over 1960 consists of North Carolina, South Carolina, Illinois, and New Jersey. Would it have been a gain for him to "out-Wallace Wallace"? Not likely, in view of the heavy margins piled up by Wallace in the states he did carry and his inability to do very well elsewhere. Would it have been a gain for Nixon to repudiate all possible anti-civil rights votes? Not likely, in view of the near unanimity against him of the black vote and probably of most strongly pro-civil rights white liberals. In short, did his strategy of equivocation almost win or almost lose the Presidency for Richard M. Nixon in 1960 and/or 1968?

We have previously dealt with Nixon's decision to engage in television debates with Kennedy. Let us take a look at his decision on timing the 1960 campaign. Nixon calculated that the election was going to be very close because the Democrats were the majority party in the country, and the Republicans lacked a candidate with the special appeal of a national hero like Eisenhower. Nixon reasoned, therefore, that the candidate who closed his campaign with the strongest spurt would be the winner.[52] Consequently, he held his fire somewhat until the latter part of October, hoping thereby to peak his campaign while Kennedy's was falling off. This is precisely what he did, and Kennedy's supporters were worried that he had lost and Nixon had gained impetus in the last two weeks. Nevertheless, Kennedy won. What lesson might a future candidate derive from this experience? Nixon's strategy of timing has a common sense ring to it. Yet it is really difficult to say whether it had meaning. Would he have done better to come to a peak earlier? Might the general public not have gotten tired of a full-blast effort straight through? There is no way of knowing. It is possible that Nixon lost because of his strategy, that he gained though not enough, or that the strategy had no effect whatsoever. It would have been possible to use a successive survey of the same voters to check on whether votes were changed in his favor during the period he put on the steam, but other factors could also affect the outcome of such a study. Further, there is no way of measuring how well he might have done had he pursued a different strategy.

Should the candidate arrive at a coherent strategy which fits reasonably well with what is known of the political world, he still will find that the party organization has an inertia in favor of its accustomed ways of doing things. The party workers, upon whom he is dependent to some extent, have their own ways of interpreting the world, and he disregards their point of view at some risk. Should the candidate fail to appear in a particular locality as others have done, the party workers may feel slighted. More important, they may interpret this as a sign that the candidate has written off that area and they may slacken their own efforts. Suppose the candidate decides to divert funds from campaign buttons and stickers to polls and television or to campaign trains? He may be right in his belief that the campaign methods he prefers may bring more return from the funds that are spent. But let the party faithful interpret this as a sign that he is losing—where, oh where, are those familiar signs of his popularity?—and their low morale may encourage a result which bears out this dire prophecy. An innovation in policy may shock the loyal followers of the party. It may seem to go against time-honored precepts which are not easily unlearned. Could a Republican convince his party that a balanced budget is not sacred? A selling job may have to be done on the rank-and-file, or otherwise they may sit on their hands during the campaign. It may make better political sense (if less intellectual sense) to phrase the new in old terms and make the departure seem less extreme than it might actually be. The value of the issue in the campaign may thus be blunted. The forces of inertia and tradition may be overcome by strong and persuasive candidates; the parties are greatly dependent on them and have little choice but to follow them even if haltingly. But in the absence of a special effort, in the presence of enormous uncertainties and the inevitable insecurities, the forces of tradition may do more to shape a campaign than the overt decisions of the candidates possibly can.

APPENDIX: PREDICTING ELECTIONS

As the time for voting draws closer, more and more interest focuses on attempts to forecast the shape of the outcome. This process of forecasting elections is not at all mysterious; it depends on well-settled findings about the behavior of American electorates, many of which have already been discussed. But it may be useful for citizens to understand how the "experts" go about picking the winner.

There are several ways to do it. One way, popularized by journalists Joseph Alsop and Samuel Lubell, is to interview the residents of neighborhoods where there are people who in the past have voted with great stability in one pattern or another. There are neighborhoods. for example, that always vote for the Republicans by a margin of 90% or better. Let us say that the interviewer finds that only 50% of the people he talks to tell him they are going to vote for the Republicans this time, but when he visits areas voting heavily Democratic, respondents continue to support the Democratic nominee heavily. A finding such as this permits the reporter to make a forecast, even though it is only based on a very small number of interviews, which may not at all represent the opinions of most voters.

Reporters who use this technique very rarely make firm predictions about election outcomes. Instead, they concentrate on telling about the clues they have picked up: what they learned in heavily Negro areas, what the people in Catholic areas said, what Midwest farmers say, what people from localities that always vote with the winner report, and so on.[53] This technique is impressive insofar as it digs into some of the dynamic properties of what goes into voting decisions. It reports what the issues are that seem to be on people's minds. It examines the different ways in which members of different sub-groups see the candidates and the campaign. It is also a technique which can be executed at relatively low cost. But it is unsystematic, in that people are not polled in proportions reflecting the distributions of their characteristics in the population (so many men, so many women, so many white, so many black and so forth) and thus the results of this technique would be regarded as unreliable in a scientific sense, even though they may enhance people's intuitive grasp of what is going on. The results are also unreliable in the sense that two different journalists using this method may come to drastically different conclusions, and there is no certain way of resolving the disagreement, nor any prescribed method for choosing between their conflicting interpretations.

A second technique has been used most extensively by the economist and statistician Louis Bean and does not rely on interviews at all.[54] Bean, it will be remembered, contradicted all the polls and predicted that President Truman would be re-elected in 1948. The Bean method relies principally upon assumptions about 1) the stability of voting habits, 2) the stability of the relationship between turnout and the two-party vote, 3) the stability of the relationship between the two-party distribution of the vote in one area and the two-party distribution of the vote in another, and 4) the continuation of trends in voting in whatever direction they may be heading. Some of these assumptions are quite dubious, as we shall

see, and Bean customarily hedges his predictions by claiming that
they will hold unless some issue or another intercedes to upset
them. His method does not provide a way for the impact of issues
to be examined, and, in fact, Bean does not demonstrate how the
effects of issues have sustained or failed to sustain his predictions.

The basic material out of which Bean constructs his forecasts is
a historical record of two-party voting. Let us suppose the Democratic percentage of the two-party vote has risen in each of the last
five elections. The Bean technique continues the line on the graph
in a simple extrapolation. Even when the percentage of the two-
party vote does not describe a straight line on a graph, it is possible to make an extrapolation by assuming that the historical
pattern of fluctuation will be followed in the future.

Another type of analysis done by Bean made use of the September election results in Maine. This became unusable when Maine
moved its election day from September to November, thus bringing
its election day into line with practice in the rest of the country.
But for many years it was possible to make a forecast based on the
Maine results. Maine's distribution of the two-party vote, Bean
said, bore a historically consistent relation with the national two-
party vote distribution, rising and falling at about the same rate
(but always somewhat below the nation on the Democratic graph,
and above the nation on the Republican graph). And so it was
possible to forecast the outcome nationwide, or in any state, by
noting the two-party ratio in the early Maine results and correct-
ing it for two-party voting habits in the area whose result he
wanted to predict.

The strength of forecasting from historical voting statistics
arises out of the marvelous stability of American voting habits.
But the weakness of such a technique is also manifest. Sometimes
gross changes in population, through immigration, or changes in
the appeals of the parties to different voting groups, will throw
the historical two-party vote ratios in the sample area out of joint.
When a forecast made with this technique is wrong, it is usually
quite difficult to tell whether transitory or lasting causes are at
the root of it. This limits the usefulness of the forecast greatly,
since, in the end, it rests on assumptions which have only partial
validity in any one election, and nobody can say precisely how or
where or to what extent they may be valid.

A third technique is a variant of the two foregoing types of
analysis and is used by electronic computers at the radio and television networks on election night. The basic principle of these machines, for our purposes, can be described simply. They are given
information about the past voting history of various locales. As
these locales report their returns on election night, the machine

compares this year's result with the information about previous years and arrives at a prediction of how this year's election will turn out, when all the votes are counted. The system is exactly the same as we have already described for Alsop and Lubell, only the machine can be loaded with historical information about many localities: precincts, wards, and so on, and then the machine compares this historical information, not with voting *intentions* as expressed by a few interviewees, but by voting *results* as expressed by the whole voting population of the area. The method the machine uses to predict the outcome early in the evening is roughly the same as Louis Bean's technique, only, once again, instead of the Maine election, the machine has results from a great many early reporting areas and can therefore correct discrepancies arising out of one or two purely local situations.

Interestingly enough, at least one of the network machines on election night in 1960 was not programmed in the way described above. The IBM system set up for CBS began election night in 1960 with the erroneous prediction that Richard Nixon would win the Presidency—a prediction that was later corrected as more and more returns came in.[55] It is useful to pause for a moment to look at this mistake, because it demonstrates clearly that these machines, like any other tools, are only as good as the people who use them.

The IBM computer was fed information based not on the geographic locale of the vote, but rather on the order in which the vote was reported to election headquarters. Thus, all the machine knew in 1960 was how many Democratic votes and how many Republican votes had been reported at 7 p.m. in previous elections, at 7:15, and so on. But it did not know *where* these votes had come from. The introduction of a faster method of vote-counting in Kansas between 1956 and 1960 was the reason for the IBM computer's early mistake. A flood of Kansas Republican votes arrived earlier than ever before. The computer, not knowing where they came from, compared them with the early returns in 1956, which were from the "swing" state of Connecticut and drew a false conclusion.

Since the order in which states report their vote varies quite a bit more than the voting habits of people living in specific early-reporting places, all the computers seem likely in the future to be working on geographic assumptions. It will, in all probability, be almost impossible to find out what assumptions the computers are using during election night coverage, however, because of the network reporters' dislike of imparting "complicated" information. It is so much friendlier to give the machine a nickname and ask it to "do tricks" and to bat one's eyelashes helplessly at the TV camera while the "mysterious" machine does its prosaic work.

The final method for predicting elections is the most controversial, and by all odds the most famous: polls. These are based on a few simple assumptions that have been found to be quite correct over the years. One is that people will generally tell you the truth if you ask them how they are going to vote. Another is that it is not necessary to ask everyone what he is going to do in order to get as accurate a forecast as if you had asked nearly everyone.

The polls are commercial operations and, these days, they are big business. In addition to the publicly available polls, such as the Gallup and Harris newspaper reports, politicians commission private polls. They are expensive. They entail writing up a list of questions and asking them all, and all in the same way, to several thousand people, spread all over the country, collecting the answers, and figuring out what it all means. Each of these phases of the operation—question writing, selecting the sample of the total population to be interviewed, interviewing, organizing the answers, and interpreting the results—is a job requiring skill and training. It is this that commercial polling organizations provide.

Some of these organizations, regrettably, treat the technical aspects of their operation as trade secrets (which they are not) and persist in leaving the impression that their forecasts are the result of a particularly efficacious kind of witchcraft. Since the fiasco of 1948, when pollsters were so sure of the result that they became professionally careless, there has been less ballyhoo. But the general reader will do well to keep a sharp eye on the following points as the polls begin reporting early in the campaign.[56]

1) How big is the population which is reported to be "undecided"? There are some elections in which members of this group cast the crucial ballots. In reporting their results pollsters have a rule which goes this way: "If the undecided people were to cast their ballots in the same proportion as those who have made up their minds. . . ." But wait. If these people *were* like the decided, they too would have made up their minds. Sometimes they *do* vote like early deciders. But sometimes they don't. Unfortunately, not enough is known about when they do and when they don't; the best advice we can give is to pay close attention to what the pollster says he is doing about them, and if they are more than 10 to 15 per cent of the population sampled, then place little confidence in the poll report. Until these people make up their minds, it is too early to tell about the outcome.

2) What is the stability of general sentiment in the population? Very often, the polls will report wide swings of sentiment from week to week. In 1960, The Gallup organization began averaging one week's totals with the previous week's part-way through the campaign—without telling its readers.[57] This tended to depress the

extent of an apparent shift of sympathy from Nixon to Kennedy, and it also tended to make the figures appear a great deal more stable and settled than they actually were. In general, wide swings of sentiment from week to week mean that opinions have not crystallized sufficiently for a reliable prediction to be made.

3) Remember that the polls are based on a gross, overall nationwide sample, but that Presidential elections are decided by the distribution of votes in the Electoral College. Thus a really reliable prediction would have to include a state-by-state breakdown. This is prohibitively expensive, and so it is not done. If it were done, it would be possible to detect situations like the following:

Candidate A has 49% of the popular vote in polls taken in all the populous states and 75% of the popular vote in sparsely settled states. He loses badly to Candidate B in the Electoral College, although it looks like a close election.

Pollsters generally caution that they are trying only to forecast the percentage distributions in the popular vote. Here again, if the result is closely divided around 50%, then the poll may be quite close to being perfectly accurate, but still forecast the wrong winner.

4) Some people never show up to vote on Election Day; these tend to be undecideds and Democrats (in that order) more often than Republicans, but in any event some sort of grain of salt has to be taken with results in order to account for the phenomenon of differential turnout. Most experienced polling organizations do build some sort of correction into their results based on assumptions about how many people in their sample will actually vote. It is important to know precisely what this assumption is and what the resulting corrections are.

5) Many people are plagued with the feeling that the samples used by pollsters—of two to five thousand people—are inadequate to represent the feelings of the millions of Americans whose voting they are supposed to represent. This, by and large, is a false issue. Experience has shown that very few of the errors one makes with a sample of 3,000 are correctable with a sample of 15 or 20 thousand, although the expense of polling such a population rises steeply.[58]

Generally, it is not a sampling error that is at fault nowadays when pollsters' predictions go awry, but illicit "cooking" of the data or incompetent interpretations of findings. There is one famous instance of a sampling error, when polling was in its most rudimentary stages. In 1936 the *Literary Digest* predicted a landslide victory for the Republican Alfred Landon.[59] When Franklin D. Roosevelt won overwhelmingly, the *Digest* became a laughingstock and soon thereafter went out of business. What had happened was simple enough. The magazine had sent out millions of postcards to telephone subscribers asking them how they intended to vote. The returns showed a huge Republican triumph. Surely, the *Digest* must have thought, we cannot possibly be wrong when our total response is so large, and so one-sided. But, of course, something was terribly wrong. And that stemmed from the fact that in the Depression years only the relatively wealthy had telephones. So the *Digest* got its returns from that group in the population most likely to vote Republican and completely ignored the much larger number of poorer people who were going to vote Democratic. Moreover, there is a much greater tendency for people of wealth and education to return mail questionnaires so that the bias in favor of people likely to vote Republican was further enhanced.[60]

In 1948, a whole series of errors were made, but none of them seem to have been connected with the size of the sample. In that year, the Gallup, Roper, and Crossley polls all predicted that Governor Dewey would unseat President Truman. Among the problems with the polls that year, the following were uncovered by a committee of social scientists after the event.[61]

a) The pollsters were so sure of the outcome that they stopped taking polls early in the campaign, assuming that the large population of undecideds would vote, if they voted, in the same way as those who had made up their minds early in the campaign.

b) The undecideds voted in just the reverse proportions.

c) Many instances were revealed where polling organization analysts, disbelieving pro-Truman results, arbitrarily "corrected" them in favor of Dewey. The methods of analysis employed were not traced in any systematic way, however, because they could not systematically be reconstructed from records of the polling organizations.

d) Sampling error occurred, not because of the size of the samples, but because respondents were selected by methods that gave interviewers too much leeway to introduce biases into the sample. The so-called "quota-control" method (which instructs interviewers, for example, out of 20 interviews to pick ten men, ten women, fifteen Protestants, four Catholics, one Jew, seventeen whites and three blacks, and so on) has been replaced with "stratified random samples" in which geographic areas are picked randomly, and neighborhoods and houses within neighborhoods are selected randomly with controls so that areas representing a variety of economic levels are sure to be selected. This gives the people in charge of the poll greater control over who is going to be in their sample and prevents interviewers from asking only people who live near them, or who are conveniently accessible in some other way, and are likely to be similar to them in social standing and political outlook.

Predicting Presidential elections is largely a matter of satisfying curiosity. It is a great game to guess who will win, and we look to the polls for indications of the signs of the times. But the importance of this kind of prediction is not great. After all, we do get to know who has won very soon after Election Day with much greater detail and accuracy than the polls can supply. The bare prediction of the outcome, even if it is reasonably correct, tells us little about how the result came to occur. More may be learned if it is possible to break down the figures to see what kind of groups—ethnic, racial, economic, regional—voted to what degree for which candidates. Yet our enlightenment at this point is still not great. Suppose we know that in one election Catholics voted Democratic 60% of the time and in another election this percentage was reduced to 53. Surely this is interesting; but unless we have some good idea about why Catholics have switched their allegiance, our knowledge has hardly advanced. The polls often tell us "what" but seldom "why." There is, however, no reason why polling techniques in the future cannot be used to answer "why" questions.

The usual polling technique consists of talking to samples of the population at various points in time. The samples may be perfectly adequate but *different* people constitute each successive sample as the interviewers seek out people who meet their specifications. It is difficult to discover with any reliability why particular individuals or classes of people are changing their minds because interviewers ordinarily do not go back to the same people who gave their original preferences. A panel survey is used to overcome this difficulty.[62] In a panel survey, a sample of the voting population is obtained and the very same people are interviewed at various intervals before Election Day and perhaps afterwards. This technique makes it possible to isolate the people who make up their minds early and those who decide late. These groups can be reinterviewed and examined for other distinguishing characteristics. More important, perhaps, those voters who change their minds during the campaign can be identified and studied. If a panel of respondents can be reinterviewed over a number of years and a series of elections, it may become possible to discover directly why some people change their voting habits from election to election.

NOTES

1. See Seymour M. Lipset, Paul F. Lazarsfeld, Allen H. Barton, and Juan Linz, "The Psychology of Voting: An Analysis of Political Behavior," in *Handbook of Social Psychology*, ed. Gardner Lindzey (Cambridge, Mass., 1954), pp. 1124–1175; Paul F. Lazarsfeld, Bernard Berelson, and Hazel Gaudet, *The People's Choice*, 2nd ed. (New York, 1948), pp. 87–93; and Bernard Berelson, Paul F. Lazarsfeld, and William N. McPhee, *Voting* (Chicago, 1954), pp. 16–17.

2. See Angus Campbell, Philip E. Converse, Warren E. Miller, and Donald E. Stokes, *The American Voter* (New York, 1960), pp. 124, 532-553. Table 6-1 on p. 124 summarizes the highly consistent results of seven separate national sample surveys taken by the Survey Research Center from October 1952 to October 1958. Here are S.R.C. figures for October 1958 and November 1968 (the latter figures are taken from unpublished S.R.C. tables).

PARTY AFFILIATIONS ARE STABLE

	October 1958	November 1968
Strong Republicans	13%	10%
Weak Republicans	16%	14%
Independent Republicans	4%	9%
Independents	8%	11%
Independent Democrats	7%	10%
Weak Democrats	24%	25%
Strong Democrats	23%	20%
Apolitical, don't know	5%	1%

See also Warren E. Miller, "The Political Behavior of the Electorate," *American Government Annual: 1960–61*, ed. E. Latham (New York, 1960), pp. 40–61, and Fred I. Greenstein, *The American Party System and the American People* (Englewood Cliffs, 1963), Chapter 3, both of which give findings of surveys conducted primarily under academic auspices. Gallup data also bear out the same general conclusion: "If every potential voter in the country had to register with either party, the figures projected by survey findings would be Democrats: 56,800,000; Republicans: 40,020,000; Undecided: 6,200,000." (American Institute of Public Opinion News Release, "Republicans Outnumbered by 16 Million, Poll Finds," October 16, 1960.) The number of "undecideds" may have been reduced by assigning a party affiliation to people who expressed a faint preference for one or the other party.

3. There is another possibility: that voters who turn out only by being dinned at by the media are likely to be less stable in their political orientations and will therefore vote less for the party and more for the candidate whose name or personality seems more familiar to them. This, in a year when an Eisenhower is on the ticket, might well mean Republican votes.

4. See Philip E. Converse, Angus Campbell, Warren E. Miller, and Donald E. Stokes, "Stability and Change in 1960: A Reinstating Election," *American Political Science Review* 55 (June 1961), 269–280, esp. p. 274.

5. See Campbell *et al., The American Voter*, pp. 537–538 and Herbert H. Hyman and Paul B. Sheatsley, "The Political Appeal of President Eisenhower," *Public Opinion Quarterly* 19 (Winter 1955–56), 26–39.

6. For indications that this strategy is feasible despite the existence of general stereotypes, see Campbell *et al., The American Voter*, pp. 44–59, 179–187. See also American Institute of Public Opinion News Releases, February 6, 1963, October 9, 1964, and October 25, 1964.

7. For a striking demonstration of this, see Ithiel de Sola Pool, Robert P. Abelson, and Samuel Popkin, *Candidates, Issues and Strategies* (Cambridge, Mass., 1964), pp. 117–118.

8. Recall Senator Dirksen's famous castigation of Thomas E. Dewey at the Republican Convention of 1952: "We followed you before, and you took us down the path to defeat." Richard Nixon in 1968 did pursue a modified "me-too" strategy. The main thrust of his compaign, however, was more like the first strategy we discussed: emphasizing dissatisfaction with a new issue, "law and order." Furthermore, there is some reason to suppose that rather than scoring a clear win what Nixon really did was sneak through to victory because the Democrats tore themselves apart. See our discussion of Nixon in this context on pp. 118 – 119, 121.

9. For indications that this is so, see in particular Herbert McClosky, Paul J. Hoffman, and Rosemary O'Hara, "Issue Conflicts and Consensus Among Party Leaders and Followers," *American Political Science Review* 54 (June 1960), 406–427.

10. Good accounts of debates over strategy among Republicans can be found in such sources as Charles O. Jones, *The Republican Party in American Politics* (New York, 1965); Robert Donovan, *The Future of the Republican Party* (New York, 1964); Malcolm

C. Moos, *The Republicans: A History of Their Party* (New York, 1956); Robert Novak, *The Agony of the G.O.P. 1964* (New York, 1965); and Conrad Joyner, *The Republican Dilemma* (Tucson, 1964).

11. *Congressional Quarterly,* November 20, 1964, p. 2709, estimated that Republicans lost more than 500 seats in state legislatures in the 1964 election. Republicans gained one Governor (for a total of 17), lost two United States Senators (reducing their Senatorial representation to 32), and sustained a net loss in the House of Representatives of 38 seats (reducing their strength to 140 members, the lowest since the Roosevelt landslide of 1936).

12. See, for example, Charles O. Jones, *The Republican Party in American Politics* (New York, 1965), pp. 66–71. The Michigan Survey Research Center estimates that an overwhelming 96% to 98% of such Republicans typically vote. Philip E. Converse, Aage R. Clausen, and Warren E. Miller, "Electoral Myth and Reality: The 1964 Election," *American Political Science Review* 59 June 1965), 322–323.

13. This point has been confirmed as often as any in the entire literature of voting behavior. See Bernard Berelson, Paul F. Lazarsfeld, and William McPhee, *Voting* (Chicago, 1954), pp. 333–347, e.g., propositions 39, 50, 51, 66, 68, 69, 70, 71, 78, 79; Angus Campbell, Philip E.. Converse, Warren E. Miller, and Donald E. Stokes, *The American Voter* (New York, 1960), pp. 142–145.

14. The study of right-wing ideologues and their supporters is more speculative than empirical. Nevertheless, there are a few straws in the wind, and all blow in the same direction. In 1962, Raymond E. Wolfinger and his associates administered a questionnaire to 308 "students" at an anti-Communism school conducted by Dr. Fred Schwarz's Christian Anti-Communism Crusade in Oakland, California. Among the findings of this study were that 278 of the 302 persons in this sample who voted in 1960 (or 92% of those who voted) had voted for Nixon, and that 58% of those who answered the question chose Goldwater over Nixon for 1964. At about the same time, a nationwide Gallup poll showed Goldwater the choice of only 13% of Republicans. Raymond E. Wolfinger, Barbara Kaye Wolfinger, Kenneth Prewitt, and Sheilah Rosenhack, "America's Radical Right: Politics and Ideology" in *Ideology and Discontent,* ed. David Apter (New York, 1964), pp. 267–269. Analysis of various election returns and of a 1954 Gallup poll suggests that support for the late Senator Joseph McCarthy was importantly determined by party affiliation, with Republicans far exceeding Democrats or independents in the

ranks of his supporters. See Nelson W. Polsby, "Towards an Explanation of McCarthyism," *Political Studies* 8 (October 1960), 250–271.

15. AIPO News Releases of September 6, 1964 and October 16, 1964 suggested that Republican defections would run as high as 30%, but the Release of December 11 indicated that a 20% defection figure was more accurate. This compares with defections by Republican voters of 5%, 4%, and 8% in the three previous elections. Democratic defections in this election were also high—13% of those calling themselves Democrats voted for Goldwater—but these were confined mostly to the Southern states.

16. In early July, the Gallup poll (AIPO News Release, November 11, 1964) showed the following figures among Republican voters:

Preferring:

Goldwater 22%	Scranton 20%
Lodge 21%	Rockefeller 6%

Just before the Republican Convention, the figures among Republicans were:

Scranton 60%	Undecided 6%
Goldwater 34%	

Goldwater received 23% of the vote in the New Hampshire primary; 18% in Oregon; 8% in Pennsylvania (fourth in a field of five write-ins); 10.5% in Massachusetts; 71% in Indiana, where Harold Stassen received the remainder; only 49% in Nebraska, where Goldwater's name alone was on the ballot; 51.4% in California; 76% in Texas, running in a trial heat with only Rockefeller; 31.9% in South Dakota; and a bit better than 60% in Illinois, where he was opposed on the ballot only by Margaret Chase Smith and where there is no law requiring election officials to tabulate write-in votes.

Gallup trial heats (AIPO News Release, July 1, 1964) before the Republican Convention showed Goldwater running a poorer race against President Johnson than either Scranton or Nixon, e.g.:

Goldwater 18%	Scranton 26%	Nixon 27%
Johnson 77%	Johnson 69%	Johnson 70%
Undecided 5%	Undecided 5%	Undecided 3%

17. AIPO News Release, September 13, 1964.

18. Louis Harris Survey News Releases, July 13, 1964, and September 14, 1964. Some of the Harris survey findings on foreign affairs were:

ISSUE		VOTERS DESCRIBE GOLDWATER POSITION		DESCRIBE OWN POSITION	
		July	Sept.	July	Sept.
Go to war over	For	78%	71%	29%	29%
Cuba	Against	22%	29%	71%	71%
Use atomic bombs	For	72%	58%	18%	18%
in Asia	Against	28%	42%	82%	82%
United Nations	For	42%	50%	82%	83%
	Against	58%	50%	18%	17%

19. Jules Witcover, *The Resurrection of Richard Nixon* (New York, 1970), Chapter 8.

20. Phillip E. Converse, Warren E. Miller, General Jerrold G. Rusk, Arthur C. Wolfe, "Continuity and Change in American Politics: Parties and Issues in the 1968 Election," *American Political Science Review* 63 (December 1969), p. 1084.

21. See the discussion in *ibid.*, pp. 1090–1104.

22. *Congressional Quarterly*, November 22, 1968, p. 3177.

23. The report of the speech in the New York *Times*, October 6, 1956, gives no indications of how it was received. The authors heard it delivered.

24. Thomas Flinn, "How Nixon Took Ohio," *Western Political Quarterly* 15 (June 1962), 276–279.

25. Witcover, *op. cit.*, pp. 237–239.

26. See, for example, the American Institute of Public Opinion News Release of September 3, 1964, in which 53% of a national sample said that the Democrats were the party best able to keep the country prosperous. Only 21% picked the Republicans. See also, Campbell *et al.*, *The American Voter*, pp. 44–59.

27. See, for example, *The Joint Appearances of Senator John F. Kennedy and Vice-President Richard M. Nixon, Presidential Campaign of 1960*, Report 994, Part III, 87th Congress, 1st Session, U.S. Senate (Washington, 1961). Especially see Mr. Nixon's opening remarks in the first joint television debate, pp. 75–78.

28. See, for example, Campbell *et al.*, *The American Voter*, pp. 44–59 and Angus Campbell, Gerald Gurin, and Warren E. Miller, *The Voter Decides* (Evanston, 1954), pp. 44–45, especially Table 4-3, p. 45.

AIPO surveys show the twenty-year trend on this issue indicated in the graph on page 220. The graph is remarkably consistent in several ways. First, it testifies to the continuing perception (with ten of these years under Republican Presidents and ten under Democrats) that the Republican party is more "the party of peace"; there may have been a slight erosion of the Republican position and a gain by the Democrats over this period as a whole, although in March 1970 the Democrats were only one percentage point above where they had been twenty years earlier, while the Republicans were only four points below their 1951 reading. Second, and very revealing, is the clear periodicity of the relationship; there is a sharp peak and maximum difference between the parties as November of every Presidential election year approaches, followed by a convergence over the next two years, followed by divergence toward the Presidential election peak again. Just before elections we would expect voters' expressions of their accustomed stereotypes to be at their strongest, owing to the polarization in the attitudes of voters that normally takes place during the heat of a campaign. Senator Goldwater's extreme foreign policy positions caused the lone reversal in the positions of the two parties, but, despite the fact that both major candidates in 1968 were pledged to "end the war" and despite what was probably the more "dovish" position by Humphrey, the Republican advantage on this issue had reasserted itself within four years of the Johnson landslide.

29. The most well-publicized clashes over foreign policy occurred in the second and third television debates; see the New York *Times,* October 8, 1960, pp. 1, 12; October 9, 1960, Pt. IV, p. 10; and October 14, 1960, p. 22. The impression of journalists and political observers that Nixon gained in these confrontations (see, for example, the New York *Times* for October 17, 1960) was corroborated by surveys of the viewers (see the references in footnote 31, following) and by Pool, Abelson, and Popkin, *Candidates, Issues, and Strategies,* p. 118.

30. Converse *et al.,* "Stability and Change in 1960: A Reinstating Election," 269–280.

31. Elihu Katz and Jacob J. Feldman, "The Debates in the Light of Research: A Survey of Surveys," in *The Great Debates,* ed. Sidney Kraus (Bloomington, 1962), pp. 201–202. Bear in mind, however, that *issues* as such do not strongly influence voting behavior. Katz and Feldman conclude: "First of all, it seems safe to say that the debates—especially the first one—resulted primarily in a strengthening of commitment to one's own party and candidate. This was much more the case for Democrats than Republicans, but the former had much greater room for improvement" (p. 208).

Party More Likely to Keep the United States Out of World War III

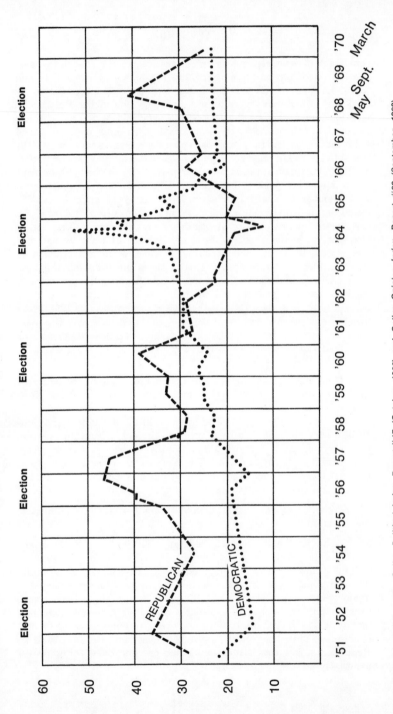

Source: Adapted from the *Gallup Political Index*, Report #17 (October, 1966) and *Gallup Opinion Index*, Report #39 (September, 1968),
Report #41 (November, 1968) and Report #58 (April, 1970).

32. Richard Scammon and Ben Wattenberg, *The Real Majority* (New York, 1970) p. 39. See also pp. 37–43.

33. Harris Survey, published September 21, 1970, *The Washington Post*, A2.

34. See Theodore H. White, *The Making of the President, 1960* (New York, 1961), pp. 269–275 and his, *The Making of the President, 1964* (New York, 1965), *passim*.

35. Department of Marketing, Miami University, Oxford Research Associates, *The Influence of Television on the Election of 1952* (Oxford, 1954), pp. 151–160.

36. Witcover, *op. cit.*, pp. 237–239.

37. See White, *The Making of the President, 1960*, pp. 282–283, and Herbert A. Seltz and Richard D. Yoakum, "Production Diary of the Debates," in *The Great Debates*, ed., Sidney Kraus, pp. 73–126.

38. *Ibid.*; see also Richard Nixon, *Six Crises* (New York, 1962).

39. Earl Mazo, *Richard Nixon* (New York, 1959), pp. 21–22, 362–369.

40. See Katz and Feldman, "The Debates in the Light of Research: A Survey of Surveys," pp. 173–223.

41. See William L. Rivers, "The Correspondents After 25 Years," *Columbia Journalism Review* 1 (Spring 1962); Nixon, *Six Crises;* and especially White, *The Making of the President, 1960*, for a discussion of two candidates' contrasting attitudes toward their "camp" of reporters. For the 1964 election, see White, *The Making of the President, 1964*. For 1968, See White, *The Making of the President, 1968*, pp. 327 ff.

42. For further examples see Hugh A. Bone, *American Politics and the Party System*, pp. 457–469. Readers may not be aware that Al Smith had thought of moving the Vatican to Washington or that Herbert Hoover had a Negro concubine, yet these ridiculous allegations were made (p. 458).

43. Robert E. Sherwood, *Roosevelt and Hopkins* (New York, 1948), p. 821.

44 The effectiveness of underhanded tactics remains unknown. Dan Nimmo argues that deviating from a vague sense of "fairness" that exists in the electorate may backfire. *The Political Persuaders* (Englewood Cliffs, 1970), p. 50. There is plenty of evidence on the other side as well. For a treasure trove of such material, see Stanley Kelley, *Professional Public Relations and Political Power* (Baltimore, 1956).

45. See Flinn, "How Nixon Took Ohio."

46. New York *Times*, August 1, 1948, p. 49.

47. See Jules Abels, *Out of the Jaws of Victory* (New York, 1959).

48. Robert Alford, "The Role of Social Class in American Voting Behavior," *Western Political Quarterly* 16 (March 1963), 180–194; Campbell *et al.*, *The American Voter*, Chapter 13.

49. White, *The Making of the President, 1960*, pp. 203–204.

50. *Ibid.*, p. 315.

51. White, *The Making of the President, 1968*, p. 331.

52. See Nixon, *Six Crises*, pp. 315–461.

53. See, for example, Samuel Lubell, *The Future of American Politics* (Garden City, 1956), and his, "Personalities and Issues," in *The Great Debates*, ed. Sidney Kraus, pp. 151–162, and Joseph Alsop, "The Negro Vote and New York," New York *Herald-Tribune* (and elsewhere) August 8, 1960.

54. Louis H. Bean, *Ballot Behavior* (Washington, 1940).

55. IBM published a pamphlet, *The Fastest Reported Election*, in 1961 describing their operations.

56. These suggestions are drawn in part from a reading of the Report of a Committee of the Social Science Research Council, Frederick Mosteller *et al.*, *The Pre-Election Polls of 1948*, Social Science Research Council Bulletin 60 (New York, 1949). The misfortunes of the British polls in the 1970 general election underscores the usefulness of these suggestions.

57. Joseph Alsop, "The Wayward Press: Dissection of a Poll," *The New Yorker* (September 24, 1960), pp. 170–184.

58. There are several sources about the technology and tactics of polling. George Gallup has published *A Guide to Public Opinion Polls* (Princeton, 1948). More recently, see *Opinion Polls, Interviews by Donald McDonald with Elmo Roper and George Gallup* (Santa Barbara, 1962).

59. Sherwood, *Roosevelt and Hopkins*, p. 86.

60. As a matter of fact, this method produced a correct prediction in 1932, when the *Literary Digest* said that Roosevelt would win. Sampling error is tricky; an atypical sample may still give the correct prediction—by luck, but sooner or later, the law of averages is bound to catch up with it.

61. Mosteller *et al.*, *The Pre-Election Polls of 1948*.

62. See Paul F. Lazarsfeld, "The Use of Panels in Social Research," *Proceedings of the American Philosophical Society* 92 (November 1948), pp. 405–410.

chapter four

reform?

The political processes we have been describing have, from time to time, come under severe criticism from people who believe that our political system can be made more responsive to popular demands, more equitable and more effective. One clarion call asserts: "The American government today suffers from three weaknesses:

1) its difficulty in generating sustained political power;
2) its difficulty in developing a flow of imaginative, informed, consistent and power-related responses to pressing national and world issues;
3) its difficulty in making policy truly accountable to a national popular majority."[1]

If these implied goals were enunciated in the abstract, few people would disagree with them, assuming that they could be achieved at all, or at a less than exorbitant cost. It is to the credit of critics of the party system that they have recommended specific changes in specific institutions. A particularly perceptive commentator has a list which includes recommendations (1) to centralize electoral campaign finance in the hands of national party leaders, (2) to expand two-party competition in Congressional elections by strengthening the role of the national (i.e., Presidential) party in campaign finance and other campaign services, (3) to enlarge the staffs of the party national committees and to create permanent advisory councils to the national committees, (4) to build offices for the two major political parties on Federal land, situated in Washington between the White House and Capitol Hill, (5) to repeal the 22nd amendment to the Constitution, which limits the President to two terms, (6) to amend the Constitution so that Congressmen and Senators are always elected at the same time as Presidents, (7) to centralize the Congressional parties by means of frequent party caucuses and effective policy committees, and (8) to "find a mathematical formula for computing Congressional seniority which will give added weight to those legislators who come from competitive two-party districts and states."[2]

There is a kind of fascination to a list such as this one. Sweeping constitutional amendments and trivial building programs are suggested with equal seriousness. Machinery, such as Congressional party caucuses, is proposed which already exists but does not do the job contemplated by reformers. Other machinery, such as the "mathematic formula," would undoubtedly do the job assigned to it, but how would such machinery be put into effect? On this question, reformers customarily are silent, relying only on the extremity of the national "need," as they interpret it, to evaporate any possible opposition to their schemes.

Taken all together, the position of party reformers constitutes a coherent picture or view of the functions of a party system. The concreteness of their proposals makes it possible for others to examine them and to ask questions such as whether or not they will in fact accomplish the ends in view, whether they can be achieved under the political conditions which prevail, or whether changing these conditions would not lead to consequences more costly than the alleged mischiefs of the status quo. This general view can also be compared and contrasted with an alternative view, whose implications for party reform would diverge from the party reformers' ideal model.

THE POLITICAL THEORY OF PARTY REFORM

There is a general political theory implied in the proposals of party reformers, a theory that contains a conception of the proper function of the political party, which evaluates the legitimacy and the roles of the Congress and the President, and which embodies a particular definition of the public interest. Different advocates of reform have stated this theory with greater or less elaboration; some reformers leave out certain features of it, and some are disinclined to face squarely the implications of the measures they espouse. We shall try here to reproduce correctly a style of argument which, though it ignores the slight differences separating party reformers one from another, gives a coherent statement of the party reform theory and contrasts it with the political theory that critics of the party reform position appear to advance.[3]

Party reformers suggest that democratic government requires political parties which 1) make policy commitments to the electorate, 2) are willing and able to carry them out when in office, 3) develop alternatives to government policies when out of office, and 4) differ sufficiently between themselves to "provide the electorate with a proper range of choice between alternatives of action."[4] Party reformers thus come to define a political party as "an association of broadly like-minded voters seeking to carry out common objectives through their elected representatives."[5] In a word, party is based on policy.

Virtually all significant party relationships are, for reformers, mediated by policy considerations. The electorate is assumed to be policy motivated and mandate conscious. Policy discussion among party members is expected to create widespread agreement upon which party discipline will then be based. Pressure groups are to be resisted and accommodated only as the overall policy commitments of the party permit. The weaknesses of parties and the disabilities of governments are seen as stemming from failure to develop and support satisfactory policy programs. Hence it seems sensible to refer to the theory of party reform which predominates in this country

as a theory of "policy government." This theory suggests "that
the choices provided by the two-party system are valuable to
the American people in proportion to their definition in terms
of public policy."[6]

Opponents of party reform believe that democratic government in the United States requires the minimization of conflict
between contending interests and social forces.[7] Their ideal
political party is one which serves as a mechanism for accom-
plishing and reinforcing adjustment and compromise among
the various interests in society to prevent severe social conflict. Where reformers desire parties which operate "not as
mere brokers between different groups and interests but as
agencies of the electorate," their critics see the party as an
"agency for compromise." Opponents of party reform and policy government hold that "the general welfare is achieved by
harmonizing and adjusting group interests."[8] In fact, they
sometimes go so far as to suggest that "the contribution that
parties make to policy is inconsequential so long as they maintain conditions for adjustment."[9] Thus, the theory of the political party upheld by critics of the party reform position is
rooted in a notion of "consensus government."

A basic cleavage between advocates of policy government
and consensus government may be observed in their radically
opposed conceptions of the public interest. For advocates of
consensus government, the public interest is defined as whatever emerges from the negotiations, adjustments, and compromises made among conflicting interest groups. They suggest
no external criteria by which policies can be measured in order
to determine whether or not they are in the public interest. So
long as the process by which decisions are made consists of
intergroup bargaining, within certain specified democratic
"rules of the game," they regard the outcomes as being in the
public interest.

For advocates of policy government, the public interest is
held to be a discoverable set of policies which represents "something more than the mathematical result of the claims of all
the pressure groups."[10] While they suggest that there are, in

principle, ways of judging whether a policy is in the public interest, apart from the procedural test applied by supporters of consensus government, these methods are never identified. This lack of concrete criteria spelling out the public interest would not present great difficulties if it were not for the fact that policy government advocates demand that an authoritative determination of party policy be made and that party members be held to it. Information about the policy preferences of members is supposed to flow upward and orders establishing and enforcing final policy decisions are supposed to flow downward in a greatly strengthened pyramid of party authority. Without criteria of public interest clearly in mind, however, the party leaders are in a position to define the public interest in any terms they find convenient.

It would be wrong to suppose that policy government advocates do not believe in the advisability of some compromise, or that consensus government supporters do not recognize the necessity that the parties sponsor some policies and programs. Nonetheless, each gives heavy stress to its own particular concern and admits qualifications only with reluctance. The respective positions are clearly a response to their adherents' deeply held views on the most basic needs of our times.

"In an era beset with problems of unprecedented magnitude at home and abroad," party reformers declare, "it is dangerous to drift without a party system that helps the nation to set a general course of policy for the government as a whole."[11] The failure to establish policy government may well "lead to grave consequences in an explosive era."[12] Reformers seek to awaken the people to untold dangers that lie ahead, to "growing public cynicism" that may lead to the "disintegration of the two major parties," and to the eventual destruction of constitutional government.[13] It is no wonder that with the apparent need so great, the supporters of policy government feel that a way must be found to institute their essential life-or-death reforms of our present system.

The advocates of consensus government do not evidence so great a sense of urgency, because our present party system comes much closer to meeting their requirements. This is to a certain extent an artifact of their whole mode of argument, which tends to define that which is as inevitable and that which is inevitable as good. "It is the party system, more than any other American institution," they assert, "that consciously, actively and directly nurtures consensus."[14]

While advocates of policy government fear the continuation of the present party system, their opponents fear that the introduction of policy government would destroy the underlying social consensus and perhaps even lead to civil war. They hold that while our nation possesses "a degree of consensus that is more than adequate for maintaining the present political system . . . [it] might be quite inadequate for maintaining a different system . . ." such as reformers suggest.[15] Americans are agreed, in general, upon the rules governing the exercise and transfer of political power, the main outlines of our economy, and the desirability of maintaining the conditions under which they can continue to enjoy their material prosperity. But civil war is still possible because this consensus could be threatened by sharp disagreement over economic issues ("The domestic battles of American practical politics are not sham battles"[16]); by the diversity of our economic, racial, religious, ethnic, and sectional groupings; by our "restless and immoderate people"; and by the tendency of a nontraditional society to "push political conflict to its most unfortunate logical conclusion."[17]

The civil war is a living nightmare to those who insist that we maintain consensus government. But as in the case of party reformers, there is less proof of the factual assumptions lying behind their arguments that one might like. "Greater differences in party platform than those . . . [in 1948]," one writer assured his readers, "would impose a burden which politicians in a republican system could not be expected to bear."[18] In the same vein, other advocates of consensus parties have argued, "the day that some major elements completely desert one party in favor of the other, the stage will have been set for the kind of conflict that leads to civil war."[19] But we are never told in detail why policy government would lead to severe social conflict under other than the most extreme conditions.

THE BIAS BEHIND PARTY REFORM

It should be obvious that party reforms are generally not politically neutral. They are designed almost entirely to strengthen the President and to weaken Congress, especially as Congress is presently constituted. More specifically, reforms of the party system are in general designed to help Democrats and weaken Republicans. The reasoning is this: Republican Presidents represent a party generally unsympathetic to innovation and increased activity by the Federal government. Hence, they will be inclined to ask less of Congress, and thus they run less risk of being stymied by a recalcitrant Congress. Democratic Presidents, on the other hand, in behalf of the more liberal, more activist, and more innovative party, ask much more of Congress and customarily have to settle for much less of what they ask for.

It seems to us quite understandable that agitation for party reform, which during the late 1940's so excited the liberal academicians who are its chief proponents, died away to a whisper during the Eisenhower decade. In the early 1960's frustrated liberals took up their cudgels in the cause of righteousness, "responsibility," and Presidential prerogative. The underlying aim, it seems to us, was to speed up social changes that they desired by trying to rig the rules of the game more in favor of that political institution, the Presidency, which shared their policy preferences.

The close connection between the desire for party reform and the policy preferences of reformers was again illustrated in the late 1960's. Reformers could no longer complain about the failure of a conservative Congress to enact New Deal-type welfare measures: the 89th Congress had taken care of that. Their attention now became focused on foreign policy because they were outraged by America's continued involvement in the war in Vietnam. It turned out that Presidents were, if anything, more in favor of this policy than were many congressmen. The frustrations of reformers were centered on the inability of Senators who favored an anti-war policy to persuade the President to withdraw American troops and commitments as fast as they would have liked. Hence, it was no longer feasible to advocate reforms that would enable Presidents to pursue Presidential foreign policies despite the reluctance of Congressmen. Instead, reformers began to entertain notions of limitations on Presidential prerogatives. It is, unfortunately, exceedingly difficult to stop Presidents from doing things one doesn't like (such as, for example, in Indochina) without also preventing them from taking actions of which one approves (such as, conceivably, in the Middle East).

Since it is not feasible to limit the damage Presidents can do without also limiting the good they can do, the attention of many current party reformers has been focused on making the Presidential selection procedure more responsive to their preferences. They believe that if the nomination procedure is opened up to more party voters in primaries and to party activists in district and state conventions, they will have a better chance of nominating a man they prefer. Their immediate frame of reference is the 1968 Democratic convention in which they believe the fortunes of nominees like McCarthy and McGovern were damaged by undemocratic modes of delegate selection. In view of the commanding margin of victory for Hubert Humphrey it seems doubtful that different procedures, even if they had been enforced at the time, would have changed enough delegate votes to make a difference in the outcome. The assumption behind the views of new reformers, who represent generally left-wing views within the Democratic party, is that if the people were given a choice they would support candidates with policy preferences more like their own.

At the moment, of course, many rules of the game favor policies defending the political, economic, and social status quo, and we are ourselves sympathetic to many—perhaps most—of the social measures covertly advocated by party reformers. Rent supplements, universal medical health insurance, and the negative income tax are three examples. But as political scientists, rather than political advocates, we think it proper to spell out the political implications of proposals such as those put forward by party reformers, and not pretend, as party reformers sometimes do, that their suggestions can make everyone happy.

IS BROAD-GAUGED PARTY REFORM POSSIBLE?

If we were to have parties that resembled the ideal of the party reformers, what would they be like? They would be coherent in their policies, reliable in carrying them out and accountable to the people, sharply differentiated and in conflict with each other, disciplined and hierarchical internally. Let us see, then, what it would take to create a party system of this kind.

For the parties to carry out the promises they make, the people responsible for making promises would have to be the same as (or in control of) the people responsible for carrying them out. This means, logically, one of two alternatives: 1) either the people who controlled party performance all year round would have to write the party platforms at the national conventions; or 2) the people who wrote the platforms would have to be put in charge of party performance. In the first case, the party platforms would have to be written by leaders such as the Congressmen who presently refrain from enacting laws favored by both national conventions. State and local political leaders would write their respective platforms. Thus, very little formal, overall coordination or policy coherence seems likely to emerge. Since logically coherent, unified policy is the main point of policy government, we must reject the first alternative as a possible way to fulfill the demands of party reformers.

In fact, it is the second alternative which is most often recommended by advocates of policy government. National conventions must be newly arranged to make policy that will be enforced on national, state, and local levels by means of party discipline, and the people who write the convention platforms must be put in charge. This arrangement also has a fatal defect: it ignores the power of the people who do not write the platforms. How are independently elected Congressmen to be

bypassed? Will present-day sectional and state party leaders acquiesce in this rearrangement of power and subject
themselves to discipline from a newly constituted outside
source? Generally, we assume they will not. Getting politicians
to exchange some political power for none is a task the magnitude of which has surely been underestimated. When reforms
have to be carried out by those who would stand to lose the
most from them, their practicality is dubious. A Democratic
Congressman has written of the institutional factors which, in
the House of Representatives, make his party leaders shy of
party cohesiveness: "The Democrats don't meet to talk things
over, to be persuaded, to be sold. We don't meet in caucus because the Leadership fears that it would irreparably breach the
tenuous links with the South. . . . [House leaders] lead, but
they lead only because they win. If they cannot be certain of
winning, they don't want to go. Latent power, negative power,
is so much better than power committed that lacks victory as a
capstone. Hence the legislative timidity of the Congress. . . .
Hence the great time lags for consideration of legislation . . .
while the Leadership waits for the pressures to build. . . .
Hence the distaste for short cuts . . . distaste for battle just for
the sake of battle, distaste for The Discharge Petition, and for
Calendar Wednesday, and for the Democratic Caucus."[20]

One reformer says: "As for the clash of personal political
ambitions in the United States, they are being completely sub-
merged by the international and domestic concerns of the
American public. War and peace, inflation and depression are
both personal and universal issues; tariffs, taxes, foreign aid,
military spending, federal reserve policies, and hosts of other
national policies affect local economic activities across the
land. Politicians who wish to become statesmen must be able to
talk intelligently about issues that concern people in *all* constituencies. . . ."[21]

But is it necessarily the case, as party reformers suggest,
that the increasing importance of national issues will inevitably lead to placing greater power in the hands of party
leaders with national (that is to say, Presidential) constituencies? There is no necessary connection between political power

in the national arena and the national scope of issues. National political power may rest upon local control of nomination, alliances with locally based interest groups, and many other bases. Even if national issues become more important, this may only enhance the powers of the local interests best able to influence national policy—such as, for example, the people in Arkansas who reelect Chairman Wilbur Mills of the House Ways and Means Committee.

The people who have the most to lose from party reforms are, of course, the leaders of Congress. As of now, the major electoral risks facing national legislators are local. This does not mean that they will necessarily be parochial in their attitudes and policy commitments. But it does mean that they are not necessarily bound to support the President or national party leadership on issues of high local saliency. In order to impose discipline successfully, the national party must be able either to control sanctions presently important to legislators, such as nomination to office, or to impose still more severe ones upon him. At the moment, our system provides for control of Congressional, state, and local nominations and elections by geographically localized electorates and party leaders. Presidents are not totally helpless in affecting the outcomes of these local decisions, but their influence is in most cases quite marginal.

In the light of this, one obvious electoral prerequisite of disciplined parties is that the local voters must be so strongly tied to national party issues that they will reward rather than penalize their local representatives for supporting national policy pronouncements, even at the expense of local advantage. The issues on which the national party makes its appeal must either unify a large number of constituencies in favor of the party or appeal at the least to some substantial segment of opinion everywhere. But even if this could be accomplished, it would be strategically unwise for parties to attempt to discipline their members who lived in areas which were strongly against national party policy. This would mean reading the offending area out of the party. Thus, reformers must show how they intend to contribute to the national character of political parties by enforcing national policies upon members of Congress whose local constituencies are drastically opposed to national party policy, or whose constituents do not pay attention to issues but care more for the personality or the services of the Congressman.[22] Insofar as leeway exists, let us say, for Republicans in the Northeast to support liberal programs and for Southern Democrats to oppose civil rights, the parties shall, in fact, have retained their old, "undisciplined," "irresponsible" shapes. Insofar as this leeway does not exist, splinter groups of various kinds are encouraged to split off from the established parties, which happens to be a consequence regarded as undesirable by most party reformers.

IS BROAD-GAUGED PARTY REFORM DESIRABLE?

Although comprehensive reform of the party system may be impractical, this does not necessarily mean that it is undesirable. If we believed that such reform were a vital necessity, we might still advocate it and hope that the unfolding of events would lead others to share our viewpoint. But we suspect that achievement of many of the specific objectives of party reformers would be detrimental to their aims and to those of most thoughtful citizens. Let us consider, for example, three specific reforms of governmental machinery, commonly advocated to make the parties more responsive to popular will and more democratic; two of these reforms might well have the exactly opposite effects. Party reformers often advocate a variety of changes in the nomination process, simplification of the process of registering voters, and modification or abolition of the Electoral College.

An Appraisal of the Nomination Process
In order to evaluate the nominating process, it would be helpful to suggest a set of goals which most Americans would accept as desirable and important.[23] The following six standards appear to meet this test: any method for nominating Presi-

dents should 1) aid in preserving the two-party system, 2) help secure vigorous competition between the parties, 3) maintain some degree of cohesion and agreement within the parties, 4) produce candidates who have a likelihood of winning voter support, 5) lead to the choice of good men, 6) result in the acceptance of candidates as legitimate.

We may first look at some suggested alternatives to the system that presently relies so heavily upon decision-making by party leaders at national conventions.

A national direct primary has often been suggested. Many people took heart in 1968 from the way in which the piecemeal primaries around the country facilitated the expression of anti-war sentiment, and they noted that non-primary states were less responsive to persons whose participation in party activities was largely precipitated by strong feelings about the war. This led to a conclusion that primaries were rather a good thing and that, therefore, a national primary was in order.

We believe this would have serious disadvantages. First of all, it would have been self-defeating as far as the professed goals of many anti-war people who advocated it were concerned. By contesting primaries one at a time in 1968, Senator McCarthy, and later Senator Kennedy, were able to construct "test cases." We doubt that McCarthy, given the limitations of his resources before New Hampshire, could have even entered a national primary.

This merely points to a more general problem of financing national primary elections. It is quite probable that many candidates—perhaps as many as ten of them—might obtain enough signatures on nominating petitions to get on the ballot. Imagine a crowd of challengers hustling all over the United States, campaigning in a national primary. It would take, of course, enormous amounts of money. The parties could hardly be expected to show favoritism and in any event they would have to protect their treasuries for the campaign to follow. So nationwide challengers in a national primary would have to be rich or personally have access to very large amounts of money. They would also have to be quite sturdy physically. It is not hard to forecast that nobody would win a clear majority in a primary with a large number of contenders. Since all contenders would be wearing the same party label, it is hard to see how voters could differentiate among candidates except by already knowing one or two of their names in favorable or unfavorable contexts, by liking or not liking their looks, by identifying or not identifying with their ethnic or racial characteristics, or by some other means of differentiation having nothing whatever to do with ability or inclination to do the job, or even with their policy positions. Since patents on policy positions are not available, it is reasonable to suppose that more than one candidate would adopt roughly the same set of positions. The intellectual content of the campaign thereafter would consist of quibbling about who proposed what first, and, more relevantly, who could deliver better.

Suppose, then, that the primary vote was divided among several candidates. Suppose, as is the case in some Southern states, that ten or twelve aspirants divided the votes. One possibility is that the party nominee would be the man with the highest number of votes, say 19 percent of those cast, a much less democratic choice than we now have. Another possibility would be for the two highest men to contest a 50-state run-off after the first primary and before the general election, in a campaign that would begin to remind observers who can remember that far back of a marathon jitterbug contest. The party might end up with a good candidate, of course, if there was anything left of him to give to his party in the *real* election campaign, which would follow. Then if the poor fellow was elected he would have to find the energy to govern. By following this procedure, the United States might have to restrict its Presidential candidates to wealthy athletes. No man without enormous financial resources could ever raise the millions required for the nominating petition, the first primary, the run-off primary, and the national election; and no one who was not superbly conditioned could survive the pace of all these campaigns.

It is also possible that the parties would emerge with candidates no better on the average than those currently being

picked to run for high office. And perhaps they would be worse
on the average, because the national primary provides for no
consideration of the criteria of fitness to hold office that can
best be applied by those who actually know the candidates, who
have themselves a heavy investment of time and energy in
making the government work, and who know that they may
have to live at close quarters with the results of their deliberations. It is difficult to persuade those who participate only
casually in politics, and those who tend to do so when moved
by a great issue of the day, that the intensity of their feelings
does not confer a sweeping mandate. These feelings, no matter
how worthy, do not make occasional participants more worthy
than steady participants. They do not confer a special moral
status upon late-comers to politics as compared with people
who are already active. Party activists or even party leaders
are not necessarily excludable on grounds of moral inferiority
from decision-making in the Presidential nomination process.
The great virtue of primaries is, of course, that they provide
a means—increasingly supplemented by polls—of gauging the
popularity of various candidates and their effectiveness in public speaking under adverse circumstances. On the other hand,
the virtue of conventions and state caucus systems is that by
living at closer quarters than ordinary citizens with the results
of the collective choice party leaders may bring to the choosing
greater knowledge and even, sometimes, a higher sense of
responsibility.

It is generally conceded that Adlai Stevenson would have
made a rather better President than Estes Kefauver, who ran
and won in most of the primaries in 1952. Stevenson, for his
entire career in elective office, was the product of selection by
party leaders—in some cases even by "bosses"—who were
knowledgeable and continuously involved in the political process, acquainted with what governing demanded and with the
personal capabilities of the men among whom they chose.

This is not *per se* an evil system. Unchecked by the ultimate
necessity to appeal for votes it would no doubt deteriorate. It
is certainly not always a system that responds easily to short-
run opinions of high intensity in the electorate, but sometimes

this sort of system will pick a popular man over a man in whose personal capacities the delegates have more faith. This, we think, is what delegates to the Republican Convention of 1952 did when they nominated Dwight Eisenhower over Robert A. Taft. Still, conventions and caucuses of party leaders can invoke criteria of judgment unavailable to mass electorates.

In short, we believe that as long as there are many things we demand of a President—intelligence as well as popularity, integrity as well as speaking ability, private virtue as well as public presentability—we ought to foster a selection process that provides a mixture of devices for screening according to different criteria. The mixed system we now have is not perfect, of course, but it is greatly superior to the unmixed non-blessing of the national primary.

We are not ready, therefore, to give up the substantial but not overwhelming number of state primaries we now have. It is eminently desirable that it be possible in a number of states, separated geographically and in time, for test cases to be put to voters and for trial heats to be run among aspirants for high office. But a national primary would be like a steady diet consisting exclusively of dessert.

National primaries might also lead to the weakening of the party system. It is not unusual for a party to remain in office for a long period of time. If state experience with primaries is any guide, a prolonged period of victory for one party would result in a movement of interested voters into the primary of the winning party where their votes would count more.[24] As voters deserted the losing party, it would be largely the die-hards who were left. They would nominate candidates who pleased them but who could not win the election because they were unappealing to a majority in the nation. Eventually, the losing party would atrophy, thus seriously weakening the two-party system and the prospects of competition among the parties. The winning party would soon show signs of internal weakness as a consequence of the lack of opposition necessary to keep it unified.

A national primary might lead to the appearance of extremist candidates and demagogues who, unrestrained by allegiance to any permanent party organization, would have little to lose by stirring up mass hatreds or making absurd promises. A George Wallace might well find a fertile field in a national primary, an opportunity sufficient to raise the temperature of American politics to explosive levels even if he did not win. On the whole, the convention system rules out these extremists by placing responsibility in the hands of party leaders who have a permanent stake in maintaining the good name and integrity of their organization. Some insight into this problem may be had by looking at the situation in several Southern states where most voters vote only in the Democratic primary and where victory in that primary is tantamount to election. The result is a chaotic factional politics in which there are few or no permanent party leaders; the distinctions between the "ins" and "outs" become blurred; it is difficult to hold anyone responsible; and demagogues sometimes arise who make use of this situation by strident appeals.[25] The fact that under some primary systems an extreme personality can take the place of party in giving a kind of minimal structure to state politics should give pause to the advocates of a national primary.

We believe, in short, that widespread use of direct primaries would weaken the party system because only the wealthiest candidates could possibly enter a large number of them; they would encourage prospective candidates to bypass regular party organizations in favor of campaigns stressing personal publicity; and they would throw nominations entirely into the hands of persons whose stake in the workings of the political process is not great enough to ensure that the eventual nominee would be qualified for the Presidency by experience, qualities of mind, or by virtue of political alliances with others professionally engaged in political activity. The use of primaries at the state level has produced a variety of anomalous experiences: totally unqualified candidates whose names have resembled famous politicians have been nominated by innocent voters; ethnic minorities concentrated in one party have defeated attempts by party leaders to offer "balanced tickets," thus dooming to defeat their entire ticket in the general election; and palpable demagogues have defeated responsible candidates for public office. All of these consequences may not persuade reformers that an increase in the use of direct primaries is not a good idea, but they must be faced. If we value political parties, as reformers often profess, then we must hesitate to cut them off from the process of selecting candidates for public office, to deprive them of incentives to organize, and to set them prematurely at the mercy of masses of people whose information at the primary stage is especially poor.

This is not, we suggest, an elitist doctrine. Responsible political analysts and advocates must face the fact that party identification for most people provides the safe cognitive anchorage around which political preferences are organized. Set adrift from this anchorage as they are when faced with an intra-party primary election, most voters have little or nothing to guide their choices. Chance familiarity with a famous name or stray feelings of ethnic kinship under these circumstances seem to provide many voters with the only clues to choice.[26] Given the conditions of popular interest and participation which prevail, we would question throwing the future of the party system entirely and precipitously into the hands of primary electorates.

Another alternative is nomination by one of the branches of Congress. This, though, would be out of the question. The caucus system of nomination has been rejected since Andrew Jackson's time, because it did not give sufficient representation to the large population groups whose votes were decisive in the election.[27] Furthermore, the large fluctuations of party membership in Congress lead to serious difficulties. If a party happened to do very poorly for a few years in several sections of the country, the representation in Congress from those areas would be small and they would, in effect, be deprived of a voice in nominating a President. Thus, if Northern Democrats suffered a serious reversal one year, the Southern members of that party would be in complete control. This nominating procedure would advertise itself as being national in scope, but it would be far more likely than the present system to produce candidates with a limited sectional appeal. The attempts of leaders in areas where the party is weak to strengthen themselves by nominating a candidate who might help increase their vote would be stymied.

Perhaps, it may be argued, what is required is not some radically new method of nominating candidates, but reform of some of the more obnoxious practices of the present system. High on the list of objectionable practices would be the secret gathering of party leaders in the smoke-filled room. Some liken this to a political opium den where a few irresponsible men, hidden from public view, stealthily determine the destiny of the nation.[28] Yet it is difficult to see who, other than the party's leaders, should be entrusted with the delicate task of finding a candidate to meet the majority preference. Since head-on clashes of strength on the convention floor usually do not resolve the question, the only alternative would be continued deadlock, anarchy among scores of leaderless delegates splitting the party into rival factions, or some process of accommodation.

Let us suppose that the smoke-filled room were abolished and with it all behind-the-scenes negotiations. All parleys would then be held in public, before the delegates and millions of television viewers. As a result, the participants would spend their time scoring points against each other in order to impress the folks back home. Bargaining would not be taking place since the participants would not really be communicating with one another. No compromises would be possible; leaders would be accused by their followers of selling out to the other side. Once a stalemate existed, breaking it would be practically impossible, and the party would probably disintegrate into warring factions.

An extensive system of state primaries in which delegates were legally compelled to vote for the candidate who won in the state would lead to the disappearance of the smoke-filled room without any formal action. Since delegates could not change their positions there would be little point in bringing their leaders together for private conferences. But sharply increasing the number of pledged delegates would introduce great rigidity into the convention because of the increased likelihood of stalemates which could not be overcome because no one would be in a position to switch his support. It would also decrease the power of state party leaders to control the votes of their delegations, and increase the power of potential candidates to bargain with one another.

· Much criticism has been leveled at the raucousness of demonstrations that take place on the convention floor while candidates are being nominated.[29] Criticism of demonstrations on the grounds that they are unseemly and vulgar seem to us to be trivial. There is no evidence which would substantiate a claim that the final decision would be better in some way if demonstrations were banned.

In still another way the demonstrations help meet the need of many delegates for an active function which they can perform.[30] As in almost any large political gathering (the number of delegates and alternates were approximately 2,700 for the Republicans and 6,500 for the Democrats in the 1968 convention), only a small number actively participate in planning strategy or in trying to influence other people. The rest often find that they have no well-defined political role other than casting one vote out of many and they may feel at a loss to explain their lack of activity to themselves as well as to the people back home. The demonstrations provide an opportunity for the delegate to enhance his feelings of importance by active participation in a colorful event which he can recount when he returns. Since one of the advantages of the convention is to gather the party faithful and imbue them with a sense of belonging to a national party, a mechanism which increases the delegate's sense of satisfaction is by no means unimportant.

Undoubtedly, the demonstrations have been overdone and might be cut short. This task can safely be left to the requirements of television. As the conventions of the last few years have shown, television dictates briefer demonstrations to retain the attention of the vast audience which the party would like very much to influence in its favor.

The television coverage of the 1968 national conventions raised a number of questions concerning their future management. We wonder if all the things that went wrong at the

Democratic Convention were the result of willful mismanagement or whether at least some of the difficulty can be accounted for by the increasing unwieldiness of the convention. Delegates complained of an inability to attract the attention of the chair. The microphones allocated to each delegation on the floor were turned on and off at the rostrum, so it was impossible to use the microphone to get the chair's attention. Attempts to telephone the chair from the floor were often ignored. Attempts to approach the rostrum were repulsed by security guards. Attempts to signal the chair were defeated by the noise and movement in the hall.

It is hard to see how such a huge and chaotic organization can conduct itself as a parliamentary body. In fact, plenary sessions of the convention have two functions—ceremonial and business. We think it is time to consider a separation of these functions. Ceremonial activities can take place in an amphitheatre or a stadium. The general public can be invited. On such occasions there are two classes of people, performers and spectators.

When the convention is conducting its business, however, a different division of labor is involved and a different decorum should prevail. If it is not possible for a convention to conduct itself as a parliamentary body when all members are present, perhaps some democratic and equitable means could be found to restrict the number of official delegates so as to make communication among them feasible. If, let us say, 1,000 delegates met at business meetings, much of the paraphernalia associated with meetings of 10,000 could be dispensed with. The number of guards and security officers could be cut. The business of keeping order could be placed where it belongs— in the hands of the chair who directs sergeants-at-arms publicly, rather than in the hands of an anonymous functionary who at Chicago apparently felt free to dispatch security officers to harass delegates on the floor.

A smaller number of people on the floor, the possibility of spontaneous communication with the chair and with other members, and parliamentary decorum would unquestionably facilitate and properly dignify the business of the convention. It would also provide a warrant for the reexamination of the role of television cameras at national conventions.

We believe television and other news media should continue to cover national party conventions with all the care and energy they have always used. But we question the propriety of wandering television and newspaper reporters on the floor of a convention. To be sure, so long as conventions continue in their present overblown form, reporters may as well be on the floor, since everyone else is. But if conventions were reduced in size and for business purposes maintained parliamentary decorum, perhaps it would be possible to consider the problems created by news media representatives at national conventions. Neither Democrats nor Republicans alone will take the lead in grappling with this problem, because both fear the wrath of the media. Thus, academic observers are ideally situated to open this discussion.

We want to increase respect for Presidential nominations by having them conducted in a serious atmosphere conducive to mature deliberation. The presence of hordes of correspondents on the convention floor introduces a discordant note somewhere between individual breast-beating and mass hysteria. The very presence of numerous reporters, with their microphones and television cameras, creates a carnival atmosphere. No one would ordinarily make an important decision surrounded by people hurriedly throwing questions at him. No one would take seriously a decision made by people constantly distracted from the main proceedings by side conversations.

A superabundance of TV cameras on the convention floor plays up to the worst instincts of the political men gathered there. It is hard for ordinary mortals to resist publicity; it is asking too much for politicians to forego an opportunity for national exposure. Yet the purpose of the convention is not to make the delegate look good at home, but for him to make a wise choice where he is.

The mass media not only report events, they create news. They are always after sensational stories. If conflict and controversy is not inherent in a situation, they will seek to create it. A momentary misunderstanding on the floor might be cleared up later on, but reporters will jump in immediately to widen the breach.

Imagine what football games would be like if they were reported under the same rules that prevail at national conventions. Suppose that Joe Namath is getting clobbered in the next Super Bowl. His line is weak and defenders are pouring all over him. After the fifth interception, Namath receives a fearful blow. Before he can pick up his shattered bones a dozen TV reporters stick their microphones and cameras in his face, shouting questions at him. "Did you get good protection today, Joe?" "Anybody let you down, hey?" A few answers on the spot and Namath's team might never be able to work together again.

Is it asking too much for nominations of future Presidents to be conducted with at least the same dignity as presently obtains at football games? The press, radio, and TV can broadcast the proceedings and report events from booths above the convention floor. No one but delegates and elderly sergeants-at-arms should be allowed on the floor while the convention is at work.

Ample interview facilities should be provided just off the floor. When a delegate is wanted for an interview, a young page should be sent to fetch him just as is done in Congress. "Mr. Smith," the page might say, "a network wants to harass you in room nine," and if he wants to be harassed he can walk off the floor to accomplish that mission.[31]

The American people deserve full reporting of the national conventions. No one wants to limit the media in any legitimate coverage. But improving the conduct of national conventions and increasing public respect for their decisions are reasons enough to ask the media to pay a small cost for a large public benefit.

The convention, as we have said, normally aids party unity in a variety of ways. It provides a forum in which initially disunited fragments of the national party can come together and find common ground as well as a common nominee. The platform aids greatly in performing this function. In order to gain a majority of electoral votes, a party must appeal to most major population groups. Since these interests do not want the same thing in all cases, it is necessary to compromise and, sometimes, to evade issues which would lead to drastic losses of support. And since the parties must contain somewhat conflicting interests, internal accommodation is essential to avoid splits. A perfectly clear, unequivocal, consistent platform on all major issues presupposes an electorate and a party system which divides neatly and more or less evenly along ideological lines, and that is not the case in this country.

The concern of reformers with party platforms stems primarily from two assumptions: first, that there is a significant demand in the electorate for more clear-cut differences on policy; second, that elections are likely to be a significant source of guidance on individual issues to policy-makers. Yet both these assumptions are either false or highly dubious. On a wide range of issues, leaders in both parties are much further apart than are ordinary members who, in fact, are separated by rather small differences.[32] To the degree that party platforms do spell out clear and important differences on policy, and these were considerable in 1960 and extraordinarily large in 1964, this probably results far more from a desire of party leaders to please themselves or from misinformation about what the voters desire than from any supposed demand from the electorate. It is, of course, possible for a party to meet at least three of the four prerequisites for policy government reform (making policy commitments to the electorate, developing alternatives to governmental policy when out of office, and differing sufficiently to provide "a choice, not an echo") if a large enough majority of its own activists so desire. We have argued that such activists are unlikely to be rewarded with victory if they force a unilateral movement of one of the major parties far away from the position of the other on a great number of issues at the same time and then campaign vigorously on this new position. The Republican experience of 1964 makes it clear that such a strategy can be pursued, but the outcome of that election stands as a warning to political activists who entertain such notions again. In any event, it is exceedingly difficult (if not impossible) to discover just what an election means in terms of the policy preferences of a majority. About all that one can expect from a platform is an indication of the general direction in which a candidate and the dominant factions in his party intend to go, and the present party platforms do reasonably well in this respect.

Some critics object to the normal convention's stress on picking a winner rather than the "best man" regardless of his popularity. This doctrine is not compatible with the democratic notion that voters should decide who is best for them and communicate this decision in an election. Only in dictatorial countries do a set of leaders arrogate unto themselves the right to determine who is best regardless of popular preferences. An unpopular man can hardly win a free election. An unpopular President can hardly secure the support he needs to accomplish his goals. Thus, popularity can be regarded as a necessary element for obtaining consent in democratic politics. Only if one assumes that it is the characteristic behavior of parties in a two-party system to disregard their chances of winning, does it make sense to speak of popularity in a derogatory way.

Although popularity is normally a necessary condition for nomination, it should not be the only condition. The guideline for purposes of nomination should be to nominate the best of the popular candidates. But "best" is a slippery word. A great deal of what we mean by "best" in politics is "best for us" or "best represents our policy preferences" and this can hardly be held up as an objective criterion. What is meant by "best" in this context are certain personal qualities such as experience, intelligence, and decisiveness. Nevertheless, it is not at all clear that an extreme conservative would prefer a highly intelligent liberal to a moderately intelligent candidate who shared his conservative policy preferences. Personal qualities are clearly subject to discount based on the compatibility of interests between the voter and the candidate.

Insofar as the "best man" criterion has a residue of meaning, we believe that it is possible to argue that the criterion has largely been followed in recent times. Looking at the candidates of both parties since 1940—Roosevelt, Truman, Stevenson, Kennedy, Johnson, Humphrey for the Democrats, and Willkie, Dewey, Eisenhower, Nixon for the Republicans— there is not one man among them who could not be said to have had some outstanding qualities or experience for the White House. Without bothering to make a formal declaration of the fact, American political leaders and their followers have apparently agreed on at least one hidden requirement of availability. They have restricted their choice to those popular candidates who give promise of measuring up to the formidable task of the President as preserver of the nation and guardian of prosperity. The nominee whose sole virtue is his innocuousness or pleasant smile seems to have disappeared.

As usual, Goldwater presents a special problem because in many important ways he is a man of extreme views, something, we have argued, the present nominating process normally discourages. It is unlikely that any system of nomination—total primary, total convention, mixed, or even action by Republicans in Congress—would have resulted in a different choice. For the nomination of Goldwater is, in part, the result of an underlying trend, working since the New Deal period, through which Republican activists have become separated in their preferences from Republican voters and from the electorate as a whole. It required only the temporary disarray of the moderate opposition within the Republican party for this trend to manifest itself in Senator Goldwater's visible presence on the ticket. No system of nomination, indeed no political system, can be expected to forever run counter to the desires of the activists who have the most say about running it. It is not the convention system but the desires of the activist core of the Republican party that produced an exception to the rule in 1964.

It might be argued, however, that the criterion of ability has been violated because nominations have come to be determined by popularity, that is, by expressions of mass preferences as reported in polls and state primaries.[33] Merely defining the candidate who won the nomination as most popular is not sufficient to prove the thesis; it must be shown that the voters agreed who was the most popular candidate, that this was communicated to the delegates, and that they nominated him. It would be hard to say that William Howard Taft, Warren Harding, Alfred Landon, Wendell Willkie, and Thomas Dewey, to name a few, were indisputably the most popular Republican candidates. (Goldwater was clearly an *un*popular candidate.) Dwight Eisenhower might fit in this category (though he had to fight for the nomination), but he represents just one case and is counterbalanced by the very popular Theodore Roosevelt's failure to obtain the nomination in 1912. There is no evidence to suggest that, among Democratic candidates, Woodrow Wilson was more popular than Champ Clark in 1912, that James M. Cox and John Davis fitted the most popular criterion, or that Franklin Roosevelt could have been placed in that category with certainty before his first nomination. If any Democrat was most popular in 1952 it was Estes Kefauver and not Adlai Stevenson.

A surface view of the 1960 Democratic Convention might suggest that John F. Kennedy's nomination was due to an irresistible current of public opinion. When other factors are taken into account, however, this "mass popularity" thesis loses much of its force. To begin with, Kennedy's excellent organization was not matched by any other candidate. We must also take into account the difficulty which Democratic leaders would have faced in refusing the nomination to a Catholic who had won important primaries, and whose defeat in the convention might easily have been viewed as a sign of religious prejudice which would damage the party's chances for years to come. Still a third factor operative in securing Kennedy's nomination is suggested indirectly by the 1960 Republican race for the Presidential nomination. We have never discovered whether or not Nelson Rockefeller was more popular with the voting public than Richard Nixon, because the latter had such strong support among party professionals that Rockefeller decided it was not worth running. A crucial difference between the two conventions was that there was no Democrat to oppose Kennedy who could claim a widespread preference among party leaders as was the case with Nixon in the Republican party.

We have already dealt at length with the idea of a national primary. Now we must consider some difficulties with the primaries currently in operation. What, we may ask, is the overall effect of the primary in Presidential nominating politics? In theory, the primary election is supposed to bring the nominating process to the people, but in practice it does not work quite that way at all. What really happens in primary elections is governed by a number of contingencies not at all anticipated by those who advocate primaries as the solution to a variety of political problems.

First, not all serious candidates run in primary elections. The primaries are held at widely separated intervals so that some candidates do not declare themselves in time to enter and others are exhausted by a grueling series of campaigns. Some candidates may not even want to run the risk, although they are avowed candidates. They may not wish to tip their hand, if they are not. They may not have the time to make what they regard as an adequate campaign, or they may not be able to raise the money to do so. If primaries were all held at the same time they would take on the aspect of a national primary with all its disadvantages and without the one great advantage of being open to all interested voters in the nation. Candidates like Estes Kefauver and Eugene McCarthy could not afford the enormous expenditures required to put their views before the public in so many places at once.

Second, many people do not vote in primary elections. These stay-at-home voters tend to be less well-educated, less informed and less interested, and less closely tied to regular party organizations. The voting in primary elections is, in other words, a rather imperfect representation of public sentiment.

President Truman, after hearing the results of the 1952 New Hampshire primary, which Estes Kefauver had just won without serious opposition, referred to primaries (with unexpected mildness) as "eyewash." In this sense he was correct: primaries are far from what their proponents would like them to be. But they do serve the useful purpose of providing politicians at national conventions with some information about the relative popularity of candidates in a series of admittedly artificial "trial heat" settings. Most often, so it seems, primaries kill off promising contenders before the convention. This, at any rate, seems to have been the fate of Hubert Humphrey, who was a casualty in West Virginia in 1960, Harold Stassen, who lost in Oregon in 1948, Wendell Willkie in Wisconsin in 1944, and Nelson Rockefeller in California in 1964. Kennedy's long-shot parlay paid off in 1960, it is true, but the rather discouraging example of Kefauver was the best recent historical evidence he had on the fate of primary winners.

The conclusion we would draw is that the primaries, together with other methods of delegate selection which give predominance to party activists, provide one reasonably viable balance between popularity and other considerations which party leaders deem important. Without denying an element of popular participation, the decision is ultimately thrown into the hands of the men who ought to make it if we want a strong party system—the party leaders.

For some critics the defects of conventions lie not only in their poor performance in nominating candidates but also in their failure to become a sort of "superlegislature" enforcing the policy views in the platform upon party members in the executive branch and Congress. We have previously indicated that such enforcement is most unlikely to be achieved.

Let us suppose, nevertheless, for the purposes of argument, that the conventions could somehow become much more influential on matters of national policy. How could either party retain a semblance of unity if the stakes of convention deliberations were vastly increased by converting the platform into an unbreakable promise of national policy? If one believes that an increase in heated discussion necessarily increases agreement, then the problem solves itself. Experience warns us, however, that the airing of sharp differences, particularly when the stakes are high, is likely to decrease agreement. For example, at the 1964 Republican Convention, black delegates, bitter about the defeat of Governor Scranton's proposed amendment on civil rights to the GOP education plank, held a protest march around the Cow Palace and, when Goldwater was nominated, announced that they would sit out the campaign.[34] The fact that platforms are *not* binding permits the degree of unity necessary for the delegates to stay long enough to agree on a nominee. By vastly increasing the number of delegates who would bitterly oppose platform decisions, and who would probably leave the convention, the proposed change would jeopardize the legitimacy of its nominating function. Paradoxically, in such circumstances, the temptation to make the platform utterly innocuous so as to give offense to no one would be difficult to resist.

There are also good reasons for opposing the desires of those who love the conventions so well that they would like to see them convene once every year or two years. For without a Presidential candidate to nominate, they would have little to do. If the purpose of these meetings is to give free advice, there would seem to be little point to them. Congressmen are likely to pay as little attention to convention talk as they would to the pronouncements of any advisory committee that does not appreciate the context within which they operate. After all, Congressmen are subject to different risks and sanctions than are most delegates, get little help from the national party in securing nomination and election, and have no reason to be beholden to it for suggesting policies which may get them into trouble. As they have uniformly decided in the past, Congressional leaders will probably refuse to participate in organizations whose policies they cannot control but whose proposals they are committed to support. The notion of getting delegates together under circumstances where their disagreements are certain to come out into the open, merely for the purpose of making recommendations, does not seem promising. It is doubtful whether most delegates, who could not be expected to take an active part in formulating proposals, would feel it worthwhile to participate in a convention which lacked its major rationale and interest—the choice of a Presidential candidate.

Although we hope to have avoided the error of assuming that whatever is, is right, the superiority of national conventions to the available alternatives is clearly demonstrable. Only the convention permits us to realize in large measure all the six goals —the two-party system, party competition, some degree of internal cohesion, candidates attractive to voters, good men, and acceptance of nominees as legitimate—which we postulated earlier would commonly be accepted as desirable. It is a rare occasion indeed when we fail to get good candidates rather than extremists who would threaten our liberties or convert our parties into exclusive clubs for party ideologists. Leaders are usually motivated to choose popular candidates who will help maintain vigorous competition between the parties but who are unlikely to split them into warring factions. As a matter of fact, the two major party splits in this century occurred while an incumbent was securing his own renomination. The Progressive split in the Republican party which Theodore Roosevelt led against President Taft in 1912 and the revolt Dixiecrats led against President Truman in 1948 indicate that incumbent Presidents, as hierarchical leaders, are perhaps more prone to underestimate the costs of their actions to party unity than are the party leaders who are forced to bargain with one another in the smoke-filled rooms.

The element of popular participation in the present nomination process is strong enough to impress itself upon party leaders but not sufficiently powerful to take the choice out of their hands. The convention is sufficiently open to excite great national interest, but it is not led into perpetual stalemate by pseudo-bargaining in public. Voters have a choice between conservative and liberal tendencies—a choice which is not absolute because a two-party system can be maintained only if both parties moderate their views in order to appeal to large population groups in the country. In our view, the very unusual experience of 1964 only serves to reinforce strongly this conclusion.

An Appraisal of Permanent Voting Enrollment

One reform that has received increasing attention and that would presumably have at least marginal effects on all stages of Presidential elections without directly altering either the means of nominating candidates or the ways in which they campaign is universal automatic voter enrollment. One of the distinguishing features of American national elections is the low share of the potential electorate that actually gets to the polls and votes. In 1968, the number of non-voters (47,000,000) was one and one-half times the number of voters for each of the two major candidates; the turnout percentage lagged ten to fifteen points behind those for other major democracies such as Britain, France, and West Germany. The most detailed study of the matter yet available traces both of these facts to the American system of voter registration; it shows that the level of voter registration is easily the greatest influence (accounting for 80% of the variance) on the percent of the population that actually votes, far greater than any other single factor usually pointed to in studies of voting by those registered, and in fact greater than all such factors put together.[35]

Unlike the citizens of foreign democracies where the government takes responsibility for registration, the American must prepare himself for the eventual vote by registering sometimes months before the election, at a time when his political information and interest are at a low point.[36] Since interest and information are the important factors, the level of registration can be advanced or retarded by altering the time of year when voter registration rolls are closed or the physical ease of reaching a registration point, and practicing political leaders are well aware of the fact.[37] As Stanley Kelley and his collaborators observe: "Local differences in the turnout for elections are to a large extent related to local differences in rates of registration, and these in turn reflect to a considerable degree local differences in the rules governing, and the arrangements for handling, the registration of voters."[38]

Proposals for universal automatic voter enrollment differ according to administrative arrangements for the enrollment, the time when it would occur, the duration of enrollment, and the levels of government to which it would apply. The basic idea, however, is that the U.S. would be divided into election districts, and deputy registrars within them would go door-to-door, enrolling every citizen who did not refuse to be registered.[39]

At present there are not nearly enough registration drives to enfranchise a high percentage of the electorate, and most such drives fail; a major New York City drive in 1969, for example, spent $310,000 but added only 70,000 voters, 3% of the electorate, for a total registered of only 35% of those eligible.[40] Some U.S. areas use universal automatic enrollment already. They get striking results; the state of Idaho makes an aggressive search for new registrants, and as the following table shows, the consequences for voting turnout are impressive. The table also compares U.S. national figures with those in Great Britain, and it is apparent that the percent registered is strongly associated with the percent of the potential electorate voting.

The Rules for Registration are an Important Influence on the Proportion of the Electorate That Actually Votes

	ALL U.S. (1968)	IDAHO (1968)	GREAT BRITAIN (1970)	(1966)
Persons of Voting Age (Thousands)	120,773	400	40,778	36,936
% Registered	74.5%	91.8%	91.5%	97.4%
% Registered Who Vote	81.3%	79.4%	72.0%	75.8%
% Persons of Voting Age Who Vote	60.6%	72.8%	69.5%	73.8%

While the rest of the U.S. now lags behind the Idaho performance, there was once a time, in an era when the impact of the President was remote, mass communication absent, and electronic voting equipment unheard of, when more than 70% of *potential* (not just registered) voters turned out in Presidential elections; in the election of 1876, 82% of the possible voters turned out for the nation as a whole. Soon thereafter, however, harsh registration restrictions were introduced, cloaked in rhetoric about stopping corruption but aimed at keeping down the vote of "undesirable elements" (immigrants and blacks)—which they did. "In short," Kelley observes, "turnout in presidential elections in the U.S. may have declined and then risen again, not because of changes in the interest of voters in elections, but because of changes in the interest demanded of them. . . . [Not] only . . . [are] electorates . . . much more the product of political forces than many have appreciated, but also . . . to a considerable extent, they can be *political artifacts*. Within limits, they can be constructed to a size and composition deemed desirable by those in power."[41]

The effect of universal automatic enrollment on Presidential politics seems relatively straightforward. We know that those who are disenfranchised by current practices are generally those with lower levels of political information and interest, and these are traditionally the young, the less well-educated, those lower in income, and black citizens.[42] We also know how these groups behave politically; they are much more Democratic than Republican, but far less stable in all aspects of their participation than other groups in the electorate. Their effective entry into politics would serve to intensify the need for the parties to follow the Presidential strategies we have already outlined; Democrats could afford even more to try to emphasize party identification through partisan appeals, while Republicans would be forced even more to follow "me-too" strategies, obscure party lines, claim they could better deal with the domestic problems on which the Democrats focus, and emphasize foreign affairs.

Whether this expanded electorate would have any direct effect on primaries and delegate selection would depend on the particular enrollment plan adopted. At one extreme, if enrollment were held every four years in October and provided for continuation on the rolls only if the registrant voted in each election held in the district—state and municipal elections, as well as federal—the reform would have little direct effect. If the canvass occurred in the spring, however, and registrants had to vote only once every four years to stay on the rolls, there would be a significant addition to the Presidential electorate. Some have argued that this portends new strength for non-party-organization activists, since this new group would be far less tied to any political organizations than the already enfranchised groups.

Both black and white former non-voters are likely to favor increased expenditures on policies designed to benefit lower-income people. But on questions of political style—protest, demonstrations, etc.—the young, white voters (who greatly outnumber the blacks) will undoubtedly favor more traditional standards of seemly behavior.[43]

While universal automatic voter enrollment deals with the means by which the share of the potential electorate which gets to the polls can be changed, there are a whole series of lesser reforms which deal with changes in the size of the potential electorate itself. The major limiting factors on this potential electorate are legal requirements concerning: (1) Residence, (2) Age, (3) Literacy, (4) Criminal Conviction, (5) Mental Incompetence, (6) U.S. Citizenship.

The most notorious of these restrictions is the residence requirement; in a nation noted for the geographic mobility of its population, a majority of states require one year within the state, three months within the county, and thirty days within the precinct to vote in any election, including Presidential. The best available estimate of the number of persons thus disenfranchised in a Presidential election year was 5%, or 5,400,000 voters, for 1960.[44] A.I.P.O. surveys suggest that this group is disproportionately in the 21–30 age group, since 4 out of 10 in this group moved during 1968, and that therefore it is residence requirements rather than lack of interest which keep them from voting.[45] We know that voters in this age group are more Democratic than Republican but less identified with any party than are older voters, that they have less political information and are less interested, and that they participate less in all forms of political activity. Thus if residence requirements for Presidential voting were dropped, the potential electorate would expand by a part of the population less likely to get out to vote at all, more likely to vote Democratic in a "normal" situation if they got out to vote, but more likely to be unstable in their preferences and to move disproportionately in any one direction if there were strong forces moving that way.

The same can, of course, be said for a group which has gotten the most recent attention—18, 19, and 20 year olds. They could be expected to behave much as 21–30 year olds, only more so. In 1970 the Supreme Court upheld the right of this group to vote in national elections, but left it for individual states to decide the age requirements in state elections.[46]

There are four other major groups currently kept out of the potential electorate: (1) Travellers and the ill. William Andrews, estimates that while 3,400,000 absentee ballots were cast in 1960, another 3,600,000 voters could not vote because they had departed or become ill too late to receive an absentee ballot.[47] (2) Aliens. Aliens who could not vote in 1960 totaled 2,800,000. (3) Ex-felons. Convicted felons are permanently stripped of voting rights in most states, and there were 1,400,000 such persons in 1960.[48] (4) Illiterates. Of the 3,400,000 illiterates in 1960, 1,500,000 were literate but not in English. The analysis of whether or not such groups should be allowed to become part of the electorate must be much the same as that for non-registrants; to the degree that voting is a means to distribute the political goods of a society, they presumably have as much (perhaps more) stake in its outcome as do other groups, and while they may be low in general political information, this would not be an adequate reason, in our view, to deprive them of the vote.

An Appraisal of the Electoral College

Close Presidential elections, where the new President has only a narrow margin in the total popular vote, always lead to renewed public discussion of the merits of the Electoral College, since close elections remind people of the mathematical possibility that the candidate with a plurality of all the votes will not necessarily be the one to become President. Reform interest surges even higher when a regionally-based third party such as George Wallace led in 1968 becomes strong enough conceivably to prevent any candidate from having an electoral vote majority, thus threatening to drive the decision into the U.S. House of Representatives, which under the Constitution decides such matters when the Electoral College cannot.

The number of reform plans generated in the aftermath of the 1968 elections, including all their permutations and combinations, was legion. There were, however, three basic alternatives proposed to the present system, and the rest were variations. One would abolish the Electoral College outright and weigh votes equally everywhere. The net effect of such a proposal would be to undermine slightly the current strategic advantage enjoyed by populous, two-party, urbanized states; it might also have some long-run effects on the two-party system itself, but these would depend on other changes in the social situation within the country. The second proposal would retain the apportionment of the Electoral College (which gives numerical advantage to the smaller, rural states) but abolish the unit rule electoral vote (which operates strongly in favor of populous states). This proposal is quite extreme in its import, which would be to confer an additional political bonus upon states already overrepresented in positions of Congressional power. A third, quite similar proposal, also retains the apportionment of the Electoral College but distributes an Electoral College vote for the plurality vote winner in each Congressional district and two additional electoral votes for the winner in each state. This system maximizes the strength of one-party states, and of those forces which are most important in the U.S. House of Representatives; in fact, it could realign the Presidential coalition in very fundamental ways.[49]

The Constitution provides that each state, regardless of its population, shall be represented in the Senate by an equal number of Senators. This means that the eight largest states, with just over 50% of the voters in 1968, have just sixteen Senators. In the course of legislative proceedings, these Senators' votes can be canceled by the sixteen votes of the Senators from the eight least populous states, with 2.2% of the voters in the 1968 Presidential election. Before the series of Supreme Court decisions beginning with *Baker* vs. *Carr*, and extending through *Wesberry* vs. *Sanders* and *Reynolds* vs. *Sims*,[50] the less populous, more rural states had been similarly favored in the distribution of seats in the House of Representatives; at one point in the early 1960's an average vote in Nevada was worth 85 times as much as an average vote in New York in elections for the House. The requirement that each state have at least one representative still gives the smaller states a slight edge over the big states in Congressmen per capita (about 300,000 per congressman in the smaller states, and well over 400,000 in the large states), and the distribution of one-party, "safe" districts within the smaller states augments this further by tending to give House leadership positions to Representatives from these areas. The imbalance is comparatively far less than it was as recently as ten years ago; it roughly corresponds to the advantage which more populous, urbanized, two-party states enjoy in the Electoral College, and thus in access to the Presidency.

The present Electoral College system, with its votes apportioned according to the total of Senate and House seats a state has, and awarded on a "winner take all" basis, does provide a clear advantage to two groups of states.

It yields a secondary advantage to the smallest states, since their overrepresentation in the Senate and the House guarantees them overrepresentation in the Electoral College; in 1968, all five states with three electoral votes each had a ratio of 150,000 or fewer citizens per electoral vote, while every state with thirteen or more electoral votes had a ratio of 350,000 or more citizens per electoral vote. But it is primarily the larger states, through the unit-rule principle, who benefit from the Electoral College. A candidate who can get a narrow majority in New York state can get almost as many electoral votes (42) as he could by carrying all of the sixteen smallest states (58); he can, mathematically, carry New York by one vote and not receive any votes in those 16 states and do just as well. This fact alone suggests that a Presidential candidate spend his energy in the larger states and tailor his programs to appeal to their voters, provided that energy expended there is nearly as likely to yield results. In fact, the larger states are usually quite close in their division of the major party vote, while the smaller states are more nearly "sure" for one party or the other. In 1968, the average share of the vote for the winner in the 16 smallest states was 55%, and 8 out of the 16 states gave the winner a 10% margin of victory; in the 8 largest states, on the other hand, the average share of the vote for the winner was 47%, with none of these states giving as much as 55% to the winner and none of them giving him a 10% margin. The large states are the home of many organized minorities, especially racial and ethnic minorities, and this has traditionally meant that both Presidential candidates have had to pitch their appeals to attract these groups, or at least not to drive off significant proportions of them. This is a major reason why U.S. Presidents, Republicans as well as Democrats, have been more activists, welfare-oriented, minority-oriented—in a word, more liberal—than their congressional party counterparts.[51]

Some of the critics of the current system have pointed to this advantage for the larger states, and especially their urban minorities, as a drawback of that system, to be reformed out of existence,[52] but most have concentrated their fire on the possibility of "deadlock," the possibility of the "wrong winner," and the "undemocratic" nature of the unit rule.

Allowing a majority (or plurality) of voters to choose a President has a great deal to commend it. This is the simplest method of all; it would be most easily understood by the greatest number of people; it is the plan favored by the majority of Americans; and it comes closest to reflecting intuitive notions of direct popular sovereignty through majority rule. But to end the matter there would be too simple-minded. There is more than one political lesson to be learned by a closer examination of the Electoral College and available alternatives to it.

The outright abolition of the Electoral College, and the substitution of the direct election of the President, would certainly reduce the importance of the larger states. It would

mean that the popular vote margin which a state could provide, not the number of electoral votes, would determine its
importance; for example, under the present system a candidate who carries California by 220,000 votes (as Nixon did
in 1968) has garnered about 1/7 of the support he needs to
win, while under the direct vote system states like Massachusetts or Alabama can generate three and four times that much
margin. In the two-party states, in which category most of the
larger states fall, voters are cross-pressured in many ways, and
a candidate can seldom count on defeating his opponent by a
very large margin. The reason, then, that the large states
lose influence is that this system switches influence from
the close states to one-party states; in some states where one
party's organization is weak, large majorities for the other
party are easier to turn out at election time, and special
rewards would be forthcoming for party leaders who could
provide a large margin of victory for their candidate. As
candidates currently look with favor on those who can bring
them support in the large states, because this spells victory,
so might they be expected to look with favor on those who
can bring them large popular margins in the one-party states,
should that become the criterion. The emphasis would not
be on which candidate was going to win the state, already a
foregone conclusion, but by how many votes he was going to
win. The small states do not gain, however, because even
when they are one-party, they are not large enough to generate substantial voting margins. Direct election thus changes
the advantage from the biggest and the smallest two-party
states to the medium-sized one-party states, and these, in the
U.S., happen most commonly to be located in the South.[53]

The chart on the next page lists all states having more than
fourteen electoral votes, and all states having more than a
margin of 100,000 votes for the winner in 1968, and shows
clearly that the major gainers under a direct election system
would be Southern states, for six out of the eight Southern
states that were not "big states" on an electoral vote basis are
now "big states" because of their vote margin (along with

POPULAR VOTE MARGIN, 1968

	Small (less than 100,000)	Large (more than 100,000)
Large (14 +)	21-Ohio-90,000 17-New Jersey-61,000 25-Texas-39,000	14-Massachusetts-702,000 43-New York-371,000 40-California-223,000 21-Michigan-222,000 14-Florida-210,000 29-Pennsylvania-169,000 26-Illinois-135,000 17-Mississippi-265,000
Small (13 −)		10-Alabama-495,000 13-Indiana-261,000 10-Louisiana-221,000 10-Minnesota-199,000 7-Kansas-176,000 12-Georgia-169,000 5-Nebraska-151,000 12-Virginia-148,000 8-Oklahoma-143,000 9-Iowa-142,000 13-North Carolina-131,000 4-Rhode Island-124,000 11-Tennessee-121,000 3-D.C.-109,000

(ELECTORAL VOTE (MARGIN))

eight other randomly assorted states); conversely, three of the ten "big states" by the Electoral College standard are now "small," and all but one of the ten lag behind Alabama in their importance to a Presidential candidate.

This does not, of course, settle the matter, for one of the reasons that direct election is touted is that third parties cannot deadlock the process. In fact, those Southern states with the largest 1968 margins were not powerful but weak, for they did not contribute to a winner, but a third-place loser. If the same chart is redrawn to show only the two-party vote and excludes votes for Wallace, the Southern influence disappears.

TWO-PARTY POPULAR VOTE MARGIN, 1968

	Small (less than 100,000)	Large (more than 100,000)
Large (14+)	21-Ohio-90,000 17-New Jersey-61,000 25-Texas-39,000	14-Massachusetts-702,000 43-New York-371,000 40-California-223,000 21-Michigan-222,000 14-Florida-210,000 29-Pennsylvania-169,000 26-Illinois-135,000
Small (13−)		13-Indiana-261,000 10-Minnesota-199,000 7-Kansas-176,000 5-Nebraska-151,000 8-Oklahoma-143,000 9-Iowa-142,000 13-North Carolina-131,000 4-Rhode Island-124,000 11-Tennessee-121,000 3-D.C.-109,000

(left margin: ELECTORAL VOTE (MARGIN))

How one feels about this situation, however, depends on 1) how one still feels about the diminution of large state influence and the gain by sundry other smaller states, 2) how much of a plurality one feels a newly elected President should have, 3) how this plurality limit will affect others in the system.

Clearly, third-party votes under a direct election system are wasted if the candidate with a plurality wins, no matter how small that plurality; if this is how the system is made to work, it is quite possible that future "Dixiecrat"-type movements will disappear, or merge into Southern Republicanism. At best, voters could express only their anger by voting for third party candidates and this would be at the cost of foregoing the chance to decide an election. We suspect, however, that most Americans would feel uncomfortable with a President who, even though he won a plurality, was elected by say, only 35% of the voters; one of the virtues of the present electoral vote system is that it magnifies the margin of a Presidential victory (as, for instance, in 1960, Kennedy's .1% victory margin gave him 57% of the electoral vote), presumably conferring added legitimacy and with it acceptance of the new President's responsibility to govern in fact as well as in title. Any system of direct election would almost have to eliminate the majority principle in favor of some plurality, or it would clearly lead to much more, not less, deadlock; in three out of our last six Presidential elections the winning candidate was without an absolute majority.

Reformers have generally agreed, though, that the winner must win by at least a substantial plurality; consequently the Electoral College reform amendment which passed the House in late 1969 provided for a run-off between the top two candidates if no one secured as much as 40% of the popular vote in the initial election.[54] The first effect of this change would be to hand segregationist (and other) third parties back their influence; if your friends are going to have a second chance to win the office anyway, there is an incentive for any sizable organized minority to contest the first election on its own. That the run-off would likely be used if it were provided is suggested by the 1968 figures. A fourth candidate, perhaps a "peace" advocate, would have needed to pull only 6 or 7% of the national total to keep either candidate from having the required 40% (Nixon won with only 43.4%, although he had 56.2% of the electoral vote); a large enough minority was significantly concerned about this one issue to make this a real possibility.[55] Once this becomes even a plausible expectation, there is no reason for other intense minorities not to do likewise; visions of a segregationist party, a black party, a labor party, even a Catholic party, a farmers' party, etc., appear. Where one of the strong points of the present system is that it enforces a compromise by penalizing all minorities that will not come to terms, the direct election system could well approximate a Continental European model, in which numerous groups contest the first election and then recombine for the second; at the very least, severe changes would be worked on the present convention system.[56] Should such a result have occurred in 1968, or should it occur in the future, the simplicity, ease of comprehension, and inherent majoritarian rightness of the direct election solution would quickly disappear.

The direct election plan passed by the House received a warmer reception in the Senate than the last time it appeared there, in 1956, when it was voted down 66 to 17, but there were, not surprisingly, two major opposition groups. The first were the liberal Senators from the biggest states, who had most to lose. The second were some of the conservative Senators from the smallest states, whom we named as the group deriving second greatest benefits from the current system. They argued that direct election would be a complete breach of the federalism underlying our Constitution, since it would *de facto* abolish state boundaries for Presidential elections.[57]

Another proposal, once embodied in the unsuccessful Lodge-Gossett Resolution, is seen by some reformers as an acceptable "compromise" between outright abolition of the Electoral College and its retention.[58] In this scheme, the electoral vote in each state is split between the candidates according to their proportion of the state's popular vote. This may seem to be a procedural compromise, but it is a rather extreme reform in political terms. As the chart on the next page shows, the large, urban, two-party states are nearly eclipsed, in a way that direct election could not do; four out of the ten largest states would not in 1968 have been able to provide their winner with even one full electoral vote margin, while fifteen other states *would* have been able to do so.

The bargaining position of the large states at national conventions would be drastically reduced, and Presidential nominees would have to follow a different strategy in their campaigns, giving special attention to those states in which they felt a large difference in electoral votes could be attained. Once again, the proposed reform throws the emphasis on the amount of difference within the state between the winner and the loser. In this case, however, it is the electoral votes of the states which are divided rather than the popular votes. This effectively cancels out the advantage of the large states entirely. The fact that the Electoral College underrepresents the

PROPORTIONAL ELECTORAL VOTE MARGIN, 1968

	Small (1.00—)	Large (1.00+)
Large (14+)	26-Illinois-0.75 21-Ohio-0.60 17-New Jersey-0.36 25-Texas-0.30	14-Massachusetts-4.22 43-New York-2.36 21-Michigan-1.41 14-Florida-1.33 29-Pennsylvania-1.30 40-California-1.21
Small (13—)		10-Alabama-4.74 7-Mississippi-2.84 10-Louisiana-2.01 3-D.C.-1.90 12-Georgia-1.63 7-Kansas-1.41 12-Virginia-1.31 13-Indiana-1.30 4-Rhode Island-1.29 10-Minnesota-1.25 8-Oklahoma-1.21 9-Iowa-1.08 13-North Carolina-1.07 7-Idaho-1.04 5-Arizona-1.00

ELECTORAL VOTE (MARGIN)

large states in the first place even further reduces their influence. The beneficiaries are again the one-party states, as well as the smaller states, since in any particular election Idaho and Arizona, for example, may have more to contribute than Illinois, New Jersey, Ohio, or Texas.

There are two versions of this plan, one which divides electoral votes to the nearest vote and one which divides them to the nearest tenth of a vote. Most proponents favor the plan to divide them to the nearest tenth, since the nearest whole vote still in many cases would understate the closeness of the vote in a large number of states, especially those with five or fewer electoral votes to divide, and "representativeness" is the primary theoretical support for the plan. Since preventing deadlock is supposed to be one of the goals of Electoral

College reform, it is interesting to note that with the majority vote victory required by proponents of both plans, either the whole or the tenth-vote system would have thrown the 1968 election into the House of Representatives (Nixon 235, Humphrey 221, Wallace 74; or, Nixon 233.8, Humphrey 223.2, Wallace 78.8, others 2.2) ; and the system allotting electoral votes to the nearest tenth would even have deadlocked the election of 1960 (Kennedy 264.8, Nixon 263.5, others 7.7).

The reduction in influence suffered by the large states under this proposal might mean, in effect, that the already overrepresented sparsely populated and one-party states in the Congress would entirely dominate the national lawmaking process, unchecked by a President obliged to cultivate urban and two-party constituencies. It is perhaps gratuitous to point out that the same plurality problem is present if the deadlock is dealt with by letting the plurality candidate win. Even with a plurality provision, splintering is facilitated under this plan because a party need only pull a fraction of a percentage point of a major state's total vote in order to get some electoral votes. The present system at least cuts off splinter groups without a strong regional base.

A third plan, the district plan, has been proposed as still another "political compromise" between the other two major reform proposals, on the grounds that since thirty-eight states must ratify a Constitutional Amendment on electoral reform, the fifteen states with four or three electoral votes are not likely to support either of the first two proposals because each dilutes their current strength. The district plan would give a Presidential candidate one electoral vote for every congressional district he carried, plus two more for every state. It has been pushed largely by conservative Senators; it is clearly the most radical of all the reform proposals in its effect on the U.S. political system, and it is least advantageous to the big states. This system would have given Nixon victory in 1968 (289-192-57), but if it had already been in effect he probably would not have been running, since he would have won the election of 1960 (Nixon 278, Kennedy 245). Since the goal of electoral reform is supposedly to prevent the wrong man from winning, to avoid deadlock, and to do away with winner-take-all arrangements, it is hard to see how much is offered by a system which would have given the less popular man victory, provides no more guarantee against deadlock than the present system (Wallace in 1968 got forty-five under the present system, but would have received fifty-seven under this one), uses a winner-take-all principle, and which has the incidental feature of ending the activist character of the American Presidency and giving control to one-party areas for the foreseeable future.[59]

Under the present Electoral College system, there is no time since 1876 when any splinter group has been able to make good its threat to throw the election into the House, and in fact this is quite unlikely to occur since it requires all of the Deep South (Louisiana, Arkansas, Mississippi, Alabama, Georgia, South Carolina, North Carolina) to vote for a third party, plus a very even division in non-Southern votes. Even in 1948 Harry Truman won an electoral majority despite threats from both a third and a fourth party. In spite of the mathematical possibilities, not once in this century has the loser of the popular vote become President. On the other hand a direct election plan which required a 40% plurality might well have gone to a run-off in 1968, and both the proportional and district plans would have created deadlocks in the past decade. In view of this analysis of the effect of electoral reforms, it is curious that many liberal reformers support changes in the Electoral College, presumably in order to thwart Southern, racist party movements.

Underlying all of the above arguments, of course, is the premise that most structural reforms "tend" to shift influence in certain ways; there may well be situations of social polarization which electoral system alternatives by themselves cannot paper over. But while we have argued that there is no better system than the current one, from the standpoint of the professed goals of most reformers, there is one minor change that would aid them. Under the present plan the electors who make up the Electoral College are in fact free to vote for whomever they wish; as an almost invariable rule, they vote for the winner in their state, but abuses are possible, and two within the past decade come to mind: 1) the unpledged electors chosen by citizens in Mississippi and Alabama in 1960 decided for whom they would vote only after the election— this clearly thwarts any popular control; 2) this liberty allowed George Wallace to hope that he could run for President, create an electoral deadlock, and then bargain with one of the other candidates for policy concessions in exchange for his electors. An amendment making the casting of electoral votes automatic would dispel both of these possibilities.

We have argued that there is in fact no major reason to quarrel with the major features of the present system, since in our form of government "majority rule" does not operate in a vacuum but within a system of "checks and balances." The President, for example, holds a veto power over Congress, which, if exercised, requires a two-thirds vote of each House to override. Treaties must be ratified by two-thirds of the Senate, and amendments to the Constitution must be proposed by two-thirds of Congress or of the state legislatures and ratified by three-fourths of the states. Presidential appointments, in most important cases, must receive Senatorial approval. The Supreme Court passes upon the constitutionality of legislative and executive actions. Involved in these political arrangements is the hope that the power of one branch of government will be counter-balanced by certain "checks" from another, the result being an approximate "balance" of forces. In our view, it is not necessarily a loss to have slightly different majorities preponderant in different institutions, and it is definitely a loss to have the same majority preponderant in several branches while other majorities are frozen out. In the past the Electoral College had its place within this system. Originally designed to check popular majorities from choosing Presidents unwisely, the Electoral College provided a "check" on the overrepresentation of rural states in the legislative branch by giving extra weight to the urban constituencies of the President.

Electoral Outcomes Under Various Plans

	PRESENT PLAN	DIRECT PLAN	PROPORTION PLAN	DISTRICT PLAN
1968	Nixon Wins	Nixon Wins	Nobody Wins	Nixon Wins
	Nixon 302	Nixon 43.4	Nixon 233.8	Nixon 289
	Humphrey 191	Humphrey 42.7	Humphrey 223.2	Humphrey 192
	Wallace 45	Wallace 13.5	Wallace 78.8	Wallace 57
1960	Kennedy Wins	Kennedy Wins	Nobody Wins	Nixon Wins
	Kennedy 303	Kennedy 49.7	Kennedy 264.8	Kennedy 245
	Nixon 219	Nixon 49.6	Nixon 263.5	Nixon 278
	Others 15	Others .7	Others 7.7	Others 15

Majority rule should be placed in proper perspective by considering other aspects of democratic government, such as the principle of political equality. We want majority rule, but we also want all sectors of the population to have an equal voice in government. Overrepresentation of rural interests in Congress inhibited political equality. To check this inequality we either had to alter the circumstances which promoted such inequality or provide some other means of preventing rural interests from dominating the political system. Now that the method of determining the composition of Congress is undergoing change, we can consider abolishing the Electoral College and turn to majority (or plurality) voting in electing Presidents. Other things being equal a simpler and more direct method would be preferable to a device as complex in operation and as difficult to understand as the Electoral College. But the probable defects and equivalent complexities of alternatives to the Electoral College thus far proposed make us skeptical that the day has yet arrived when we can say that other things are in fact equal.

Party Differences and Political Stability

The case for the desirability of party reform often rests on the assumption that American political parties are identical, that this is confusing and frustrating to American voters, and that it is undesirable to have a political system where parties do not disagree sharply.

We would suggest, rather, that there are enough differences between the political parties to give voters a choice, but that many wide policy differences between the parties would be undesirable from the standpoint of the stability of the political system. The parties could well be somewhat further apart on a few issues, however, without necessarily decreasing the stability of the system. Our conceptual tools are too rough to say much about these small departures from the existing situation; let us consider only extreme changes of the kind advocated by the proponents of policy government.

Imagine for a moment that the two parties were in total and extreme disagreement on every major point of public policy. One group would appease the U.S.S.R.; the other would court nuclear war. One group would stop Social Security; the other would expand it drastically. One group would raise tariffs; the other would abolish them entirely. Obviously, one consequence of having clear-cut parties with strong policy positions would be that the costs of losing an election would skyrocket. If parties were forced to formulate coherent, full-dress programs and were forced to carry them out "responsibly," then people who did not favor these programs would have no recourse. Clearly, their confidence in a government whose policies were not to their liking would suffer, and, indeed, they might feel strongly enough about preventing these policies from being enacted to do something drastic, like leaving the country, or not complying with governmental regulations, or, in an extreme case, seeking to change the political system by force.

In fact, we have a political system that is kind to losers. Why? Because both Presidential parties usually agree on a wide variety of issues; because people other than the President have to pass on policies before they are enacted by law, and these people are not bound by the Presidential platform.

This is, we suggest, not necessarily a bad thing. Suppose that each major political party were composed solely of people who supported it because, and only because, it represented their views on a wide range of policies. The surface attractiveness of this idea diminishes rapidly once we consider the consequences. The most immediate results would be extraordinary instability in the party system. For as soon as people changed their minds or the party changed its position, vast numbers of its adherents would leave. Great swings in party strength might take place, leaving the minority party on occasion virtually without representation. Who, then, would take on the burdens of party opposition? Who would take the lead in introducing rival policies to compete for public favor?

The existence of a one-party system would be the least of our troubles. What would be the point in building up a party organization if it were doomed to come tumbling down with every significant change of opinion? None at all. So the function of nominating and electing candidates would become a matter for shifting groups of individuals varying from issue to issue and place to place. Naturally, those groups with the best organizations, the most money, and the greatest interest in the policies of the day would predominate. No longer would it be possible to use party identification as a shortcut, as a means of reducing information costs about candidates. Unless voters spent most of their time finding out precisely what officeholders were doing, they would have little idea how to vote. Nevertheless, their votes might be more important to them because the dizzying alternation of policy would have created such political chaos as to disrupt normal patterns of life. We need go no further to make the point that the existence of a hard core of party adherents who do not easily switch party allegiance from year to year provides an element of stability for the party system and thus for the whole political system as well. Paradoxically, the attempt to make issues all-important as a means of increasing the rationality of public decisions greatly decreases the chances for making any sort of meaningful decisions at all.

Party platforms written by the Presidential parties should be understood not as ends in themselves but as means to obtaining and holding public office. It would be strange indeed if one party found policies like Social Security and unemployment compensation to be enormously popular and yet refused to incorporate them into its platform.[60] This would have to be a party of ideologues who cared everything about their pet ideas and nothing about winning elections. Nor would it profit them much since they would never get elected and never be in a position to do something about their ideas. Eventually, ideologues have to make the choice between pleasing themselves and pleasing others.

Actually, party platforms do change over a period of time in a cyclical movement. The differences between the parties may be great for one or two elections until innovations made by one party are picked up by the other. The net change from one decade to the next, however, is substantial. Let us begin when platforms are more or less alike. Their similarity begins to give way as it appears that certain demands in society are not being met. The minority party of the period senses an opportunity to gain votes by articulating and promising to meet these demands. The majority party, reluctant to let go of a winning combination, resists. In one or two elections the minority party makes its bid and makes the appropriate changes in its platforms. Then, in the ensuing elections, if the party which has changed its platform loses, it drops the innovation. If it wins, however, and wins big, the other party then seeks to take over what seem to be its most popular planks, and the platforms become more and more alike again.

We can see this cycle clearly in the New Deal period. The 1932 Democratic platform, though hinting at change, was much like the Republican, especially in its emphasis on balancing the budget. A great difference in platforms could be noted in 1936 as the Democrats made a bid to consolidate the New Deal, and the Republicans stood pat. The spectacular Democratic triumph signaled the end of widely divergent platforms. By 1940 the Republicans had concluded that they could not continue to oppose the welfare state wholesale if they ever wished to win again. By 1952 the parties had come much closer to one another, as the Republicans adopted most of the New Deal. Though the platforms of the major parties were similar to each other in both 1932 and 1952, the differences between 1932 and 1952 for either party were enormous.[61]

Sometimes, reformers deplore what they regard as an excessive amount of mud-slinging in campaigns, but they also ask that differences among the major parties be sharply increased in order to give the voters a clear choice. The two ideas are incompatible to some extent. It would be surprising indeed if the parties disagreed more sharply about more and more subjects in an increasingly gentlemanly way. A far more likely outcome would be an increase in vituperation as the stakes of campaigns increased, passions rose, tempers flared, and the consequences of victory for the other side appeared much more threatening than had heretofore been the case. The 1936 campaign is a good case in point.

Those who claim American elections are a fraud and wish to see great things decided in these contests all the time often point to Great Britain as a shining example of the right way to do things. There, in that wiser country, where the fires of class warfare are held (fortunately) to burn more fiercely, the voters have real choices. They vote a government in or out, and the victorious party goes about making great changes in order to carry out its mandate.

This tale may be a pretty one, according to one's taste for conflict, but it is quite exaggerated. The truth in it occurs every once in a great while, much as American party platforms present sharp and profound differences about that often. Such was the case in 1945 when the Labour party staged its great bid to bring the full welfare state to Britain and to nationalize what it could. The overwhelming Labour victory did its work. The Conservatives soon decided to adopt all the most popular parts of the Labour party program—medicare, increased pensions—and left Labour holding the unpopular bag of nationalization. By 1955 the two major parties in Britain were presenting much the same program. By 1958 the only difference we could find was that Labour offered sixpence more on the pension. Most of the time, in fact, in Britain as in the United States, the great parties lean toward the undivided middle.[62]

The Labour party's reaction to the problem of nationalization is instructive. The party was reluctant to leave behind its heritage in this respect; nor was it certain that this issue alone caused its electoral defeats after 1950. Nevertheless, it moved, however painfully, away from a strident position on the subject. There were pleas from those who put ideological consistency first and felt that the lesson to be learned from each defeat was to propose more of the same. Parties do not usually choose to die in this way, however, and Labour politicians who hoped one day to gain office won out over their more ideologically inclined colleagues. Indeed, until it left office in 1970, the Labour party leadership carefully avoided a showdown in Parliament over nationalization of industry.[63]

IS PARTY REFORM RELEVANT?

Even if reform were successful and the political system did not suffer detrimental effects such as we have outlined, many of the problems at which reform is aimed still would not be closer to solution. Thus, it can be argued that the achievement of party government is beside the point.

Can we say, for example, that the present system shows marked or widespread party incoherence in Congress? This is perhaps an overstated problem for, in fact, on roll call voting, and in many other matters, party allegiance is the strongest cohesive force in Congress. It has been demonstrated that party is stronger than other bases of allegiance, stronger than sectionalism, rural versus urban, native born versus foreign born.[64] Party cohesion depends, to be sure, on the nature of the issue. On the organization of Congress itself and on patronage matters, each party is aligned 100% against the other. On a significant number of issues there is widespread agreement among members of both parties, a situation which, because it limits and focuses conflict, is usually regarded as desirable. Some issues like race relations may split each of the parties down the middle. On the economic and welfare issues, where the general label of liberal is commonly attributed to Democrats and conservative to Republicans, cohesion, while not perfect, is high; the labels make sense. If we look at votes on public housing, medical care for the aged, private versus public power, and so on, we can discover that a preponderant majority of both parties takes opposing views. Cohesion does exist and it is important. Since it is not perfect, however, and one party rarely has an overwhelming advantage, it is often necessary to gain some votes from the opposing party in order to make up a majority. Party, therefore, cannot properly be viewed as a drag on unified policy-making. It is most often a force making for greater cohesion than would be the case without it. By itself, it does not supply all the agreement necessary for the making of policy. In the American context of separated and fragmented powers, based on a population divided along many lines, this is no small accomplishment.

Consider now the realm of foreign policy, where decisions made at any moment literally involve our survival and possibly that of the human race. How would policy government help us? The answer, presumably, is that the United States government would be able to follow more consistent, less internally contradictory, policies and that these would lead to happier results. This assumes first that inconsistent policies are, in themselves, undesirable, a proposition which has never been convincingly demonstrated. In fact, inconsistency, "imbalance," and incoherence may in many instances be beneficial because of the necessity for satisfying a variety of diverse interests both at home and abroad through various policies of the government. By pursuing inconsistency in its policies the government often gains the legitimacy and support which are necessary to govern at all. A second assumption of the reformers is that the lack of party cohesion has been a major problem in foreign affairs. But this is simply not the case. In fact, it appears that virtually every major policy initiative of a President in the last twenty years—the blockade of Cuba, the Marshall Plan, NATO, the Eisenhower Doctrine, the Gulf of Tonkin resolution, intervention in Korea and Vietnam, nonintervention in Indochina in 1954—has been supported by Congress, in most cases promptly and enthusiastically. When dissent appears, it is as often from members of the President's own party as from the opposition; therefore dissent on foreign affairs is not a consequence of the party system. We also have the impression that dissent on

foreign affairs—even from members of a President's own party
—is not as unpopular with liberal reformers as it once was.

The difficulties facing the United States may be traced to
causes for which the party system cannot be blamed. The rise
of the Soviet Union and Communist China as great powers
generally hostile to America, nationalist revolutions all over
the world, the break-up of colonialism, the creation of weapons
of unparalleled destructiveness—all these developments have
neither been hastened nor delayed by the character of our
party system. American makers of foreign policy have found
that they could not solve these problems primarily because of
the enormous difficulties involved, not because Congress refused to accept the correct policies. Presidents and Secretaries
of State today find that the world is intractable; there are so
many things they can do little or nothing about. They have
to deal with a worldwide range of problems, make decisions of
enormous technical complexity, gain consent of allies with
differing interests, take account of huge forces arrayed against
them, obtain popular support at home, all largely outside the
help or the hindrance the party system can give them. If only
they can decide what to do, if only their policies prove viable,
they can expect to be strongly supported. It would be pure
fantasy to claim that our Presidents and their advisors have
had wonderful ideas for making the world a better place only
to have them frustrated by lack of ability to command support
in Congress.

The Chief Executive has unique opportunities for leadership
in foreign affairs if only he can decide in what direction the
nation ought to move. He is the single most commanding voice
in the nation. He is visible above all others. He has the information, the opportunity to deal with foreign governments, the
formal powers, and the acknowledged right to lead. Others may
clamor but in the post-World War II environment at least,
he is the one who will be heard. All of us are dependent upon
the President for guidance in a fantastically complicated world
where our personal experience rarely proves a reliable guide.
Perhaps this is why the President's popularity rises sharply
whenever he acts in an international crisis, even in cases

like the invasions of Cuba and Cambodia, and the Suez crisis, which were, from our point of view, disasters.[65] Rather than seeing danger in our President's being thwarted by hostile Congresses, the more likely danger is that few, except the President, will have much to say about the most vital foreign policy decisions which may have to be made in a terribly short time.

Perhaps the most significant area with impact on foreign policy in which some contradiction among party policies appears is in the area of tariffs.[66] The United States seeks the stability of nations like Japan, on the one hand, and sets up tariff barriers which may help undermine this stability on the other. Interests which find themselves disadvantaged seek a sympathetic hearing in Congress where members are less attuned to foreign policy considerations than is the President.

It would not, in any event, be surprising if governments were concerned about protecting the interests of domestic industries to some extent. Looking at nations like Britain, France, and Germany, whose governments can command automatic support in parliament, we find that they are also interested in protecting their domestic industries and the workers who depend on them. The negotiations on the Common Market have made this abundantly clear. If party government, let us say, on the British model were suddenly to appear in the United States, there would still be the necessity of bargaining with interests within the majority party, and no one doubts that the impact of tariff levels on industry would have to be considered. The United States has, for the most part, been moving toward a tariff position more consonant with its foreign policy objectives. At least we have done no worse than other democratic nations with different party systems.

There is an unfortunate tendency to blame the American decentralized party system for all sorts of things which cannot properly be laid at its door. In 1960, after the U-2 incident blew up the summit meeting in Paris, many recriminations were voiced about the lack of coordination in Washington. Wasn't it terrible, these critics cried, that in this crisis we were let down by our fragmented political system which permitted so many spokesmen to go off in different directions?

A careful review of these events reveals, however, that the charges were wholly erroneous. The problem was not at all one of lack of coordination. Just the opposite. All the responsible officials were following whatever instructions they had; the trouble was that these instructions turned out to be poor ones. The apparent inconsistencies, the clumsy efforts to cover up, resulted from the defective instructions. "Lack of coordination" presumably means that the officials involved all went their separate ways without regard to what the President wanted; it cannot properly be taken to mean that they did badly, because the central directions they followed turned out not to be appropriate.

When we turn to Great Britain, where policy government has long been established, we do not find that ability to command a certain majority in the House of Commons helps Prime Ministers solve foreign policy problems better than Presidents. Her Majesty's Government has, on the whole, had at least as much difficulty as ours because its problems are as difficult. The Prime Minister may be better able to disregard criticism but this is not necessarily an advantage.

The most notorious example of failure of democratic leadership in recent times comes not from the United States but from Great Britain. There, in the 1930's Stanley Baldwin and Neville Chamberlain led their country to the brink of ruin when they failed to inform the people of the growing danger of Nazi Germany, partly because they thought their people were profoundly pacifist and would defeat them at the polls. These men were patriots who wished their country well; they had devoted their lifetimes to its service. Had they realized the full implications of their actions (or failures to act), they undoubtedly would have done otherwise. Uncertain as to the course of events, prone to underestimate the fury of their foes abroad, they allowed themselves to be swayed by the notion that the people would not stand for the truth, no matter how essential that truth was. Surely the existence of a cohesive party system, with sharp policy differences between the parties, did nothing to avoid this disaster. If anything, party cohesion permitted Baldwin and Chamberlain to proceed with impunity despite attacks leveled by Churchill and others who vainly sought to alert the nation. So strong was party unity that it took the calamitous events of 1940, threatening the very existence of the nation, to bring about a change in government.

Policy government is not, however, irrelevant for purposes of domestic politics, and we will want to define more precisely its likely impact. But before we proceed in this direction, it is necessary to modify the policy government proposals so that they are more defensible. For so long as its proponents insist that the parties be both popular and extremely far apart on many policies, the contradictions in this approach do grave damage to the consistency and validity of their proposals. Let us agree to modify the reformers' proposals by stating that the major Presidential parties should be able to propose coherent policies to the electorate and to carry them out after they assume office, regardless of whether their policies are or are not similar.

Now we are in a position to write a sort of profit and loss statement on what would be involved in the realm of domestic politics if policy government were instituted. The benefits would accrue almost entirely to liberals (and the interests they represent) with superior access to the President who would have a better chance of securing the enactment of the welfare and civil rights measures they prefer. Conservatives would stand to lose their power and their policy preferences as their Congressional bastion was weakened if not rendered wholly useless. Liberals in Congress would gain more of their preferred policies but their power, as Congressmen, would suffer as Congress lost power. Where the present system enables them to maintain their power as Congressmen while achieving some of their policies, they would have to choose between power and their other preferences under policy government. People who prefer more welfare policies and a traditionally powerful Congress would have to weigh their competing preferences carefully. Beyond this point we see dimly at best. In order to achieve somewhat greater party cohesion on domestic affairs we would risk an unspecified increase in social conflict and a somewhat greater likelihood of producing splinter parties. What the citizen has to decide is whether the benefits are worth the costs.

We think that the supporters of policy government over-estimate by far the magnitude of the problem from their own viewpoint. It is not true that the parties are basically lacking in cohesion and certainly not true that no welfare legislation is passed by Congress. What is true is that medical care for the aged, aid to education, and greater attention to problems besetting urban areas have had a rough road in Congress. The recent passage of much forward-looking legislation dealing with these problems weakens the argument that there was a serious need for basic reform of the party system. It seems excessive to us to contemplate far-reaching changes in the party system which are exceedingly difficult to achieve and whose desirability is at least questionable, when there are much less drastic and much more desirable means available for securing the kinds of legislation which the proponents of policy government want so badly.

A basic difficulty is that the policy government people are so enchanted with the mystique of the Presidency, and so annoyed with Congress, that they do not perceive the excellent opportunities available to them for altering the pattern of legislation. Let us consider some of the activities which give promise of bearing results: (1) continued attack on the problem of apportionment toward the end that metropolitan areas receive greater representation in Congress; (2) efforts to secure from liberal strongholds in the cities candidates who will make a career out of service in Congress, rather than regarding their service as a stepping-stone toward a judgeship or some other such position. There is no need for conservatives to enjoy their present superiority of seniority, skill, and dedication; (3) greater attention by national party leaders to the distribution of Congressional committee positions so that liberal majorities on crucial committees may be more readily achieved. The success at the start of the 88th Congress in permanently expanding the House Rules Committee and putting men favorable to welfare legislation on House Ways and

Means and Appropriations Committees are good examples of what might be done; (4) development of strategies which show the mass of people, especially urban people, the stake they have in welfare legislation and which bring home to them the importance of presenting their views to their Congressmen. No doubt it seems easier to talk blithely about a revolution in the party system than actually to do something to increase the support which the mass of people give to legislation presumed to benefit them. Action in any one or all of these directions would, in our opinion, do more to secure welfare legislation than talking about policy government or taking actions which are bound to be futile. Knowing what we know now, we can well understand why the clamor for Congressional party reform died down after the 89th Congress passed an enormous amount of the legislation that liberals had tried so hard to get in the 1940's and 1950's. The major reason these bills passed was that the Democrats were able to elect an extraordinary majority (particularly in the House) in 1964. Indirectly, of course, Barry Goldwater's candidacy was responsible for putting enough liberal Democrats in Congress to complete virtually the entire New Deal. It should also be said, however, that years of effort, begun half a decade before, that altered the composition of crucial Congressional committees, were also important in securing this result.

To summarize: Most of the reforms suggested by students of the party system are, we believe, designed to give greater power to liberal Presidents to enact their domestic programs and to diminish, correspondingly, the power of Congress. For the conduct of foreign affairs these changes would, we believe, be largely irrelevant. With respect to the stability and inclusiveness of the two major parties themselves, the reforms might well be detrimental, owing to the encouragement they might well give to splinter parties. And finally, we observe that the case for party reform has certainly not been made. The enunciation of large national problems does not in and of itself demonstrate the linkage of these problems to the party system. The prescription of reforms does not in and of itself provide the strategy or the power or the inducements to carry them out. Until these key links in the argument are forged, the advocacy of comprehensive party reform will continue to be an academic exercise, appealing to the frustrations of unsophisticated audiences but without practical import.

NOTES

1. Stephen K. Bailey, *The Condition of· Our National Political Parties* (New York, 1959), p. 3.

2. *Ibid.*, pp. 12–16.

3. There are many examples of the party reform school of thought. See for example, Woodrow Wilson, *Congressional Government* (Boston, 1889); Henry Jones Ford, *The Rise and Growth of American Politics* (New York, 1898); A. Lawrence Lowell, *Public Opinion and Popular Government* (New York, 1913); William MacDonald, *A New Constitution for a New America* (New York, 1921); William Y. Elliott, *The Need for Constitutional Reform* (New York, 1935); E. E. Schattschneider, *Party Government* (New York, 1942); Henry Hazlitt, *A New Constitution Now* (New York, 1942); Thomas K. Finletter, *Can Representative Government Do the Job?* (New York, 1945); James M. Burns, *Congress on Trial* (New York, 1949); Committee on Political Parties, American Political Science Association, *Toward a More Responsible Two-Party System* (New York, 1950); Bailey, *The Condition of Our National Political Parties;* and James M. Burns, *The Deadlock of Democracy* (Englewood Cliffs, 1963). The work of the Committee on Political Parties, representing the collective judgment of a panel of distinguished political scientists in 1950, is the statement we shall refer to most often.

4. Committee on Political Parties, *Toward a More Responsible Two-Party System*, p. 1.

5. *Ibid.*, p. 66.

6. *Ibid.*, p. 15.

7. A sample of this literature might include Pendleton Herring, *The Politics of Democracy* (New York, 1940); Herbert Agar, *The Price of Union* (Boston, 1950); Malcolm C. Moos, *Politics, Presidents and Coattails* (Baltimore, 1952); Austin Ranney and Willmoore Kendall, *Democracy and the American Party System* (New York, 1956); David B. Truman, *The Governmental Process* (New York, 1953); John Fischer, "Unwritten Rules of American Poli-

tics," *Harper's Magazine* (November 1948), 27–36; Peter Drucker, "A Key to American Politics: Calhoun's Pluralism," *Review of Politics* 10 (October 1948), 412–426; Ernest F. Griffith, *Congress: Its Contemporary Role* (New York, 1951); Murray Stedman and Herbert Sonthoff, "Party Responsibility: A Critical Inquiry," *Western Political Quarterly* 4 (September 1951), 454–486; Julius Turner, "Responsible Parties: A Dissent from the Floor," *American Political Science Review* 45 (March 1951), 143–152; William Goodman, "How Much Political Party Centralization Do We Want?" *The Journal of Politics* 13 (November 1961), 536–561; and Austin Ranney, *The Doctrine of Responsible Party Government* (Urbana, 1954).

8. Herring, *The Politics of Democracy*, p. 327.

9. *Ibid.*, p. 420.

10. Committee on Political Parties, *Toward a More Responsible Two-Party System*, p. 19.

11. *Ibid.*, p. 17.

12. *Ibid.*, p. 92

13 See *ibid.*, and especially Burns, *The Deadlock of Democracy*, *passim*.

14. Ranney and Kendall, *Democracy and the American Party System*, p. 508.

15. *Ibid.*, p. 476.

16. Herring, *The Politics of Democracy*, p. 345.

17. Robert A. Dahl, *A Preface to Democratic Theory* (Chicago, 1956), p. 151; Don K. Price, "The Presidency: Its Burdens and Its Promises," *Strengthening America's Institutions* (Ithaca, 1949), p. 110.

18. Turner, "Responsible Parties: A Dissent from the Floor," p. 144.

19. Ranney and Kendall, *Democracy and the American Party System*, p. 509.

20. Clem Miller, *Member of the House*, ed. John W. Baker (New York, 1962), pp. 53, 91–92.

21. Bailey, *The Condition of Our National Political Parties*, p. 20.

22. This is, of course, not at all uncommon. See, for instance, examples in Raymond Bauer, Ithiel Pool, and Lewis A. Dexter, *American Business and Public Policy* (New York, 1963), Chapters 16, 18, and 19; Donald E. Stokes and Warren E. Miller, "Party Government and the Saliency of Congress," *Public Opinion Quar-*

terly 26 (Winter 1962), 531–546; Jacob K. Javits, "How I Used a Poll in Campaigning for Congress," *Public Opinion Quarterly* 11 (Summer 1947), 222–226.

23. This section is adapted from Aaron B. Wildavsky, "On the Superiority of National Conventions," *Review of Politics* 24 (July 1962), 307–319.

24. See V. O. Key, Jr., *American State Politics* (New York, 1956), Chapter 6.

25. V. O. Key, Jr., *Southern Politics* (New York, 1949), e.g., Chapter 3 (Alabama) and Chapter 9 (Arkansas).

26. Key, *American State Politics*, p. 216.

27. See Edward Stanwood, *A History of the Presidency from 1788 to 1897* (Boston, 1898), pp. 125–141.

28. A classic statement is M. Ostrogorski, *Democracy and the Party System* (New York, 1910), pp. 158–160. See also, Elmo Roper, "What Price Conventions?" *Saturday Review* (September 3, 1960), 26.

29. Ostrogorski, *Democracy and the Party System*, pp. 141–142.

30. See Aaron Wildavsky, "What Can I Do? Ohio Delegates View the Democratic Convention," in *Inside Politics: The National Conventions, 1960*, ed. Paul Tillett (Dobbs Ferry, N.Y., 1962), pp. 112–130.

31. At least one representative of the media apparently feels as we do about this problem. Walter Cronkite argues that: ". . . it is not necessary that we be admitted to the actual floor of the convention. There is a better way (such as the use of immediate off-floor interview booths) to cover the non-podium action in order to permit a more orderly convention procedure." *The Challenges of Change* (Washington, D.C., 1971), p. 75.

32. Herbert McClosky, Paul J. Hoffman, and Rosemary O'Hara, "Issue Conflict and Consensus Among Party Leaders and Followers," *American Political Science Review* 54 (June 1960), 406–427.

33. See, for example, William Carleton's argument, "The Revolution in the Presidential Nominating Convention," *Political Science Quarterly* 72 (June 1957), 224–240.

34. New York *Times*, July 16, 1964, p. 1.

35. Stanley Kelley, Jr., Richard E. Ayres, and William G. Bowen, "Registration and Voting: Putting First Things First," *American Political Science Review* 61 (June 1967), p. 362.

36. The general outline of this argument has been known in this country for at least fifty years. For example, in 1924, Harold G. Gosnell wrote, "In the European countries studied, a citizen who is entitled to vote does not, as a rule, have to make any effort to see that his name is on the list of eligible voters. The inconvenience of registering for voting in this country has caused many citizens to become non-voters." Harold G. Gosnell, *Why Europe Votes* (Chicago, 1930), p. 185.

37. In *Registration 1960: Key to Democratic Victory?* (unpublished senior thesis, Princeton University, 1964), cited in Kelley, Ayres, and Bowen, *op. cit.*, p. 375, Richard E. Ayres cites the correlation between convenience of registration and percent of the vote for the Democratic party as proof of the Daley machine's awareness of this phenomenon. By making registration extremely convenient, the state of Utah has succeeded in getting nearly total registration. (See "Registration Procedures in the State of Utah," *Election Laws of the Fifty States and the District of Columbia* (Washington, D.C., Library of Congress Legislative Reference Service, June 1968), pp. 247–248. Similarly, Costantini and Hawley estimate that turnout in California could be raised by more than 5% simply by keeping registration open until the last week before the election. Edmond Costantini and Willis Hawley, "Increasing Participation in California Elections: The Need for Electoral Reform," *Public Affairs Report* 10, Bulletin of the Institute of Governmental Studies (June 1969). A 1968 registration figure of 97.8% was attained by holding registration open until the Wednesday before election (when political interest, which would stimulate the voter to register, and which would stimulate the party activists to get him registered, is highest) and by having publicized locations in every district.

38. Kelley, *et al., op. cit.*, p. 373.

39. The latest suggestions for a comprehensive program along these lines are from the Freedom to Vote Task Force of the Democratic National Committee, *That All May Vote* (Washington, D.C., 1969), 46 pp., and are embodied in House and Senate bills: The Universal Voter Enrollment Act of 1970 (House Resolution 19010 and Senate 4238). See the statement by Representative Morris Udall in the *Congressional Record*, August 13, 1970, pp. H8319–8332.

40. Citizens Voter Registration Campaign, "Final Report (mimeo, New York, September 3, 1969). See *That All May Vote*, above.

41. Kelley, *et al., op. cit.*, pp. 374–375.

42. *Ibid.*, p. 363.

43.   Recent evidence shows that white youth who have not attended college are much more conservative on stylistic questions than are their peers with higher education. See the issue of *Esquire* (January 1970) devoted to this question. In general, young people divide more or less as their elders do, except more of them are neutral or undecided. See Jerald G. Bachman and Elizabeth Van Duinen, *Youth Looks at National Problems* (Ann Arbor, Mich., 1971), especially Table 3–2 (p. 33), which shows the results from three surveys of teenagers conducted in 1970:

MICHIGAN SURVEY 19-Year-Old Males		PURDUE STUDY High-School Seniors		HARRIS SURVEY 15–21-Year-Old Youths	
Republican	21%	Republican	14%	Republican	18%
Democratic	32%	Democratic	26%	Democratic	35%
Haven't Thought		Wallace A.I.P.	7%	Wallace	4%
About It	20%	No Difference	18%	Other or	
Neutral	14%	Undecided	30%	Not Sure	40%
Other	6%	Missing Data	5%	Will Refuse	
Missing Data	7%			To Vote	3%

44.   William G. Andrews, "American Voting Participation," *Western Political Quarterly* 19 (1966), 641–642.

45.   N.Y. *Times*, "Poll Finds Residency Rules Cut Vote of Young and Democrats," December 6, 1969. Most universal automatic voter enrollment programs include a provision whereby the enrollee could at least vote for President even if he moved within the week before election. For example, see *That All May Vote*, above.

46.   *U.S.* vs. *Arizona*, 91 S. Ct. 260 (1970).

47.   Andrews, *op. cit.*, p. 643.

48.   Although we know of no effort to review the situation, there seems no compelling reason why felons—"ex" or otherwise—should be denied the ballot. Voting may be a small way of maintaining their connection with society. Their ability to vote should make politicians more interested in their welfare, including the structure of penal institutions. The view that loss of the right to vote penalizes would-be felons and is, therefore, a deterrent to crime is hardly worth considering.

49.   There were, of course, many other plans for "reform," involving almost all possible combinations of these three alternatives. For example, President Nixon at one point recommended that the

40% plurality plank which usually goes with the direct election proposal be applied instead to the present Electoral College set-up (The Washington *Post,* Friday, March 14, 1969, p. A2). A second example is the "federal system plan" of Senators Dole and Eagleton, which states: (1) A President would be elected if he (a) won a plurality of the national vote *and* (b) won *either* pluralities in more than 50% of the States and D.C., *or* pluralities in states with 50% of the voters in the election. (2) If no candidate qualified, the election would go to an Electoral College where the states would be represented as they are today, and each candidate would automatically receive the electoral votes of the states he won. (3) In the unlikely event that no candidate received a majority of the electoral votes, the electoral votes of states which went for third party candidates would be divided between the two leading national candidates in proportion to their share of the popular votes in those states. (*Congressional Record,* Thursday, March 5, 1970, p. S3026). These plans have the following characteristics: (a) They are too complicated to solve any problems of public confusion or public perception that they are not "democratic." (b) They have no significant body of congressional support, as of late 1970.

50. *Baker* vs. *Carr,* 369 U.S. 186 (1962); *Wesberry* vs. *Sanders,* 376 U.S. 1 (1964), and *Reynolds* vs. *Sims,* 377 U.S. 533 (1964).

51. Because numbers games are such an important part of electoral reform debates, it is perhaps worth buttressing the argument about the benefits of the present system with the current figures The clearest way to see who the most powerful voters are in the current system is to divide the number of electoral votes a state has into the margin of victory in that state; this is a measure of the citizen's likelihood to swing electoral votes with his vote. In 1968, this ratio was lowest for the smallest states (Nevada 4,300:1, Delaware 2,700:1, and Alaska 700:1) and the largest states (Texas 1,600:1, Ohio 3,500:1, California 5,600:1). It was highest for the middle-sized states, with electoral votes in the 7 to 14 range (Louisiana 22,100:1, Kansas 25,000:1, Minnesota 19,900:1).

52. For example, Ed Gossett, original co-sponsor of the district plan, asked, "Is it fair, is it honest, is it democratic, is it to the best interests of anyone in fact to place such a premium on a few thousand labor votes or Italian votes or Irish votes or Negro votes or Jewish votes or Polish votes, or Communist votes or big city machine votes, simply because they happen to be located in two or three industrial pivotal states? Can anything but evil come from placing such temptation and power in the hands of political parties and political bosses? Both said groups and said politicians are

corrupted as a nation suffers." Cited in David Brook, "Proposed Electoral College Reforms and Urban Minorities," paper delivered at the Sixty-Fifth Annual Meeting of the American Political Science Association, September 2-6, 1969, p. 6.

53. In "The South Will Not Rise Again Through Direct Election of the President, Polsby and Wildavsky Notwithstanding," *Journal of Politics* 31 (August 1969), pp. 808–811, Professor Harvey Zeidenstein shows that the winner's margin of victory in eight large northern urban states—taken together—was greater than in the eleven states of the old Confederacy—taken together—in four of the six Presidential elections between 1948 and 1968. From this he concludes that the influence of northern urban states, where the votes are, is likely to be very great under a system of direct elections. We agree, but argue in the text that direct elections do improve the strategic position of one-party states (including some southern states), as compared with the Electoral College winner-take-all system. On this issue Zeidenstein is silent.

54. On September 18, 1969, by a vote of 339 to 70, a direct election plan with a 40% plurality run-off provision was passed by the U.S. House of Representatives. See *Congressional Record*, September 18, 1969, pp. H8142–H8143; for the content of the bill, see *Congressional Record*, September 10, 1969, pp. H7745–H7746.

55. The Michigan Survey Research Center finds that only 1.5% of the voters had felt that Senator Eugene McCarthy was the best man for President in the spring and still felt that way after the election, but if all participants in the system had known that he was not going to be defeated and disappear but would be a serious candidate at least through the first election, it is at least possible to conjecture that he could have picked up an additional 4% or 5%. Philip E. Converse, Warren E. Miller, Jerrold G. Rusk, and Arthur C. Wolfe, "Continuity and Change in American Politics: Parties and Issues in the 1968 Election," *American Political Science Review*, 63 (December 1969), 1092. Cf. Richard N. Goodwin, "Reflections: Sources of the Public Unhappiness," *The New Yorker* (January 4, 1969), pp. 38–58.

56. The article which deals most clearly with the Electoral College in terms of its virtues of conciliation and of broad coalition building is John Wildenthal, "Consensus After L.B.J.," *Southwest Review*, 53 (Spring 1968). He argues in part, "Rather than complain about being deprived of a choice when both parties wage 'me too' campaigns, thhe American people should be thankful that the interests of a wide variety of Americans can be reconciled by both parties with similar programs."

57. One summary of this position is given by Representative Kleppe of North Dakota, in *Congressional Record*, February 3, 1969, p. H648. An interesting sidelight, and a tribute to the change of perspective a change of office can bring, is his citing of Senator John F. Kennedy, who said, "After all, the States came into the Union as units. Electoral votes are not given out on the basis of voting numbers, but on the basis of population. The electoral votes belong to each State. The way the system works now is that we carry on a campaign in forty-eight States, and the electoral votes of that State belong to that party which carries each State. If we are going to change that system, it seems to me it would strike a blow at States rights in major proportions. It would probably end States rights and make this country one great unit."

58. Roscoe Drummond, "Perils of the Electoral System," Washington *Post*, November 14, 1960. An argument in some ways parallel to our own is contained in Anthony Lewis, "The Case Against Electoral Reform," *The Reporter* (December 8, 1960). See also Allan P. Sindler, "Presidential Election Methods and Urban-Ethnic Interests," *Law and Contemporary Problems* (Spring 1962), 213–233.

59. See Estes Kefauver, "The Electoral College: Old Reforms Take a New Look," *Law and Contemporary Problems* (Spring 1962), p. 197.

60. Despite popular misconceptions, even the 1964 Republican platform, written by supporters of Barry Goldwater, contained explicit promises to preserve these programs.

61. See Kirk H. Porter and Donald Bruce Johnson, *National Party Platforms 1840–1956* (Urbana, 1956). There are immense differences between both party platforms of 1932 and 1952. Note, for example, the subheadings under domestic policy in the 1952 platforms dealing with a range of topics entirely missing in 1932. The Democratic 1952 platform includes subheadings on full employment, price supports, farm credit, crop insurance, rural electrification, the physically handicapped, migratory workers, river basin development, arid areas, wildlife, recreation, Social Security, unemployment insurance, public assistance, needs of our aging citizens, health, medical education, hospitals and health centers, costs of medical care, public housing, slum clearance, urban redevelopment, aid to education, school lunches, day care facilities, specific steps under civil rights, and many other subjects completely absent in 1932. Most of these worthy causes were also supported in the 1952 Republican platform and were missing from the 1932 Republican platform. Nevertheless, there are differences *between*

the parties in 1952 in regard to use of the public lands, public housing, labor legislation, farm legislation, public power, aid to education, and much more. In regard to education, for example, the 1952 Republican platform reads: "The tradition of popular education, tax-supported and free to all, is strong with our people. The responsibility for sustaining this system of popular education has always rested upon the local communities and the states. We subscribe fully to this principle." The corresponding Democratic plank reads in part: "Local, State, and Federal governments have shared responsibility to contribute appropriately to the pressing needs of our education system. . . . We pledge immediate consideration for those school systems which need further legislation to provide Federal aid for new school construction, teachers' salaries and school maintenance and repair" (pp. 504, 485). See also Gerald Pomper, " 'If Elected, I Promise': American Party Platforms," mimeo, 1966.

62. This is one of the main conclusions of Arnold Rogow, *The Labour Government and British Industry* (Oxford, 1955).

63. Douglas Chalmers illustrates much the same process in the Socialist party of Germany. See Chalmers, *The Social Democratic Party of Germany* (New Haven, 1964).

64. See Julius Turner, *Party and Constituency: Pressures on Congress* (Baltimore, 1951) and David B. Truman, *The Congressional Party* (New York, 1959).

65. For a general discussion of Presidential control, see Aaron Wildavsky, "The Two Presidencies," *Transaction* 4 (December 1966), 7–14.

66. See Bauer, Pool, and Dexter, *American Business and Public Policy*, pp. 9–79.

chapter five

the ballot and the political system

We began this book by asserting that Presidential elections are important because the results are significant to us as citizens. We would now like to explore whether the act of voting in a democracy such as ours is meaningful not only in the sense that voters help choose the next President but also in the sense that their collective choice limits and shapes national policy. It seems appropriate, therefore, to begin our analysis with a brief statement of how policy outcomes are achieved in national politics. Then we shall go on to relate the act of voting in free elections to the policy process.

COALITIONS IN THE SYSTEM

In the American political system, powers and opportunities to act effectively on public policy are parceled out to the President, to Congress, to the courts, to independent regulatory agencies, to various of the Federal bureaucracies, to the political parties, and even, in some respects, to interest groups. It is clear that each of these agencies enjoys partial autonomy; but in most important areas of public policy formation, they share powers. And this means that it is possible for participants in policy making to achieve their desired ends only by entering into cooperation with other participants in the system, by making coalitions.

What sorts of behavior are encouraged in a system which requires coalitions? Coalitions mean bargaining. Participants must give something in order to get something. Those who start out with the most resources to give have an advantage. But skill also counts. The prizes tend to go to those individuals and groups who are skilled in using whatever resources they have to put together and maintain coalitions. They help themselves by finding ways in which the interests of others may also be served.

The most conspicuous problem that American political parties face is to achieve a record of advocacy and accomplishment in public policy while harmonizing the interests of Presidential and Congressional wings.

The parties that convene at the national conventions do not contain the same roster of personnel, the same coalitions of interests, or the same majorities as the parties that meet in Congress. These two different types of parties, though they bear the same party labels, represent different constituencies and perspectives. The national conventions are weighted according to the winning strategy dictated by the Electoral College; Congress is no longer so grossly weighted according to the overrepresentation in state legislatures of rural interests[1] (which determine the shape of Congressional districts), but still plays according to rules of seniority, and these tend to favor one-party areas. This explains why, for example, the conservative wing of the Republican party, though dominant in that party in Congress for many years, has, except for a brief moment of glory in 1964, failed to nominate a candidate of its own choosing at the Republican National Convention. The difference on the Democratic side between the two party coalitions was made abundantly clear in 1956 when Senator Estes Kefauver defeated Senator John Kennedy for the Vice-Presidential nomination in the convention and lost to the Senator from Massachusetts in the Senate a few months later when they contested for a place on the prestigeful Foreign Relations

Committee. Obviously, the same interests and considerations were not decisive in the national convention and the Senate.

Even when a President and a Congressional majority bear the same party identification, it may be, and often is, necessary in a Presidential election campaign to adjust their varying interests on particular policies. This is done through bargaining and the creation of a coalition including interests represented in both Congressional and Presidential parties.

Although the lack of cohesion and discipline attributed to American parties can be overemphasized, it is true that on many major policies the President cannot rely on support from the full complement of his party in Congress but must seek the support of at least some members of the other party. Thus, interparty coalitions are necessary and common in American national politics.

Power within Congress is fragmented and dispersed. Bits and pieces of influence are scattered, unequally to be sure, among committee chairmen, appropriations subcommittees, the Speaker of the House, the House Rules Committee, the Senate majority and minority leaders, the President's lobbyists, and others. How is legislation passed and defeated, then, if it is not done by a central body of cohesive leaders who are able to enforce their will on Congress?

Legislative policy is approved or rejected by building a majority coalition through a process of bargaining and the proposal of objectives appealing to a wide variety of interests. A series of bills may contain attractions for all; concessions may be offered, log-rolling may be attempted, and other bargaining techniques used. If the identical majority were required to pass every piece of legislation, however, and the diversity of interests in Congress prevented agreement on a comprehensive legislative program, the American political system could lead to stalemate and go the way of the French Fourth Republic. Actually, legislation in the various policy areas often requires somewhat different coalitions. Legislative politics, therefore, is largely concerned with constructing coalitions appropriate to each set of policies.

The President does not have sufficient power to accomplish

all his purposes, and those the nation sets for him, by issuing orders. He must obtain the support of others. Congress holds the vital power of the purse and the general legislative authority which the President needs. But much of the time he can neither help nor harm legislators because they are nominated and elected in their own constituencies at the local and state levels. Consequently, to get some of the things he wants, the President may have to trade some top-level appointments and make policy concessions to influential interests in Congress or to interest groups or local party leaders who can exert influence in Congress.

Power is also fragmented and dispersed in the executive branch. Parts are held by bureau chiefs, department heads, interest groups, members of Congress, party leaders, coordinating committees, the Executive Office, independent regulatory commissions and, of course, by the President himself. With no central authority to dictate decisions, administrative politics requires the formation of coalitions among the many dispersed centers of power.

"This does not mean," a contemporary student of the Presidency says, "that Presidents are powerless. . . ." If that were true they would have nothing with which to bargain. They do have a veto power, powers over foreign policy and the armed forces, some executive authority and other resources at their disposal. "It does mean, though, that Presidential power must be exercised *ad hoc*, through the employment of whatever sources of support, whatever transient advantages can be found and put together, case by case." [2]

We may achieve some perspective on the American situation by noting how it differs from British and French experience. In Great Britain the major parties form their coalitions of interests before the national elections and, if victorious, the same coalition that won election governs in Parliament. In the Fourth Republic of France coalitions were generally not formed before, but only after the elections. Even in the Fifth Republic the alliances of convenience formed on the second ballot bear no necessary relationship to the coalition which governs France. In the United States coalitions are formed both before and after the national elections, but electoral and governing coalitions are different.

In characterizing each of our political parties as coalitions, we do not mean to suggest that they are entirely alike. In fact, they are coalitions having slightly different components, and these differences are in turn reflected in the real differences that crop up from time to time in the platforms of the Presidential parties and in the policies the different party majorities favor in Congress.

The two political parties to a certain extent act as transmission belts for policy preferences in the general population. They perform this function partly out of choice—as partisans, party leaders know more and care more about issues—but mostly out of necessity. In order to win the great prize of the Presidency, they must gather support from a variety of groups in the population. They gain support by offering inducements to the electorate and to the organized groups which represent its various interests. By giving this support at the polls to party winners, interest groups gain opportunities to participate in party and governmental decision-making.

ELECTIONS AND PUBLIC POLICY

We would argue that free and competitive elections discourage, though they cannot provide a complete guarantee against, extreme policies and political leaders and aid in making the political system free, open, and responsive to a great variety of people and groups in the population. But it would not be correct to say that our elections transmit unerringly the policy preferences of electorate to leaders or confer mandates upon leaders with regard to specific policies. Consider the Democratic landslide of 1964, where the two major Presidential candidates had divergent, sharp, and consistent policy differences. Two years later, in the election of 1966, the Republicans regained much of the ground in Congress that they had lost.

Thus even in a landslide the mandate is at best a temporary, equivocal matter. And in any case elections which are even as clear-cut as 1964 are very rare.

It is easy to be cynical and expect too little from elections, however, or to be euphoric and expect too much from them. A cynical view would hold that the United States was ruled by a power elite—a small group outside the democratic process. Under these circumstances the ballot would be a sham and a delusion. What difference can it make how voting is carried on or who wins if the nation is actually governed by other means? On the other hand, a euphoric view, holding that the United States was ruled as a mass democracy with equal control over decisions by all or most citizens, would enormously magnify the importance of the ballot. Through the act of casting a ballot, it could be argued, a majority of citizens would determine major national policies. What happened at the polls would not only decide who would occupy public office, it would also determine the content of specific policy decisions. In a way, public office would then be a sham because the power of decision in important matters would be removed from the hands of public officials. A third type of political system—a pluralist one in which numerous minorities compete for shares in policy making within broad limits provided by free elections —has more complex implications. It suggests that balloting is important but that it does not often determine individual policy decisions. The ballot both guides and constrains public officials who are free to act within fairly broad limits subject to anticipated responses of the voters and to the desires of the other active participants.

In fact, it is evident from our description of coalition politics that the American political system is of the pluralist type. Public officials do make major policy decisions but elections matter in that they determine which of two competing parties holds public office. In a competitive two-party situation such as exists in American Presidential politics, the lively possibility of change provide an effective incentive for political leaders to remain in touch with followers.

But it would be inaccurate to suggest that voters in Presidential elections transmit their policy preferences to elected officials with a high degree of reliability. There are few clear mandates in our political system owing to the fact that elections are fought on so many issues and in so many incompletely overlapping constituencies. Often the voters elect officials to Congress and to the Presidency who disagree on public policies. Thus, as we shall show, mandates are not only impossible to identify, but even if they could be identified they might well be impossible to enact because of inconsistency in the instructions issued to officials who must agree on legislation.[3]

Presidential elections are not referenda. The relationship between Presidential elections and policies is a great deal subtler than the relations between the outcomes of referenda and the policies to which they pertain. In theory, the American political system is designed to work like this: two teams of men, one in office, the other seeking office, both attempt to get enough votes to win elections. In order to win, they go to various groups of voters and, by offering to pursue policies favored by these groups, hope to attract their votes. If there were only one office-seeking team, their incentive to respond to the policy preferences of groups in the population would diminish; if there were many such teams, the chances that any one of them could achieve a sufficient number of backers to govern would diminish. Hence the two-party system is regarded as a kind of compromise between the goals of responsiveness and effectiveness.

The proponents of a different theory would say that elections give the winning party a mandate to carry out the policies proposed during the campaign. Only in this way, they maintain, is popular rule through the ballot meaningful. A basic assumption in their argument is that the voters (or at least a majority of them) approve of all or most of the policies presented by the victorious candidate. No doubt this is plausible, but not in the sense intended because as we have seen, a vote for a Presidential candidate is usually merely an expression of a party habit and particular policy directions are not necessarily implied in the vote. Most voters in the United

States are not ideologically oriented. That is, they do not see or make connections among issues. They do not seek to create or to adopt coherent systems of thought in which issues are related to one another in some logical pattern. If this is the case, then voters can hardly be said to transmit preferences for particular policies by electing candidates to public office.

Other basic objections to the idea that our elections are designed to confer mandates on specific public policies may also be raised. First, the issues debated in the campaign may not be the ones in which most voters are interested. These issues may be ones which interest the candidates, which they want to stress, or which interest segments of the press, but there is no necessary reason to believe that any particular issue is of great concern to voters just because it gets publicity. Time and again, voting studies have demonstrated that what appear to be the major issues of a campaign turn out not to be significant for most of the electorate. In 1952, for example, three great Republican themes were Communism, Korea, and corruption. It turned out that the Communism issue, given perhaps the most publicity, had virtually no impact. Democrats simply would not believe that their party was the party of treason, and Republicans did not need that issue to make them vote the way they usually did. Korea and corruption were noticeable issues.[4] Yet how could anyone know, in the absence of a public opinion poll, which of the three issues were important to the voters and which constituted a mandate? There were, in any event, no significant policy differences between the parties on these issues—Democrats were also against Communism and corruption and also wanted an end to the war in Korea.

A second reason why voting for a candidate does not necessarily signify approval of his policies is that candidates pursue many policy interests at any one time with widely varying intensity, so that they may collect support from some voters on one issue and from other voters on another. It is possible for a candidate to get 100 percent of the votes and still have every voter opposed to most of his policies, as well as having every one of his policies opposed by most of the voters.

Assume that there are four major issues in a campaign.

Make the further, quite reasonable, assumption that the voting population is distributed in such a way that those people who care intensely about one major issue support the victorious candidate for that reason alone, although they differ with him mildly on the other three issues. Thus, voters who are deeply concerned about the problem of nuclear defense may vote for candidate Jones who prefers a minimum deterrence position, rather than Smith, who espouses the "no-city" doctrine which requires huge retaliatory forces.[5] This particular group of voters disagrees with Jones on the farm bill, on civil rights and on Federal aid to education, but they do not feel strongly about any of these matters. Another group, meanwhile, believes that farmers, the noble yeomanry, are the backbone of the nation and that if they are prosperous and strong, everything else will turn out all right. So they vote for Jones, too, although they prefer a "no-city" strategy and disagree with Jones's other policies. And so on for other groups of voters. Jones ends up with all the votes, yet each of his policies is preferred by less than a majority of the electorate. Since this is possible in any political system where many issues are debated at election time, it is hard to argue that our Presidential elections give unequivocal mandates on specific policies to the candidates who win.[6]

As we have seen, people go to the polls and vote for many reasons not directly connected with issues. They may vote on the basis of party identification alone. Party habits may be joined with a general feeling that Democrats are better for the common man or that Republicans will keep us safe—feelings too diffuse to tell us much about specific issues. Some people vote on the basis of a candidate's personality. Others follow a friend's recommendation. Still others may be thinking about policy issues but may be all wrong in their perception of where the candidates stand. It would be difficult to distinguish the votes of these people from those who know, care, and differentiate among the candidates on the basis of issues. We do know, however, that issue-oriented persons are usually in a minority while those who cast their ballots with other things in mind are generally in the majority.

Even if there is good reason to believe that a majority of voters do approve of specific policies supported by the victorious candidate, the mandate may be difficult or impossible to carry out. A man may get elected for a policy he pursued or preferred in the past which has no reference to present circumstances. One could have voted Republican because Dwight Eisenhower got rid of the rascals in the Truman administration, but this does not point to any future policy that is currently in the realm of Presidential discretion. "Corruption" in 1952 was a kind of issue where there was really no way of carrying out a supposed mandate other than determining to be honest, a course of action we may be pardoned for believing that Adlai Stevenson would have followed as well. John F. Kennedy promised in 1960 to get the nation moving. This was broad enough to cover a multitude of vague hopes and aspirations. More specifically, as President, Kennedy may dearly have wished to make good on this promise by increasing the rate of growth in the national economy, but no one was quite sure how to do this. Lyndon Johnson was able to make good many of his 1964 campaign promises on domestic policy, but saying he would be more responsible than Goldwater did not constitute a viable future policy for Vietnam.

Leaving aside all the difficulties about the content of a mandate, there is no accepted definition of what size electoral victory gives a President special popular sanction to pursue any particular policy. Would a 60% victory be sufficient? This is rarely achieved. Does 55% seem reasonable? What about 51% or 52%, however, or the cases in which the winner receives less than half of the votes cast? And is it right to ignore the multitudes who do not vote and whose preferences are not directly considered? One might ignore the nonvoters for the purpose of this analysis if they divided in their preferences between candidates in nearly the same proportions as those who do vote. But they often don't. In practice, this problem is easily solved. Whoever wins the election is allowed to pursue whatever policies he pleases, within the substantial constraints imposed by the rest of the political system. This, in the end, is all that a "mandate" is in American politics.

IS PARTICIPATORY DEMOCRACY BETTER?

Critiques of the American system from the standpoint of democratic values ordinarily take two forms. First, there are criticisms of the lack of impact which elections have on the policy outcomes of the government: these critics see no direct link between public policy and the desires of electoral majorities. Second, there is the critique of the electoral process itself which argues that policy does not represent what majorities want because elected representatives are not responsive to majority desires. These criticisms are simple-minded in one sense and cogent in another. Simple-minded, in that they ignore the immense problems that would have to be overcome if we were truly serious about transforming America or any large diverse population into a participatory democracy. Cogent, in that responsiveness to majorities on questions of policy is a fundamental value that gives legitimacy to democratic government. The connection between such criticism and the authority of government makes it important to deal at least briefly with some of the issues and problems which should be raised (and usually are not) by judgments of this fundamental nature.

The first and obvious question to ask is whether the criticisms are based on fact. Is the American system unresponsive to the policy desires of a majority of its citizens? Unfortunately, there is no unambiguous way to answer this question. If we focus our attentions, for example, on the mechanics of the policy process, we find what appears to be government by minorities. In some policy-areas a great number of people and interests, organized and unorganized, may have both a say in open hearings and some influence on the final product. But fewer individuals may be involved in areas dealing with other problems and policies, some of which will be of a specialized nature, of a limited interest, and so on. Certainly it is true that even members of Congress do not have equal or high influence over every decision: committee jurisdictions, seniority, special knowledge, party, individual reputation—all combine to weigh the influence of each member on a different scale for each issue.

So we must conclude that if we adopt direct participation in, and equal influence over the policy decisions of our government (the decisions which "affect our lives") as *the* single criterion of democracy, then our system surely fails the test. So, we might note, does every government known to us—possibly excepting two or three rural Swiss Cantons.

Another approach might focus on public opinion as an index of majority desires. Using this standard a quite different picture emerges. The vast majority of policy decisions made by the government have the support of popular majorities. In cases where this is not true, the lack of "responsiveness" may have several causes, not all of them curable: (1) conflicts between majority desires and intractable situations in the world (e.g., the desire to transform, peaceably, the Soviet Union into a liberal democratic ally), or (2) inconsistencies in public attitudes toward certain sets of policies (e.g., the desires for a very high rate of employment and very low rates of inflation). Occasionally, both problems are involved: stable majorities have existed which favored a policy of a quick, costless victory over Hanoi leading to a complete withdrawal of all American troops from a democratic, united, anti-Communist Vietnam.[7] (3) Finally, there are instances where majority desires are clear, consistent, and feasible, yet ignored by the government because the desires are unconstitutional or antithetical to enduring values of the political system to which leaders are more sensitive than popular majorities: recent surveys, for example, have revealed majorities in favor of constitutionally questionable repressive measures against dissenters and the press.

Criticisms of Presidential elections are more difficult to assess. American politics *does* respond to the application of resources which are arguably non-democratic, that is, which cause the influence of different actors to be weighed unequally. In a truly democratic system, it could be argued, each man would count for one and no man would count for more than one: the system would respond to numbers and only numbers. As we have indicated, however, money, energy and enthusiasm, ability and experience are all valuable assets within the structure of American politics. Should the system be condemned for this? Should we attempt to eradicate the influence which these resources presently command? Before joining a campaign in behalf of this cause, it may be wise to consider for a moment why these non-democratic resources are useful.

Possession of the relevant political resources could increase the influence of an individual because candidates seek the support of such individuals. Why do they do so? Because a contender needs money to publicize himself and his cause; because he needs experienced and able men to aid him get his image effectively delivered to the voter. Political resources and the men who possess them are important, in short, because campaigns are important. And campaigns are important because the general public needs to be roused and alerted to the fact that an election is near. Partisans must be mobilized, the uncommitted, convinced, perhaps even a few minds changed. Resources other than votes are important because—and only because—numerical majorities must be mobilized.

American politics responds to non-democratic resources because many, if not most, citizens are politically apathetic. If nearly everyone participated, no other resources would be necessary. Why is political apathy widespread? There are several alternative explanations. Perhaps it is because the system presents the citizenry with no real alternatives to choose among. Perhaps. As we mentioned, however, Barry Goldwater provided us with at least a partial test of this "hidden-vote" theory, and the evidence is negative. Perhaps it is because the public has been imbued with a "false-consciousness" that blinds them to their "real" desires and interests. Perhaps. This is an explanation traditionally seized upon by the enlightened few to deny value to the preferences of the ignorant many. The people, we are told, are easily fooled: this testifies to their credulity. They do not know what is good for them: this makes them childlike. But when the people cannot trust their own feelings, when their desires are alleged to be unworthy, when their policy preferences should be ignored because they are not "genuine" or "authentic," they are being deprived of their humanity as well. What is left for the people if they are deprived of judgment, wisdom, feeling, desire, and preference? Such a premise would offer little hope for democracy of any sort, for it introduces the most blatant form of inegalitarianism as a political "given": a structured (ascribed) difference between those who know what is "good" for themselves and those who must be "told." But, then, persons who make this argument do not believe in democracy.

A more hopeful and less self-contradictory explanation of political apathy might note that throughout American history a substantial number of American citizens have not wished to concern themselves continually with the problems and actions of government. Many citizens prefer to participate on their own terms, involving themselves with a particular issue-area or a specific problem. The participation of these citizens is necessarily sporadic and more narrow than that of the man interested in all public problems and actively involved in general political life. Many other citizens (surely a majority) are more interested in the problems of their own personal life than they are in any issue of public policy.[8] This, we would suggest, is the real "silent majority": citizens who meet their public obligations by going to the polls at fairly regular intervals, making their selections on the basis of their own criteria, and then supporting the actions and policies of the winners—whether their first choice or not. In the intervals, unless they themselves are personally affected by some policy proposal, most of these citizens simply wish to be left alone. Most citizens, that is, do not participate because they are concerned with other things important to them, like earning a living or painting a picture or cultivating a garden, not because they feel it is so difficult to influence outcomes.

Imagine for a moment a situation where these conditions did not hold. Consider a society where all citizens were as concerned about public matters as the most active of our party volunteers. Such a society would not require mobilization: all who were able would vote. The hoopla and gimcrackery associated with our contemporary (and past) political campaigns would have little effect: this citizenry would know the record of the party and the candidate and, presumably, would make their reasoned choice on this basis. Idle speculation? Perhaps. Should such an active society be the goal of those whose political philosophy is democratic? This question should not and cannot be answered without first addressing the problem of how such a society could be achieved and what the achievement would require.

Without attempting to be comprehensive, a few difficulties do merit some specific comment. First and foremost, political participation—as Aristotle made clear several thousand years ago—takes a great deal of time. For this reason (among others) a large population of slaves was felt to be a necessary concomitant of participatory government: it freed Athenian citizens from the cares of maintaining life and thus provided them the leisure time that made their political activity possible. But having rejected this ingenious solution to the problems related to relatively large scale participation some hundred years ago, we must deal with the fact that the vast majority of our citizens must work for a living. Most Americans lack the disposable time that permits professionals and students to choose their working hours. Most citizens lack the time, even if they had the temperament and training, to engage continually in politics. To the degree that mass representative institutions—political parties, legislatures, elected executives—are denigrated in favor of more direct modes of activity, to that degree the majority of the people will be without the means of participation through which they can most effectively make their will felt. In short, to impose requirements of direct participation on those desiring a voice in decisions would be to insure that the incessant few rather than the sporadic many would rule: thus the slogan power to the people really proposes to replace a representative few, who are elected, with an unrepresentative few, who are self-appointed.

We raise this issue not because we are opposed in principle to the idea of an active, participatory democratic society. By persuasion and political education the majority of our citizens might indeed be convinced that the quality of our shared existence could and should be improved through more continuous devotion to public activity. But to argue this is quite a different matter than to argue that the rules of the game should be changed so as to disenfranchise those who presently lack the opportunity or desire to be active in this sense. We do not favor efforts to implement ideal goals when the preconditions and the means of achieving these goals do not exist. More importantly, we do not favor actions which in the name of democracy (or under any other disguise) restrict the ability of most of the people to have their political say.

EXTREMISM

Among the most important things accomplished by a political system like ours is that it discourages the most extreme alternatives. Knowing that policies which would outrage significant groups in the country would result in a stream of protests leading to loss of the next election, the party in power is restrained from the worst excesses. For people in countries like the U.S. or Great Britain, this may be difficult to appreciate precisely because they rarely have occasion to witness these extremes; extreme policies are effectively ruled out by the party system and free elections. This is not so everywhere, and we can get an insight into what is possible when the ultimate restraint of free elections is missing. Imagine that in 1956 the United States repudiated its national debt on the ground that it was inflationary. Suppose that ten years previously our government had confiscated about nine-tenths of all savings by issuing new currency worth only a tenth of the old. No doubt there would have been riots in the streets, petitions galore, furious political participation by millions of formerly inactive citizens, and a complete change of government as soon as the election laws allowed. Can we conceive of a situation in which our government would ship millions of tons of wheat abroad while our own people were starving? All these extreme policies have been pursued by the Soviet Union. We are more fortunate than we know if we can say that it is difficult or impossible to imagine extreme policies like these being carried out. Indeed, it is hard to imagine that anyone in a responsible position would think of such policies let alone attempt to promulgate them. Here we come to a key point. No one thinks about these things seriously, because everyone understands that they simply could not be done.

Extreme policies are discouraged in a more subtle way: free elections discourage persons with extreme views from running for office because possible allies of such people know they cannot win and that, if they do, their victories will last only until the next election. Extremists deprive too many people of too many of their preferred policies to win office easily. Thus we find that would-be Presidential aspirants do not get far if they are known publicly to hold bigoted views about racial or religious minorities or if they have done or said things which suggest that they are extremely hostile to large population groups such as laborers or small businessmen. Moreover, those who do attain office and wish to enjoy its benefits find that compromise and conciliation bring greater rewards than hostility and instransigence. The political system conditions those who accept the rules of free elections to moderate behavior.

PARTY COMPETITION AND POLICY

Aside from casting extremists out beyond the pale, free elections and a two-party system operate to bring governmental policy roughly in line with intense public preferences over a reasonable span of time. Through the trial and error of repeated electoral experiences, party leaders discover that certain policies must be excluded and others included if they are to have any hope of winning. The "out" party has a built-in incentive to propose policies more popular than the "in" party in order to assume office. And the "in" party is highly motivated to respond by adopting the policy itself or by proposing others which it believes may be even more popular. Party competition for votes brings public policy into accord with private preferences. This calculus of support is far from precise; it is necessarily based more on hunch and guesswork at any point in time than on hard facts. Party leaders undoubtedly have a number of policies which they know they must include or exclude, such as Social Security and veterans' benefits. Beyond that, however, they face considerable uncertainty in determining which policies will prove to be the most popular with the largest number of voters who are in a position to help them. Policies themselves may break down, subjecting proponents to charges of ineffectiveness. There may be consequences of consequences which turn what once looked like a good thing into a disaster. John Kennedy might have been helped by a successful Cuban invasion but how was he to know that it would turn into a rout? And how could he tell that a Soviet attempt to install missiles would enable him to act decisively and recoup his fortunes? President Johnson found it possible to do much more than previous Presidents to improve relations with Communist countries in Eastern Europe. Yet the Vietnam war certainly created all sorts of additional difficulties for him in dealing with the Soviet Union. So much for the effectiveness of policy. How about the perhaps more difficult problem in our system of discovering whether particular policies are so widely preferred as to aid one's political fortunes?

Opinion polls may help the politician, but there are always lingering doubts as to the polls' reliability; it is not certain in any event that they tell the political leader what he needs to know. People who really have no opinion may give one just to satisfy the interviewer. People who have an opinion but who care little may be counted equally with those who are intensely concerned. Many people giving opinions may have no intention of voting for some politicians who heed them, no matter what. The result may be that the politician will get no visible support from a majority which agrees with him, but instead he will get complaints from an intense minority which disagrees. The people who agree with him may not vote while those who differ may take retribution at the ballot box. Those who are pleased may be the ones who would have voted for the public official anyway. And unless the poll is carefully done, it may leave out important groups of voters, overrepresent some, underrepresent others, and otherwise give a misleading impression.

Other methods of determining voter sentiment are bound to be even more unreliable. Who knows whether opinions expressed in newspaper editorials or a mail campaign are representative of the majority of the voting populace?

Let us turn the question around for a moment. Suppose a candidate loses office. What does this tell him about the policies he should have preferred? If there were one or two key issues widely debated and universally understood, the election may tell him a great deal. But this is seldom the case. More likely there were many issues and it was difficult to separate out those which did or did not garner support for his opponent. Perhaps the election was decided on the basis of personality or some events in the economic cycle or a military engagement—points which were not debated in the campaign and which may not have been within anyone's control. The losing candidate may always feel that if he continues to educate the public to favor the policies he prefers, he will eventually win out. Should he lose a series of elections, however, his party would undoubtedly try to change something—policies, candidates, organization, maybe all three—in an effort to improve its fortunes.

Let us suppose that a candidate wins an election. What does this event tell him and his party about the policies he should prefer when in office? He can take it on faith that the policies he proposed during the campaign are the popular ones. Some were undoubtedly rather vague, and specific applications of them may turn out quite differently than the campaign suggested. Others may founder on the rock of practicality; they sounded fine but they simply could not be carried out. Conditions change and policies which seemed appropriate but a few months before turn out to be irrelevant. As the time for putting policies into practice draws near, the new officeholder may discover that they generate a lot more opposition than when they were merely campaign oratory. And those policies he pursues to the end may have to be compromised considerably in order to get the support of other participants in the policy making process. Nevertheless, if he has even a minimal policy orientation, the newly elected candidate can try to carry out a few of his campaign proposals, seeking to maintain a general direction consonant with the approach that may—he cannot be entirely certain—have contributed measurably to his election.

Let us summarize. The role of Presidential elections has been found to be very important in keeping our political system open and competitive and in keeping public officials responsive to the preferences of a variety of interests in the general population. However, outcomes of these elections cannot by themselves transform the political system, nor can they register precisely all the nuances of policies preferred by the general public. In spite of this, our system of coalition politics, operating within and among the two parties, the President, Congress, state parties, and interest groups, does provide a kind of substitute for specific mandates by the electorate.

In the American political system, both inside and outside of formal government, it is necessary to receive multiple agreements and clearances from actors (bureaucrats, interest groups, legislators, the President) variously situated, having somewhat different roles to play and values to defend, in order to put new policies into effect. Alternatives which are fed into the political system and emerge as decisions are brought forth in a variety of ways, and all sorts of strategies and resources can be mobilized and focused on political decisions by interested parties. It is a system which encourages stability and discourages extremism, which sharply limits the choices available to the general public in the interests of finding agreement on only two alternatives, either of which can govern effectively. Very few people are perfectly satisfied with this framework within which our Presidential elections are held, but even fewer have devised ways of making the system better without simultaneously making it worse.

NOTES:

1. *Wesberry* vs. *Sanders*, *Reynolds* vs. *Sims*, and the wave of reapportionment of state legislatures they set off have already

begun to change the shape of Congress. For a fuller discussion, see Nelson W. Polsby, ed., *Reapportionment in the 1970's* (Berkeley, 1971).

2. Richard Neustadt, "The Presidency at Mid-Century," *Law and Contemporary Problems* 21 (Autumn 1956), 614.

3. This parallels in many respects an argument to be found in Robert A. Dahl, *A Preface to Democratic Theory* (Chicago, 1956).

4. Angus Campbell, Philip Converse, Warren E. Miller, and Donald Stokes, *The American Voter* (New York, 1960), pp. 525–527.

5. An excellent popular treatment of this set of alternatives is contained in Richard Fryklund, *100 Million Lives* (New York, 1962).

6. See Dahl, *A Preface to Democratic Theory*, pp. 124–131.

7. See Verba *et al.*, "Public Opinion and the War in Vietnam," *American Political Science Review* 2 (June 1967), 317–333.

8. For strong evidence on this point, see Samuel Stouffer, *Communism, Conformity and Civil Liberties* (New York, 1955), *passim*, and Julian L. Woodward and Elmo Roper, "Political Activity of American Citizens" in Nelson W. Polsby, Robert A. Dentler, and Paul A. Smith, eds., *Politics and Social Life* (Boston, 1963), pp. 527–537.

appendices a & b

bibliography

index

appendix a

1972 Presidential Primaries

March 7	New Hampshire
March 14	Florida
March 21	Illinois
April 4	Wisconsin
April 11	Rhode Island
April 25	Massachusetts, Pennsylvania
May 2	District of Columbia, Indiana, Ohio, Alabama, North Carolina
May 4	Tennessee
May 9	Nebraska, West Virginia
May 16	Maryland
May 23	Oregon
June 6	California, New Jersey, New Mexico, South Dakota
June 27	Arkansas
June	New York

appendix b

Convention Delegates And the Electoral College,
1964, 1968, and 1972

CONVENTION DELEGATES

STATE	REPUBLICAN			DEMOCRATIC			ELECTORAL VOTES		
	'64	'68	'72	'64	'68	'72	'64	'68	'72
Alabama	20	26		38	32	37	10	10	9
Alaska	12	12		12	22	10	3	3	3
Arizona	16	16		12	19	25	5	5	6
Arkansas	12	18		32	33	27	6	6	6
California	86	86		154	174	271	40	40	45
Colorado	18	18		23	35	36	6	6	7
Connecticut	16	16		43	44	51	8	8	8
Delaware	12	12		22	22	13	3	3	3
Florida	34	34		51	63	81	14	14	17
Georgia	24	30		53	43	53	12	12	12
Hawaii	8	14		25	26	17	4	4	4
Idaho	14	14		15	25	17	4	4	4
Illinois	58	58		114	118	170	26	26	26
Indiana	32	26		51	63	76	13	13	13
Iowa	24	24		35	46	46	9	8	8
Kansas	20	20		27	38	35	7	7	7
Kentucky	24	24		34	46	47	9	9	9
Louisiana	20	26		46	36	44	10	10	10
Maine	14	14		16	27	20	4	4	4
Maryland	20	26		48	49	53	10	10	10
Massachusetts	34	34		69	72	102	14	14	14
Michigan	48	48		92	96	132	21	21	21
Minnesota	26	26		50	52	64	10	10	10
Mississippi	13	20		24	24	25	7	7	7
Missouri	24	24		58	60	73	12	12	12
Montana	14	14		17	26	17	4	4	4

CONVENTION DELEGATES

STATE	REPUBLICAN			DEMOCRATIC			ELECTORAL VOTES		
	'64	'68	'72	'64	'68	'72	'64	'68	'72
Nebraska	16	16		19	30	24	5	5	5
Nevada	6	12		22	22	11	3	3	3
New Hampshire	14	8		14	25	18	4	4	4
New Jersey	40	40		77	82	109	17	17	17
New Mexico	14	14		26	26	18	4	4	4
New York	92	92		179	190	278	43	43	41
North Carolina	26	26		58	59	64	13	13	13
North Dakota	14	8		15	25	14	4	4	3
Ohio	58	58		99	115	153	26	26	25
Oklahoma	22	22		30	41	39	8	8	8
Oregon	18	18		24	35	34	6	6	6
Pennsylvania	64	64		125	130	182	29	29	27
Rhode Island	14	14		27	27	22	4	4	4
South Carolina	16	22		38	28	32	8	8	8
South Dakota	14	14		15	26	17	4	4	4
Tennessee	28	28		40	51	49	11	11	10
Texas	56	56		99	104	130	25	25	26
Utah	14	8		15	26	19	4	4	4
Vermont	12	12		12	22	12	3	3	3
Virginia	30	24		42	54	53	12	12	12
Washington	24	24		35	47	52	9	9	9
West Virginia	14	14		37	38	35	7	7	6
Wisconsin	30	30		46	59	67	12	12	11
Wyoming	12	12		15	22	11	3	3	3
Canal Zone				5	5	3	0	0	0
District of Columbia	9	9		16	23	15	3	3	3
Guam				3	5	3	0	0	0
Puerto Rico*	5	5		8	8	7	0	0	0
Virgin Islands*	3	3		5	5	3	0	0	0
TOTAL	1,308	1,333		2,316	2,622	3,016	538	538	538
Needed to Nominate	655	667		1,159	1,312	1,509			
Needed to Elect							270	270	270

* Puerto Rico and the Virgin Islands are entitled to participate in the National Conventions but not in the Presidential election.

bibliography

The works listed in the footnotes should prove helpful to anyone wishing to pursue a particular line of interest in depth. However, for a start, the following may be useful. On voters and political participation, there are now several thorough inventories, for example, Robert E. Lane's *Political Life* (Glencoe, 1959), and V. O. Key, Jr.'s *Public Opinion and American Democracy* (New York, 1961). The most intensive studies of voting behavior are *Voting* by Bernard Berelson, Paul Lazarsfeld, and William N. McPhee (Chicago, 1954), which is based on research done in Elmira, New York, during and after the 1948 Presidential campaign, and Angus Campbell and associates' *The American Voter* (New York, 1960), and *Elections and the Political Order* (New York, 1966), both of which are based on nationwide sample surveys conducted in 1952, 1956, 1960, and 1964. An interesting "case study" of public opinion is Herbert H. Hyman and Paul B. Sheatsley's, "The Political Appeal of President Eisenhower," *Public Opinion Quarterly* 19 (Winter 1955-56), pp. 26–39; this is reprinted in Nelson W. Polsby, Robert A. Dentler, and Paul A. Smith, eds., *Politics and Social Life* (Boston, 1963), pp. 453–464. See V. O. Key, Jr., *The Responsible Electorate* (Cambridge, Mass., 1966) for a discussion of voters in Presidential elections.

The nature of the party system in the United States has been described in a number of good texts, for example, Moisei Ostrogorski's *Democracy and the Party System in the United States* (New York, 1926), Pendleton Herring's *The Politics of Democracy* (New York, 1940), Austin Ranney and Willmoore Kendall, *Democracy and the American Party System* (New York, 1956), V. O. Key, Jr., *Politics, Parties and Pressure Groups*, 4th ed. (New York, 1958), and Fred I. Greenstein, *The American Party System and the American People* (Englewood Cliffs, N.J., 1964).

The literature on Presidential campaigns is, of course, voluminous. Two studies with historical perspective on the subject are Alexander Heard's *The Costs of Democracy* (Chapel Hill, N.C., 1960), and Eugene H. Roseboom's *A History of Presidential Elec-*

tions (New York, 1957). Among the more popular works on the 1960 campaign are Theodore H. White's *The Making of the President, 1960* (New York, 1961) and Harry Ernst's *The Primary that Made a President: West Virginia, 1960* (New York, 1962). Both of these works are highly readable, and contain a wealth of illustrations and anecdotes. More scholarly studies of the 1960 campaign include Herbert E. Alexander's *Financing the 1960 Election* (Princeton, 1962), his *Responsibility in Party Finance* (Princeton, 1963), and Sidney Kraus, ed. *The Great Debates* (Bloomington, 1962), which provide both facts and competent analysis of two important and controversial aspects of that struggle. The "official record" of the campaign, the words of the candidates themselves, is in Report 994, Parts I, II, and III, 87th Congress, 1st Session, U.S. Senate (Washington, 1961), entitled respectively *The Speeches of Senator John F. Kennedy, Presidential Campaign of 1960, The Speeches of Vice-President Richard M. Nixon, Presidential Campaign of 1960,* and *The Joint Appearances of Senator John F. Kennedy and Vice-President Richard M. Nixon, Presidential Campaign of 1960.* Two other useful analyses of the 1960 campaign are Paul T. David, ed., *The Presidential Election and Transition, 1960–1961* (Washington, 1961), and Eric Sevareid, ed., *Candidates, 1960* (New York, 1959). On the 1964 campaign, see Robert D. Novak, *The Agony of the G.O.P. 1964* (New York, 1965), Richard H. Rovere, *The Goldwater Caper* (New York, 1965), Theodore H. White, *The Making of the President, 1964* (New York, 1965), and Milton C. Cummings, Jr., *The National Election of 1964* (Washington, 1966). For the 1968 Campaign, see Richard Scammon and Ben Wattenberg, *The Real Majority* (New York, 1970), Theodore White, *The Making of the President, 1968* (New York, 1969), two excellent books by Jules Witcover, *85 Days: the Last Campaign of Robert Kennedy* (New York, 1969) and *The Resurrection of Richard Nixon* (New York, 1970), and one by Richard T. Stout, *People* (New York, 1970). Finally, a dissection of one type of argument frequently used in political campaigning is contained in Aaron B. Wildavsky's "The Intelligent Citizen's Guide to the Abuses of Statistics: The Kennedy Document and the Catholic Vote," in Polsby, Dentler, and Smith, *Politics and Social Life,* pp. 825–844.

Paul T. David, Ralph M. Goldman, and Richard C. Bain's *The Politics of National Party Conventions* (Washington, 1960) gives a voluminous historical treatment of Presidential nominating conventions. See also Nelson W. Polsby and Aaron B. Wildavsky's "Uncertainty and Decision-Making at the National Conventions," in Polsby, Dentler, and Smith, *Politics and Social Life,* pp. 370–389, and Gerald Pomper, *Nominating the President: The Politics of Convention Choice* (Evanston, Ill., 1963). For material on specific conventions, see Paul Tillett, ed., *Inside Politics: The National Conventions, 1960* (Dobbs Ferry, N.Y., 1962), Paul T. David, Malcolm C. Moos, and Ralph M. Goldman, *Presidential Nominating Politics in 1952*, Vols. I–V (Baltimore, 1954). Information on the formal aspects of the nomination and election process can be found in *Nomination and Election of the President and Vice President of the United States, Including the Manner of Selecting Delegates to National Political Conventions*, House Document #332, 86th Congress, 2nd Session (Washington, 1960) and, with the same title, Senate item #998 (January 1964).

Finally, materials on the actual election results can be found in Richard M. Scammon, ed., *America Votes*, Vols. I–VIII (New York, 1956–70), and, with analytical comments, in Malcolm C. Moos, *Politics, Presidents and Coattails* (Baltimore, 1952).

index

Abels, Jules, 170, 222
Abelson, Robert P., 105, 215, 219
"access," 69
  definition of, 106
Adams, John, 93
Adrian, Charles R., 113
Agar, Herbert, 284
Agger, Robert, 122
Agnew, Spiro, 154, 186
Alexander, Herbert E., 108, 109, 110, 111
Alford, Robert R., 106, 222
Alsop, Joseph, 222
American Institute of Public Opinion Survey (See: Gallup Poll)
American Political Science Association, 284, 285
Andrews, William G., 258, 288
Anti-Third Term Amendment, 127
Appeals, Special, 17–24
Apter, David, 101, 216
Arvey, Colonel Jack, 123, 165, 168
Associated Press, 76
Axelrod, Robert, 20
Ayres, Richard E., 286, 287

Bachman, Jerold G., 288
Bagby, Wesley, 169
Baggaley, Andrew R., 105
Bailey, John, 110
Bailey, Stephen K., 284, 285
Bain, Richard C., 6, 163, 165
Baker vs. Carr, 289
ballots and balloting
  at National Conventions, 147–153
  and the political system, 293–302
Bancroft, George, 155
bandwagons, 120, 122, 131, 144, 147

Banfield, Edward C., 106
bargaining, 127, 129–130, 138–139, 150–153
  and coalitions, 293–297
  prerequisites for, 129–130
Barkley, Alben, 166
Barton, Allen H., 105, 214
Bauer, Raymond A., 105, 285, 292
Bay of Tonkin, 81
Bean, Louis, 222, 208–209
Belknap, George, 102
Benton, Thomas Hart, 108
Benton, William, 110
Berelson, Bernard, 101, 102, 214, 216
Biffle, Leslie, 202
Blackhurst, James, 164
Blackwood, George, 109
Blumberg, Nathan B., 111
Bone, Hugh A., 106, 113, 163, 221
Bowen, William G., 286, 287
Bricker, John, 145
Brodbeck, Arthur J., 101, 102
Brody, Richard A., 16, 104
Brook, David, 290
Bryan, William Jennings, 155, 183
Burdick, Eugene, 101, 102
Burke, Fred G., 168
Burns, James M., 284, 285
Burr, Aaron, 95

Calhoun, John C., 95
campaign, the, 177ff.
  amateurs v. regulars, 35–59
  choosing a strategy, 178–179, 203–206
  contributions, 70–72
  costs, 67
  feedback of information, 199–200
  folklore pertaining to, 192

campaign, the, (*con't*)
    front porch vs. whistle stops, 203–204
    impact of mass media, 193–195
    and interest groups, 17–18
    mud-slinging, 196–199
    public apathy, 171, 305
    purpose of, 171
    raising money, 70–72
    reinforcement effect, 110, 182
    significance of the press, 190–192, 195–196
    theory of, 178–179
    uncertainty, 182–183
    what issues to stress, 184–187, 310–311
    where to campaign, 181, 204–205
    workers, 180–182
Campbell, Angus, 101, 102, 103, 104, 108, 113, 214, 215, 216, 218, 222, 313
candidates
    "availability of," 164, 247
    campaign blunders, 201–206
    campaign contributors, 70–72
    incumbents vs. challengers, 179–180, 128–129
    and information feed back, 199–203
    and issues, 12–15, 184–187, 310–311
    knowledge of internal party affairs, 119
    making bargains, 129–130, 139, 150–151
    and money, 68–73
    their organizations, 139–141, 180, 199–200
    and party unity, 35–59, 134
    popularity, 189, 247–248
    pre-convention strategies, 130–131
    preservation of self, 190–193
    and the press, 188, 195–196
    timing, 144
    use of primaries, 131–134
    and volunteer organizations, 180–181
Cantril, Hadley, 104
Carleton, William, 170, 286
Carter, John F., 168
Cass, Lewis, 95

Cater, Douglass, 168
Catholic vote, 21, 23–24, 187, 249
Chalmers, Douglas, 292
Chamberlain, Neville, 280
Chester, Lewis, 165
Churchill, Winston, 280
civil liberties, public concern for, 304, 308
Civil War, the, 10–11
Clague, Christopher, 113
Clark, Champ, 189
Clark, James, 107
Clausen, Aage, R., 216
Cleveland, Grover, 197
coalition politics, 293–297
coattail effect, 30, 119
Cohen, Bernard C., 112
Committee on Political Parties, 284, 285
Connelly, Gordon M., 101
Conservative Party in Great Britain, 275
consensus government, 225–230
conventions, national
    aids to party unity, 244–247
    atmosphere, 137–138, 244
    balloting strategies, 147–148, 158, 161–162 (Table)
    bandwagons, 120, 122, 131, 144, 147
    bargaining, 129–130, 139, 150–151
    confusion, 141, 244–245
    criticisms, 244–247
    deadlocks, 152–153
    delegates, 142–145 (selection of, 160; Table, 161-162)
    demonstrations, 146–147
    functions and future of, 248–249
    gallery, 169
    information and communication, 144–146
    platforms, 246–247
    power of Presidents and party leaders, 124–128
    selecting date and location, 137–138, 146
    selecting permanent chairman, 145–146
    self-fulfilling prophecies, 151
    smoke-filled room, 241–242
    T.V. coverage of, 244–246
    uncertainty, 151–152
    value of, 245, 248–249

the Vice-Presidential nominee, 151, 153–155
winner vs. "best man," 247–
248
conventions, state and district,
135–137
Converse, Philip E., 100, 101,
103, 104, 108, 113, 214,
215, 216, 218, 219, 222,
290, 313
Cooke, Edward F., 164
Cooper, Homer C., 102
Cornwell Elmer E., 103
correspondents, newspaper, 73–
74
Costantini, Edmond, 287
Cox, James M., 189
Crossley poll, 212
Cronkite, Walter, 286
Cuban crises, 187
Cummings, Milton C., 104, 108,
166

Dahl, Robert A., 100, 103, 166,
285, 313
Daley, Richard J., 137
dark horse, strategy of, 130–131
Daugherty, Harry, 149, 152, 169,
170
David, Paul T., 6, 109, 163, 165,
166, 167, 168
Davis, John, 189
delegates
activists, 142–143
and balloting, 147–148
control of, 120
at the convention, 143
goals of, 150–151
influencing, 150–151 (*See
also*: bargaining)
need for information, 141,
244–245
number of, 318–319
and policy preferences, 150–
152
problems of, 152
selection of, 160, 161 (Table)
and uncertainty, 151–152
Dawes, Charles, 95
democracy, 303–309
Democrats
activists, 33ff.
campaign expenditures, 68–
73
characteristics of, 19–23,
172–174

convertibility of resources
of, 181–182
Dixiecrats, 11, 253
and domestic issues, 184–
186, 188–190
and foreign policy, 186–188
ideological divisions, 35–37,
41–46
news coverage, 244–246
and party identification, 19–
22
party policies (*See*: political
parties, policy commit-
ments and statements)
problems of, 181–182 (*See
also*: turnout of voters)
raising money, 73
Southern defections, 85–90
strategies of, 72–74
and Vietnam, 15, 90–93
voting strength, 24–27, 178–
181
Dentler, Robert A., 105, 164, 313
Depression of 1929, 11, 185
DeSapio, Carmine, 127, 180
Dewey, Thomas E., 112, 145,
150, 151, 183, 203
"blunders" of, 202–203
Dexter, Lewis Anthony, 105,
285, 292
Dirksen, Everett M., 215
DiSalle, Michael, 134
Dixiecrats, 253
domestic policy, 184–186, 188–
189, 279–281
Donnelly, Thomas, 169
Donovan, John C., 164
Donovan, Robert J., 112, 215
Douglas, Paul, 123
Downs, Anthony, 105, 106
Drucker, Peter, 285
Drummond, Roscoe, 291

Editor and Publisher Poll, 112
Eighteen-year-old vote, 258
Eisenhower, Dwight David, 24,
67, 167, 238
popularity of, 12, 25, 302
presentation of self, 192
Election of 1960, 23, 66, 76–77,
249, 205–206, 249
(*See also*: Kennedy, John
F.; Nixon, Richard M.)
Election of 1964, 30
(*See also*: Goldwater, Bar-
ry; Johnson, Lyndon B.)

Election of 1968, 16, 64–65, 90–93, 201–202, 204
(*See also:* Humphrey, Hubert H.; Nixon, Richard M.)
elections
  and citizens, 303–309
  coattails, 30, 119
  money, 60–62
  predicting the outcome, 206–213
  and public policy, 297–301
Electoral College
  apportionment in, 59–60
  appraisals and proposed reforms, 258–276
  biases of, 260–261
  unit rule, 59
  urban-rural balance, 60
Elliott, William Y., 284
Elson, Robert, 168
Emery, Edwin, 111, 112
Ernst, Harry W., 109, 165, 166, 167
Erskine, Hazel Gaudet, 102, 103
Esquire, 288
ethnic groups, 10–14
extremism, 248, 308

Farley, James, 119, 136, 168
Feldman, Jacob, 219, 221
Field, Harry M., 101
Finletter, Thomas K., 284
Fischer, John, 284
Flinn, Thomas, 105, 218, 222
Ford, Henry Jones, 284
foreign policy, 186–188
Fraser, Donald, 68
Freeman, Orville, 165
Frick, Henry C., 70
front-runner, strategy of, 130–133, 147–149
Fryklund, Richard, 313

Gallup, George, 222
Gallup Poll, 24, 220
Garner, John Nance, 93, 153
Gilbert, Charles E., 113
Gill, Joseph, 123–124
Goldman, Ralph M., 6, 163, 165, 166, 167, 168
Goldwater, Barry, 11, 35, 129, 132, 135–136, 166, 167, 248, 283, 302
  and civil rights, 51–53
  and hidden-Republican strategy, 174–175

and style, 47–48
  supporters of, 37–40, 54–57
Goodman, William, 106, 163, 285
Gosnell, Harold, 163, 287
Gossett, Ed, 289
Great Britain, political system of, 275–276, 279–281
Greenstein, Fred I., 22, 102, 113, 214
Griffith, Ernest F., 285
Gurin, Gerald, 218

Halberstam, David, 165
Halleck, Charles, 151
Harding, Warren G., 149, 152, 183
Harnsberger, Caroline T., 169
Harriman, W. Averill, 127
Harrison, William Henry, 197
Harris Survey, 189
Hatch Act, 128
Hawley, Willis, 287
Hazlitt, Henry, 284
Heard, Alexander, 108, 109, 110
heckling and mud-slinging, 196–199
Helms, E. A., 163
Herring, Pendleton, 106, 163, 164, 284, 285
Herzog, Arthur, 165, 167
Hodgson, Godfrey, 165
Hoffman, Paul J., 106, 215, 286
Holtzman, Abraham, 166
Humphrey, Hubert H., 136, 191
  1960 campaign, 67, 251
  1968 campaign, 15–16, 42–44, 65–66, 71, 110, 111, 119, 154, 198, 201–202
  as Vice-President, 93–97
Huthmacher, J. Joseph, 103
Hyman, Herbert, 103, 110, 215

ideological purity
  vs. victory, 35–47
  (*See also:* "purists vs. professionals")
ideology, levels of, 11–14, 279–281, 297–301
incumbency, 81, 127
  as a liability, 93–97
  as a resource, 83–96
  (*See also:* candidates)
Independents, 12–13, 175
information
  nature and control of, 73–81, 182–183, 199–201

in the nominating process, 144–147, 148
"two-step flow" of, 76
interest groups, 17–19, 149–150, 293–297
(*See also*: bargaining, and coalitions)
IBM, 209
issues, impact of, 15–16, 184–190, 229–231, 273–275
(*See also*: platforms; policy government)

Jackson, Andrew, 155, 197
Javits, Jacob K., 286
Jefferson, Thomas, 108, 197
Jews, 24, 26
Johnson, Andrew, 153
Johnson, Donald Bruce, 291
Johnson, Lyndon B.
campaign expenditures, 62–63
and foreign affairs, 81–82, 119, 188, 302
vs. Goldwater, 52–53, 121, 154, 174, 195, 302
vs. John Kennedy, 68, 149
and liberal activists, 119, 188
and party unity, 119, 121
popularity of, 81–82, 195
and the press, 166
problems of, 119, 177, 188
refusal to debate, 195
strategies of, 121, 128–129
as Vice-President, 97, 154
and Vietnam, 81–82, 96, 119, 188, 302
Johnson, Walter, 168
Jones, Charles O., 215, 216
Joyner, Conrad, 216

Katz, Elihu, 113, 219, 221
Kefauver, Estes, 67, 155, 237, 250, 291, 294
Kelly, Stanley, 221, 254–255, 286, 287
Kendall, Willmoore, 163, 284, 285
Kennedy, John F.
campaign expenditures, 62–63, 66, 111
the effect of Catholicism, 23–24, 66, 132, 134, 250
and foreign affairs, 302
vs. Kefauver, 155, 294
vs. Nixon, 23–24, 25
in Ohio, 183, 201

the organization of, 139–140, 141
the popular vote, 26
pre-convention success, 132, 134, 139
presentation of self, 191–192
and the press, 73, 77, 79
and the primaries, 67, 132, 134
vs. Stevenson, 149
strategies of, 134, 135, 139–140, 141
and television debates, 193–195
Kennedy, Robert F., 16, 45, 141
Kent, Frank R., 170
Keynes, John Maynard, 178
Key, V. O., Jr., 100, 103, 104, 106, 107, 113, 163, 164, 286
King, Martin Luther, Jr., 203
Kraus, Sidney, 219, 222

Labour Party, Great Britain, 275–276, 279–281
LaFollette, Robert, 132
Lamb, Karl A., 165
Landon, Alfred, 211, 249
Lane, Robert, 101, 102
Larner, Jeremy, 108
Latham, Earl, 214
"law and order," 188–190
Lazarsfeld, Paul F., 101, 102, 104, 105, 113, 214, 216, 222
Levin, Murray, 109
Lewis, Anthony, 291
Liberty League, 66
Liebling, A. J., 112
Lincoln, Abraham, 153, 197
as a dark horse, 131
Lindblom, Charles E., 166
Lindzey, Gardner, 214
Linz, Juan, 105, 214
Lipset, Seymour M., 105, 214
Literary Digest, 211–212
Livingston, William S., 106
lobbyists, 25
Lockhard, Duane, 103
Lodge, Henry Cabot, 145
Lodge, Henry Cabot, Jr., 133
Los Angeles Times, 76
Louis Harris Survey (*See*: Harris Survey)
Lovett, Robert Morss, 169
Lowden, Frank, 149

Lowell, A. Lawrence, 284
Lubell, Samuel, 103, 222
Lundberg, Ferdinand, 170

McCarthy, Eugene, 16, 35, 129, 166, 235, 250, 290
    supporters of, 35, 41–46, 290
    and young people, 49–51
McCarthy, Joseph, 75, 217
McClosky, Herbert, 106, 215, 286
MacDonald, William, 284
McGovern, George S., 167, 168
McGovern Commission on Delegate Selection, 167
McKean, D. D., 163
MacMahon, Arthur, 106
McPhee, William N., 101, 214, 216
Madigan, John, 165, 168
majority rule, 302–309
mandates, 275–276, 297–303
Marshall, Thomas Riley, 93
Martin, Joseph W., Jr., 112, 145, 169
Martin, Ralph G., 166, 169
mass media, impact of, 74–79, 81–83, 193–195, 244–246
Matsu-Quemoy situation, 187
Mazo, Earl, 221
Merriam, C. E., 163
Meyers, Harold B., 108, 109, 110, 111
Michigan Survey Research Center, 20, 25, 63, 100–101, 172, 290
Miller, Clem, 285
Miller, Warren E., 101, 106, 108, 214, 215, 216, 218, 285, 290, 313
Miller, William, 156
Mills, Wilbur, 233
Mississippi Freedom Democratic Party, 121
Modern Romance, 80
Mohr, Charles, 113
money, as a campaign resource, 61–64, 110
money raiser, 63–64, 69, 72–73, 110
Moos, Malcolm C., 163, 166, 167, 168, 216, 284
Morison, Elting E., 167
Mosteller, Frederick, 222
Mott, Frank Luther, 112
Mott, Stewart, 110
Mowry, George, 167

mud-slinging (*See*: heckling)
Munger, Frank, 164
Muskie, Edmund, 154–155

Natchez, Peter B., 101
national primary, 235–237
Negro voters, 20–21
Neustadt, Richard, 313
Newfield, Jack, 167
newspapers
    and cost cutting, 73–74
    and issues, 79–80
    partisanship of, 74–75
    political impact of, 73–74
    reader interest, 76–77, 80
news services, 76
New York Times, 76, 218, 222, 286, 288
Nimmo, Dan, 221
Nixon, Richard M., 165, 166, 186, 192, 221, 222
    appeal to both Negroes and Southerners in 1960, 118
    in California (1962), 132
    campaign timing, 183–184
    and civil rights, 118, 121
    as dark horse in 1964, 130
    and domestic issues, 186, 189 (Table)
    and foreign affairs, 16, 187–188
    vs. Humphrey, 9, 15, 16, 203–204
    vs. Kennedy, 25–26, 96–97, 120
    "mistakes" of, 183–184, 203–204
    party connections, 136
    on party unity, 120–121
    popular vote (1960), 25, 26
    popular vote (1968), 201–202
    and the press, 76–77, 79, 192, 195–196
    and the primaries, 131–132
    strategies and strategy, problems of, 96–97, 120, 131–132, 205–206
    and television debates, 193–195
    as Vice-President, 96
nomination process
    alternative procedures, 131ff.
    appraisal of, 234–244
    goals of, 116–122

power of party leaders, 125–126
  steps of, 129–130
  uncertainty in, 122–124
"normal" voting patterns, 25
Novak, Robert D., 167, 216

Odegard, Peter H., 163
O'Hara, Rosemary, 106, 215, 286
Ostrogorski, Moisei, 163, 168, 286
"over-exposure" of candidate, 65

Page, Benjamin I., 16, 104
Page, Bruce, 165
parties (*See:* political parties; Democrats; Republicans)
party activists
  and party identification, 33–34
  role at conventions, 125–126
  role during elections, 34–35, 44–45, 180–181
  social identities of, 34–35
  (*See also:* "purists vs. professionals")
party identification
  distribution of voters by, 173 (Table)
  function for voters, 9, 10–11, 33
  and issue orientation, 12–13, 14, 303–306
  as party resource, 24–25, 32
party leaders
  bargaining among, 129–130
  at conventions, 125–126
  goals of, 123–124
  importance of, 125
  interdependency of, 129
  and party unity, 120–121, 176–177
  and policies, 118–120
  power of, 124–127
party reform
  bias of, 229–231
  desirability of, 234–253
  and domestic policy, 279–281, 303–309
  and foreign policy, 283–285
  political theory of, 225–229
  possibility of, 231–234
  relevance of, 276–283
party unity, 275–278
patronage, 27, 124, 127
Pauley, Edwin, 71
Peel, Roy V., 169

Peirce, Neal R., 108
Penniman, Howard R., 163
permanent voting enrollment, 253–258
Phillips, Kevin, 83, 113–114
Pillow, Gideon, 152
platforms, 231, 246, 252, 273–275, 291–292
Plant, Edward, 166
"pocketbook" issues, 185–186
policy government
  in Great Britain, 275–278
  in the United States, 279–281
political activity, 11–12
political parties
  achieving access, 27–28
  as coalitions, 20–22, 24–25, 30, 118–119
  cohesion in, 30–31, 37–40, 180–181
  competition between, 32–33, 174–177, 309
  polarization of, 47, 174, 271–272
  policy commitments and statements, 14–15, 16, 29, 32, 225–227
  power of leaders over, 29–30, 125–126, 128, 241–242
  power of national vis-à-vis state parties, 31, 252–253
  problems of, 66–67, 97–98, 173–175
  raising money, 61–64
  reconciliation of Presidential and Congressional wings, 37, 42, 252–253
  at state level, 28–29, 31
  suggested reforms of, 225–229, 276–283
  as transmission belts, 10–11
  workers for, 34–35, 44–45, 180–181
  (*See also:* Democrats; Republicans)
political power
  definition of, 27
  fragmentation of, 295–296
political resources, 61ff.
  convertibility of, 97–99
  of incumbent, 81–83
  information, 73–79
  money, 61–72
  party affiliates, 24–25, 32
political system in America
  and the ballot, 297–303

political system in America
(*con't*)
coalitions in, 293–297
criticism of, 303–309
design of, 302–303
and extremism, 308–309
suggested reforms of, 303–
309
(*See also*: party reform;
primaries)
Polk, James, 152
polls and polling, 200–201, 206–
213
(*See also*: Gallup Poll; Harris Survey; Roper Poll)
Polsby, Nelson W., 105, 113, 114,
164, 166, 217, 313
Pomper, Gerald, 163, 292
Pool, Ithiel de Sola, 105, 215,
219, 285, 292
Popkin, Samuel L., 105, 215, 219
Porter, Kirk H., 291
Pre-convention strategies, 130–
137
Presidency, the
immunity from financial
pressures, 69–70
popularity in crises, 278–
279
(*See also*: incumbency)
Prewitt, Kenneth, 216
Price, Don K., 285
primaries
appraisal of, 234–253
criticism of, 249–253
national primaries, 235–240
as sources of information,
129–130
strategies of, 131–135
privatization of politics, 51–59
(*See also*: Goldwater, Barry; McCarthy, Eugene;
"purists vs. profession-
als")
Progressive Republication split,
253
Protestants, 24–25
public opinion (*See*: voters)
"purists vs. professionals," 35–
39

Quemoy-Matsu situation (*See*:
Matsu-Quemoy situation)
"quota-control" method, 211–212

Ranney, Austin, 163, 284, 285
Reagan, Ronald, 189

Reconstruction, 13
Registration, 254, 255 (Table)
(*See also*: permanent voter
enrollment)
Republicans
activists, 36–44
amateur take-over, 37–40,
135–136
campaign expenditures, 73–
75
characteristics of, 21–22,
172–173
Congressional wing, 186
defection from (1964), 30–
31, 176–177, 283
and domestic issues, 51–52,
118–119, 184–186, 188–190
extremism, 37–40, 47, 52,
218
and foreign affairs, 81, 179,
186–188, 218
hidden vote, 174–175
ideological divisions, 35–38,
47–50, 135–136, 155, 174–
175
"me-too" Republicanism, 47–
50
news coverage, 74–75, 193–
195
organization of, 135–137
and party identification,
170–173
party policies (*See*: political parties, policy com-
mitments and statements)
Progressive split, 253
"purists vs. professionals,"
35–39
raising money, 62–64, 72
resources of, 64–65, 68–69,
98–99
strategies of, 83–87, 118–
119, 155, 173–174
turnout, 22–23
and the Vice-Presidency,
95–97, 153–157
voting strength, 90–93, 201–
202
resources, political (*See*: political resources)
Reston, James, 166
Reynolds vs. *Sims*, 289, 312
Ribicoff, Abraham, 110
Rischin, Moses, 102–103
Rivers, William L., 112, 221
Rockefeller, Nelson, 67, 68, 251
Rogow, Arnold, 292

Roosevelt, Franklin D., 79, 94, 155, 185, 197
Roosevelt, Theodore, 70
Roper, Elmo, 100, 113, 286, 313
Roper Poll, 212–213
   (*See also*: polls and polling)
Rosenhack, Sheilah, 216
Rossi, Peter H., 101
Rovere, Richard, 112
Rowse, Arthur Edward, 111
Ruml, Beardsley, 71
Rusk, Jerrold G., 108, 218, 290

Sandburg, Carl, 166
Scammon, Richard A., 22, 165, 167, 189, 221
Schattschneider, E. E., 163, 164, 284
Schelling, Thomas, 167
Schlesinger, Arthur, Jr., 169, 170
Schwartz, Dr. Fred, 216
Scranton, William, 40
selective perception, 77–78
Seltz, Herbert A., 221
Sevareid, Eric, 166
Seward, William H., 168
Shannon, Jasper B., 110, 111
Sheatsley, Paul B., 103, 215
Sherwood, Robert E., 221, 222
Simulmatics Corporation, 25
Sindler, Allan P., 166, 291
Smith, Al, 146, 150
Smith, Henry L., 111, 112
Smith, Paul A., 105, 164, 313
smoke-filled room, 241
Smoot, Reed, 145
Solid South, 85–86
Sonthoff, Herbert, 285
Soule, John W., 107
Southern Strategy, 83–87
Stans, Maurice, 111
Stanwood, Edward, 170, 286
Stassen, Harold, 251
Stavis, Ben, 165
Stedman, Murray, 285
Stevenson, Adlai, 24, 149, 191–192, 237, 320
   lack of organization, 142, 181
   and money, 71
   and the press, 192
Stokes, Donald, 101, 214, 215, 216, 285
Stouffer, Samuel, 100, 103, 104, 313

Strong, Donald S., 164
Strunk, Mildred, 104
Sullivan, Mark, 169, 170
Symington, Stuart, 68, 130

Taft, Robert A., 145, 238
Taft, William Howard, 250, 253
Tate, James, 137
television debates, 188, 193–195
"ticket balancing," 96
Tillett, Paul, 164, 165, 167, 168, 286
Truman, David B., 106, 284, 292
Truman, Harry S., 71, 78, 79, 94, 149, 166, 183, 202, 203, 269, 302
Turner, Julius, 285, 292
turnout of voters, 22–23, 303–313
two-thirds rule, 169

uncertainty of nomination, 122–125
Underwood, Oscar, 150–151
unit rule, 167–168
United Press International, 76
Unruh, Jess, 58
U.S. Civil Rights Commission, 106
U.S. vs. *Arizona*, 288

Van Buren, Martin, 155, 197
Vandenburg, Arthur, Jr., 150, 169
Van Deusen, Glynden G., 168
Van Duinen, Elizabeth, 288
Verba, Sydney, 313
Vice-President
   nomination of, 153–157
   as political liability, 93–97
Vietnam, 15ff., 187–188, 229–230, 302
Votaw, Albert, 168
voters
   behavior of, 7–8, 25–26
   campaign contributions of, 62–63
   Catholic, 21, 23–24
   and class-oriented voting, 23
   ethnic groups, 20–25
   and ideology levels of, 7–8, 15, 184, 186
   Independents, 13–14
   interest groups, 17–18
   and issue orientation, 7–8, 15, 16 (Table)

voters (*con't*)
  Negro, 10–12, 20
  and the nominating process,
    131–135, 250–251
  party affiliation of, 9–10
  party identification of, 20–
    24 (*See also*: political
    party)
  and the press, 64–65, 80
  primary interest and con-
    cern of, 305, 307
  registration, 253–258
  turnout of, 22–23, 255
voting blocs, 17–27

Wallace, George C., 11, 16, 21,
  23, 198, 204, 239
Wallace, Henry A., 155, 156
Washington Post, 221, 289
Wattenberg, Ben J., 22, 165, 167,
  189, 221
Weed, Thurlow, 168
Wesberry vs. *Sanders*, 289, 312
Westin, Alan, 166
White, E. Clifton, 135

White, Theodore H., 35, 109, 111,
  112, 165, 166, 167, 168,
  170, 204, 221, 222
White, William S., 166
Wildavsky, Aaron B., 100, 105,
  164, 166, 167, 170, 286,
  292
Wildenthal, John, 290
Williams, Irving G., 170
Willkie, Wendell, 145, 147, 251
Wilson, James Q., 103, 108
Wilson, Woodrow, 284
Witcover, Jules, 35, 111, 113,
  165, 167, 170, 218, 221
Wolfe, Arthur C., 108, 218, 290
Wolfinger, Raymond E., 113, 216
Wood, Leonard, 149
Woodward, Julian L., 100, 313
write-in votes, 133–134, 167

Yoakum, Richard D., 221
youth, 42–43
  (*See also*: eighteen-year-
    old vote)

Zeidenstein, Harvey, 290